MICRO-SERIES
TEENAGE MUTANT NINJA
TURTLES

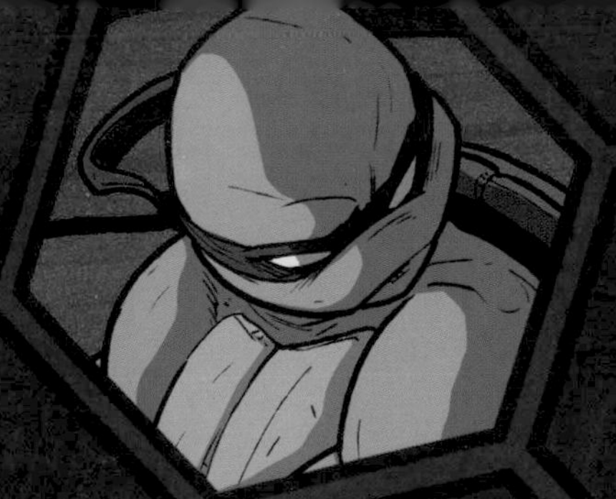

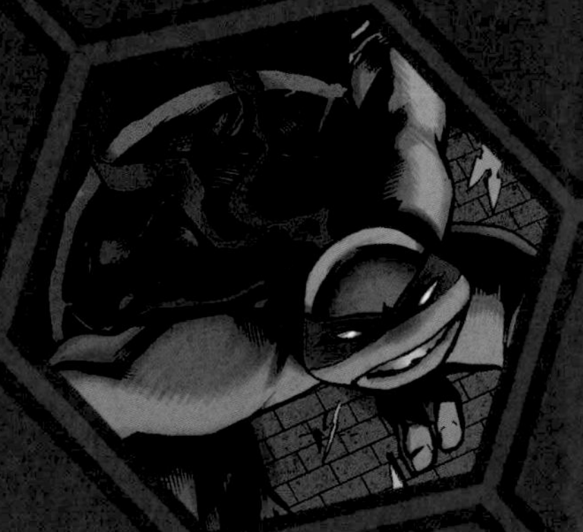

Series Edits by **Bobby Curnow**
Collection Edits by **Justin Eisinger** and **Alonzo Simon**

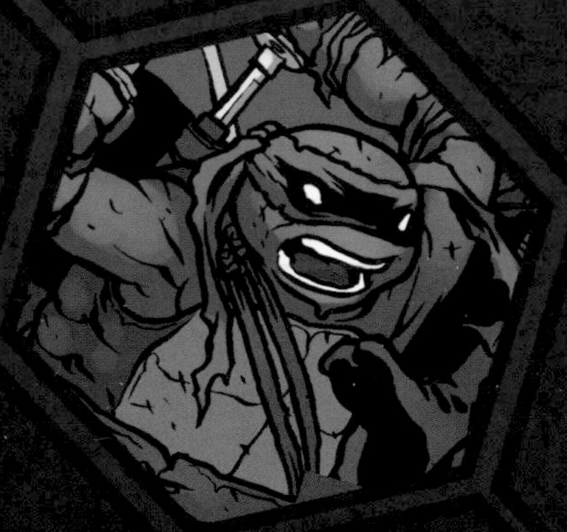

Collection Design by **Shawn Lee**
Collection Cover by **David Petersen**

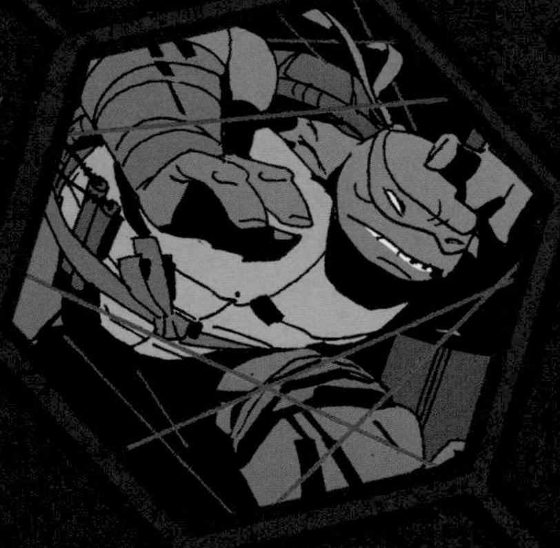

Special thanks to Joan Hilty, Linda Lee, and Kat van Dam for their invaluable assistance.

IDW founded by Ted Adams, Alex Garner, Kris Oprisko, and Robbie Robbins | International Rights Representative, Christine Meyer: christine@gfloystudio.com

ISBN: 978-1-61377-232-4

15 14 13 12   1 2 3 4

Ted Adams, CEO & Publisher
Greg Goldstein, President & COO
Robbie Robbins, EVP/Sr. Graphic Artist
Chris Ryall, Chief Creative Officer/Editor-in-Chief
Matthew Ruzicka, CPA, Chief Financial Officer
Alan Payne, VP of Sales

Become our fan on Facebook **facebook.com/idwpublishing**
Follow us on Twitter **@idwpublishing**
Check us out on YouTube **youtube.com/idwpublishing**
www.IDWPUBLISHING.com

Originally published as TEENAGE MUTANT NINJA TURTLES MICRO-SERIES Issues #1–4.

MICRO-SERIES
TEENAGE MUTANT NINJA
TURTLES

RAPHAEL .... Page 5
Written by **Brian Lynch**
Artwork by **Franco Urru**
Colors by **Fabio Mantovani**
Lettering by **Chris Mowry**

MICHELANGELO .... Page 29
Written by **Brian Lynch**
Artwork by **Andy Kuhn**
Colors by **Bill Crabtree**
Lettering by **Shawn Lee**

DONATELLO .... Page 53
Story by **Brian Lynch**
Script by **Brian Lynch** and **Tom Waltz**
Artwork by **Valerio Schiti**
Colors by **ScarletGothica** and **Ilaria Traversi**
Lettering by **Robbie Robbins**

LEONARDO .... Page 77
Written by **Brian Lynch**
Artwork by **Ross Campbell**
Colors by **Jay Fotos**
Lettering by **Shawn Lee**

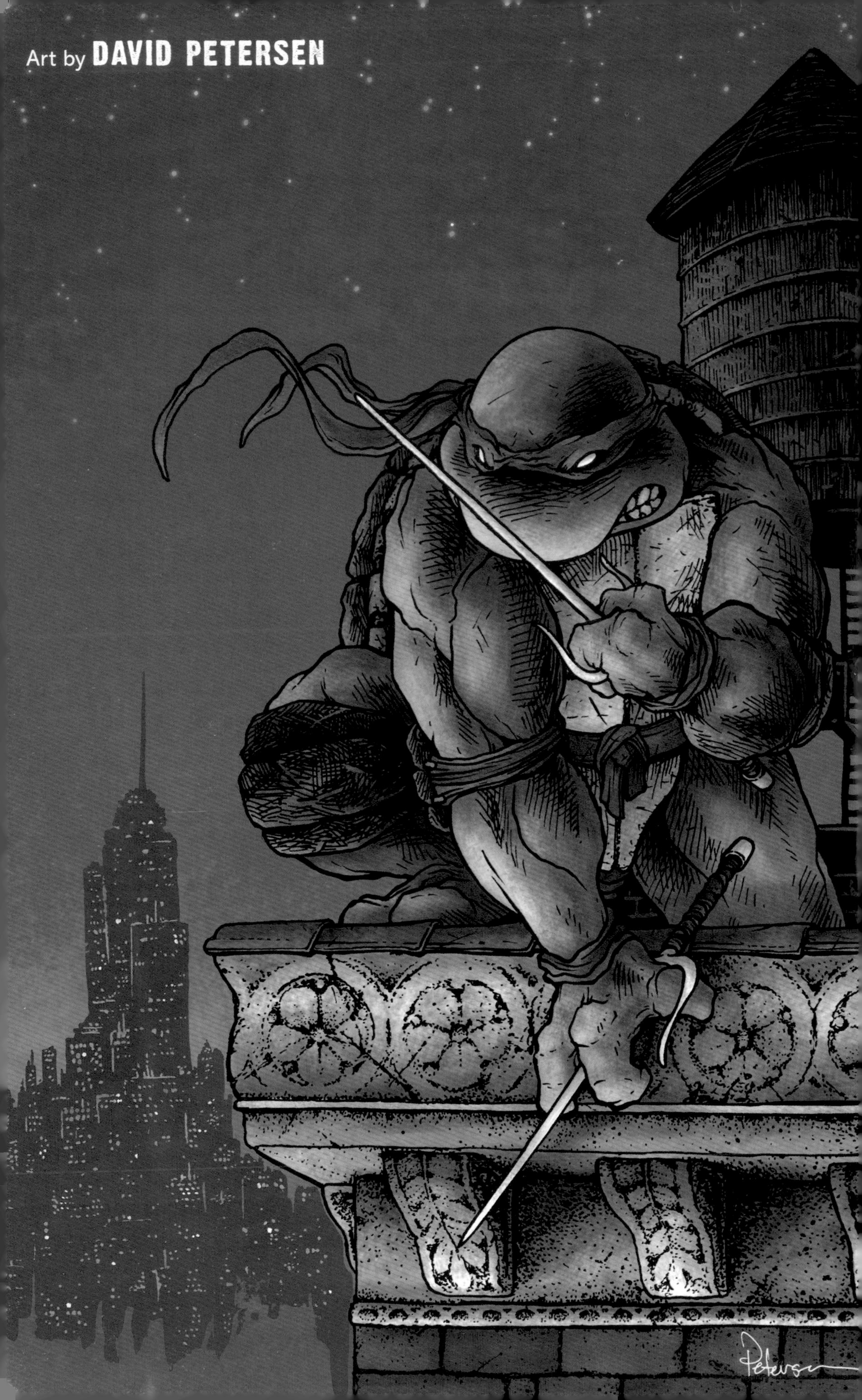

Art by **DAVID PETERSEN**

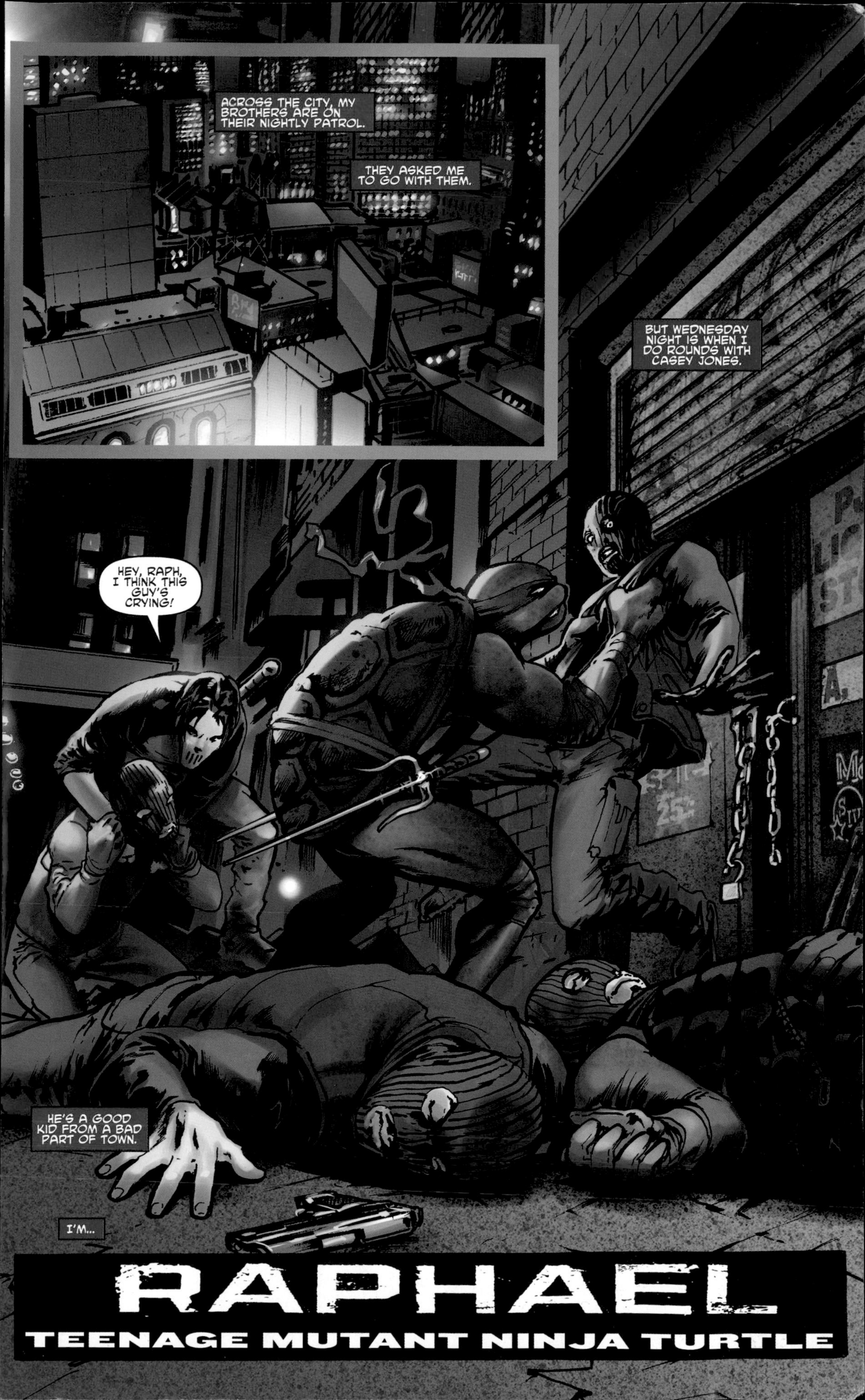

ACROSS THE CITY, MY BROTHERS ARE ON THEIR NIGHTLY PATROL.
THEY ASKED ME TO GO WITH THEM.
BUT WEDNESDAY NIGHT IS WHEN I DO ROUNDS WITH CASEY JONES.
HEY, RAPH, I THINK THIS GUY'S CRYING!
HE'S A GOOD KID FROM A BAD PART OF TOWN.
I'M...
RAPHAEL
TEENAGE MUTANT NINJA TURTLE

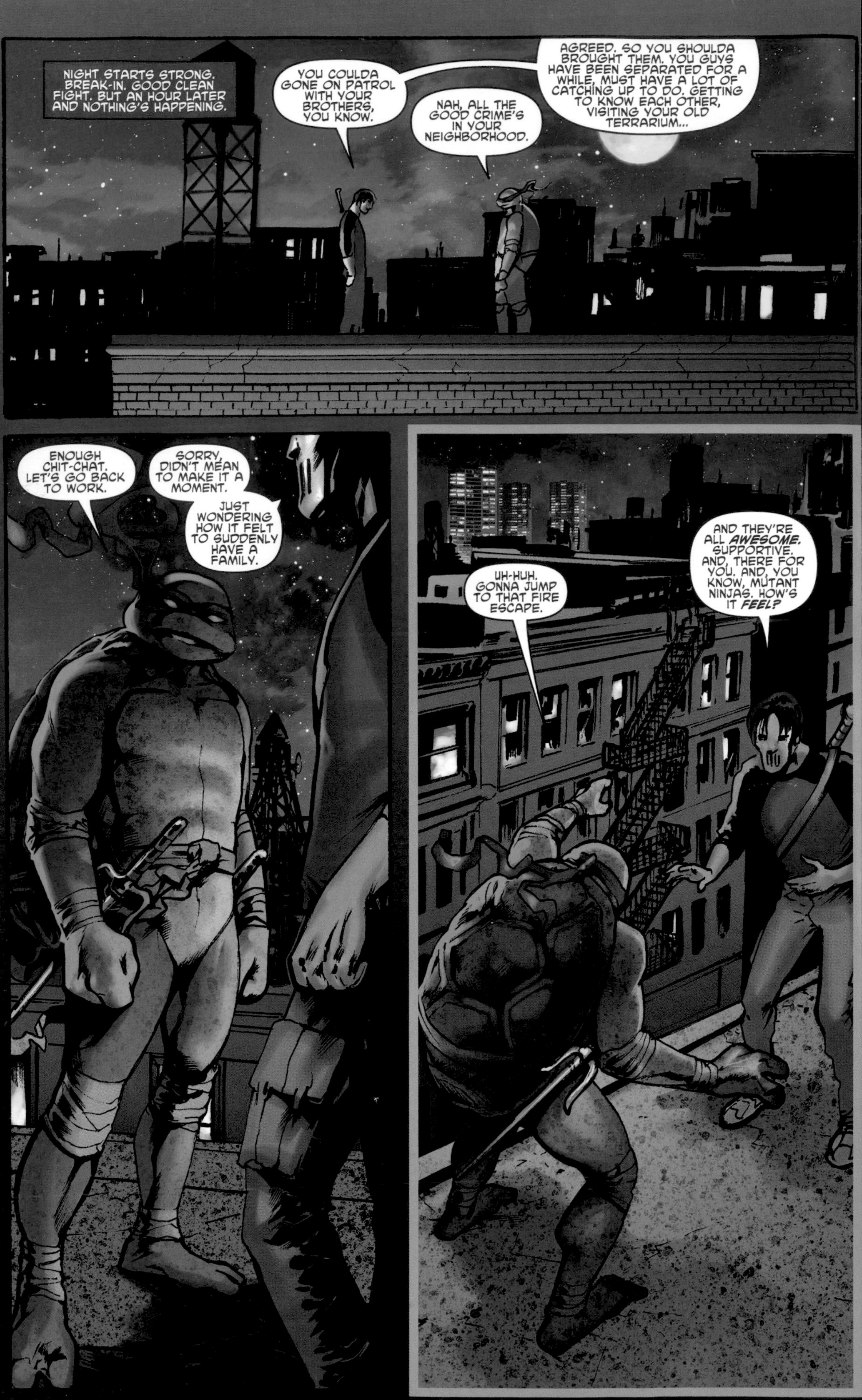
NIGHT STARTS STRONG. BREAK-IN. GOOD CLEAN FIGHT. BUT AN HOUR LATER AND NOTHING'S HAPPENING.
YOU COULDA GONE ON PATROL WITH YOUR BROTHERS, YOU KNOW.
NAH, ALL THE GOOD CRIME'S IN YOUR NEIGHBORHOOD.
AGREED. SO YOU SHOULDA BROUGHT THEM. YOU GUYS HAVE BEEN SEPARATED FOR A WHILE, MUST HAVE A LOT OF CATCHING UP TO DO. GETTING TO KNOW EACH OTHER, VISITING YOUR OLD TERRARIUM...
ENOUGH CHIT-CHAT. LET'S GO BACK TO WORK.
SORRY, DIDN'T MEAN TO MAKE IT A MOMENT.
JUST WONDERING HOW IT FELT TO SUDDENLY HAVE A FAMILY.
AND THEY'RE ALL AWESOME. SUPPORTIVE. AND, THERE FOR YOU. AND, YOU KNOW, MUTANT NINJAS. HOW'S IT FEEL?
UH-HUH. GONNA JUMP TO THAT FIRE ESCAPE.

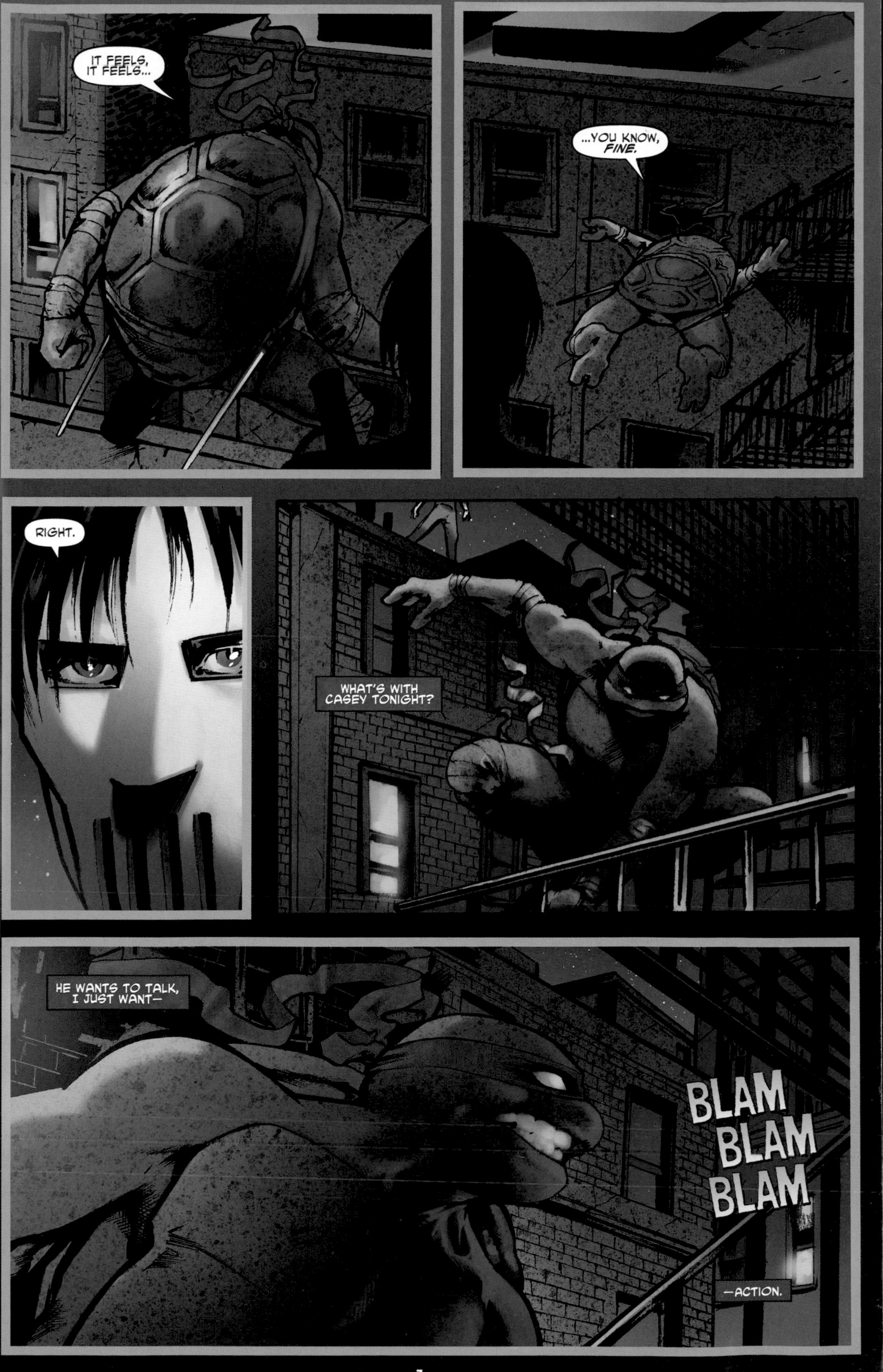
IT FEELS,
IT FEELS...
...YOU KNOW,
FINE.
RIGHT.
WHAT'S WITH CASEY TONIGHT?
HE WANTS TO TALK, I JUST WANT—
BLAM
BLAM
BLAM
—ACTION.

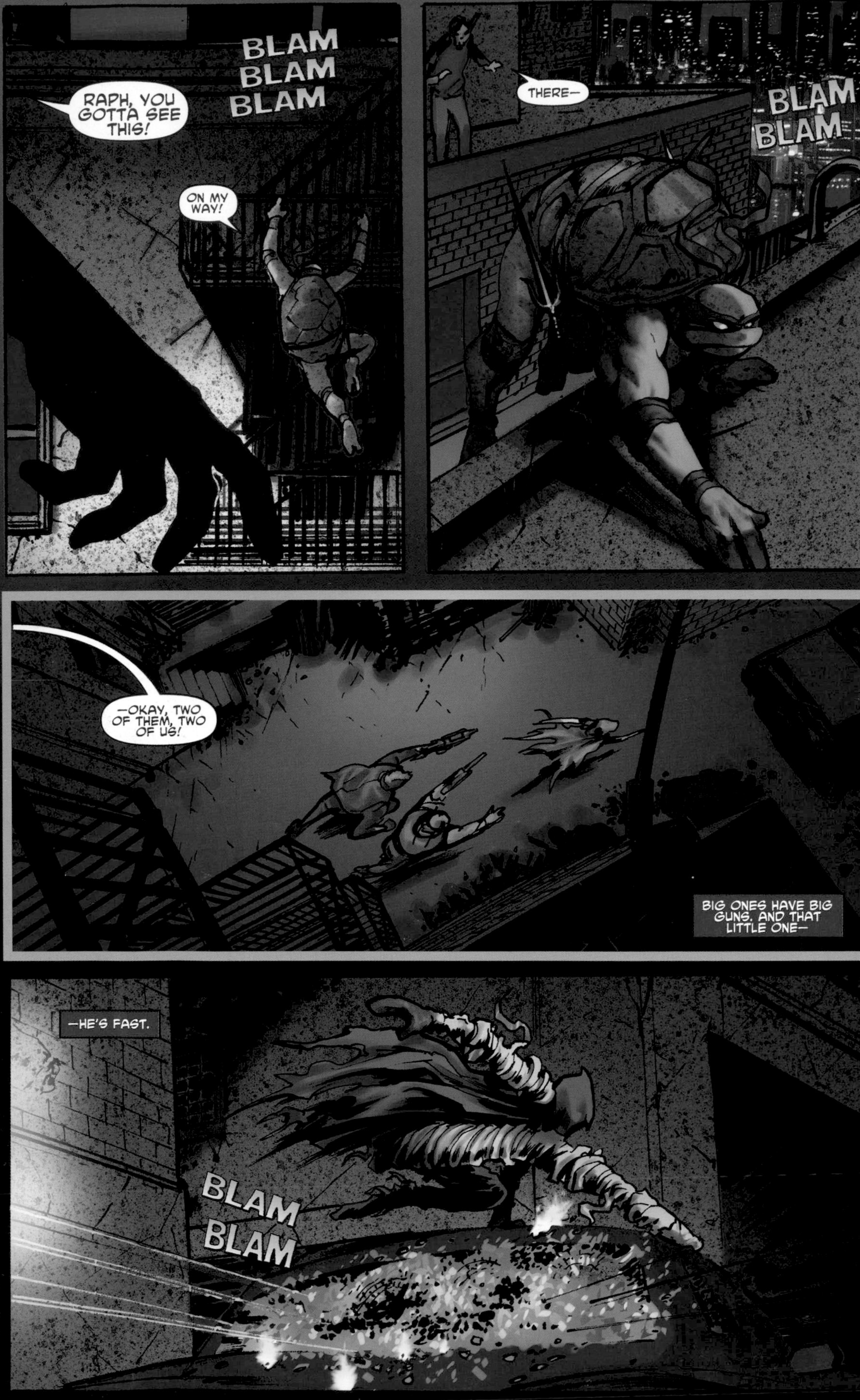
BLAM
BLAM
BLAM
RAPH, YOU GOTTA SEE THIS!
ON MY WAY!
THERE—
BLAM
BLAM
—OKAY, TWO OF THEM, TWO OF US!
BIG ONES HAVE BIG GUNS. AND THAT LITTLE ONE—
—HE'S FAST.
BLAM
BLAM

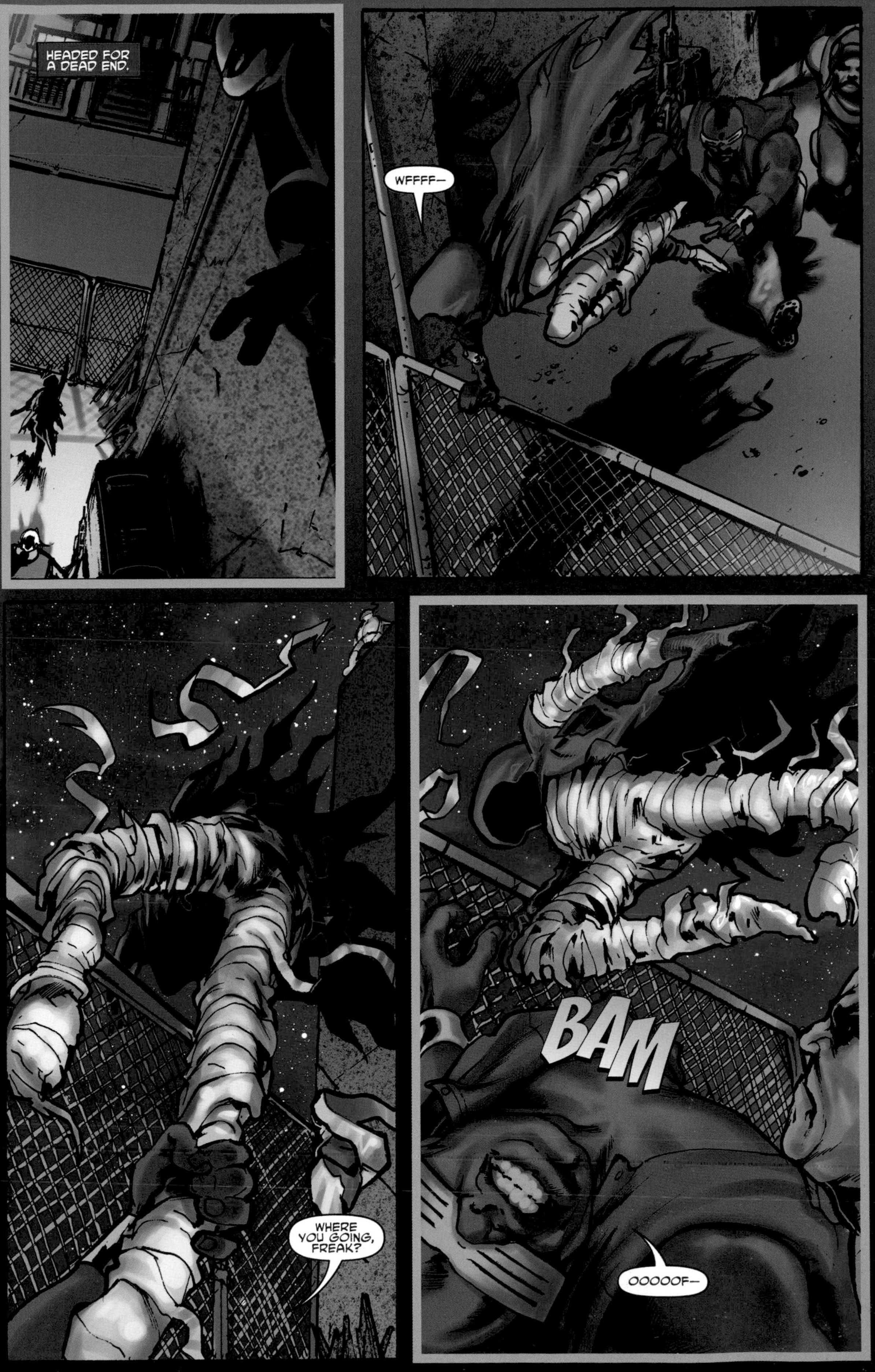
HEADED FOR A DEAD END.
WFFFF–
WHERE YOU GOING, FREAK?
BAM
OOOOOF–

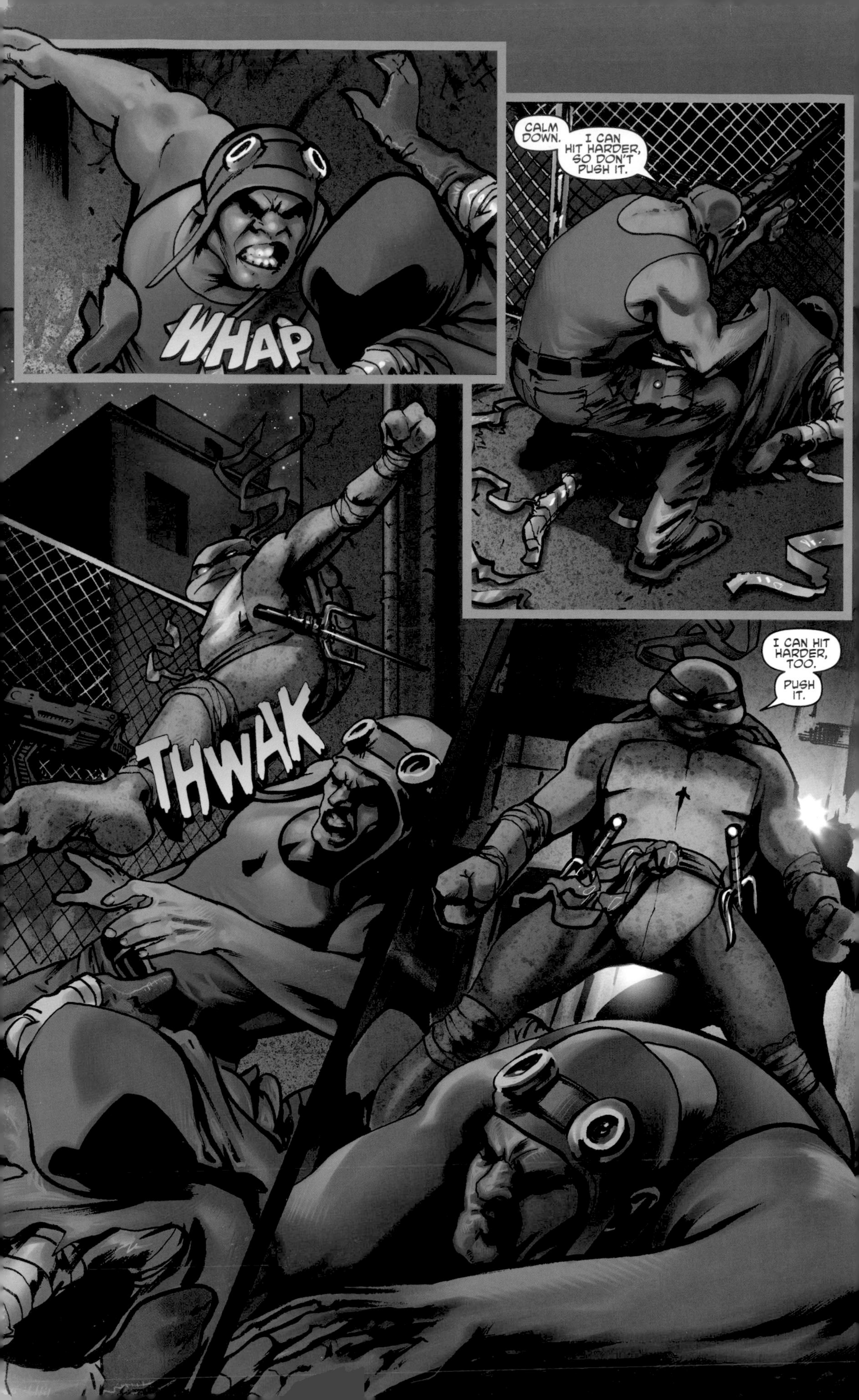
WHAP
CALM DOWN.
I CAN HIT HARDER, SO DON'T PUSH IT.
THWAK
I CAN HIT HARDER, TOO.
PUSH IT.

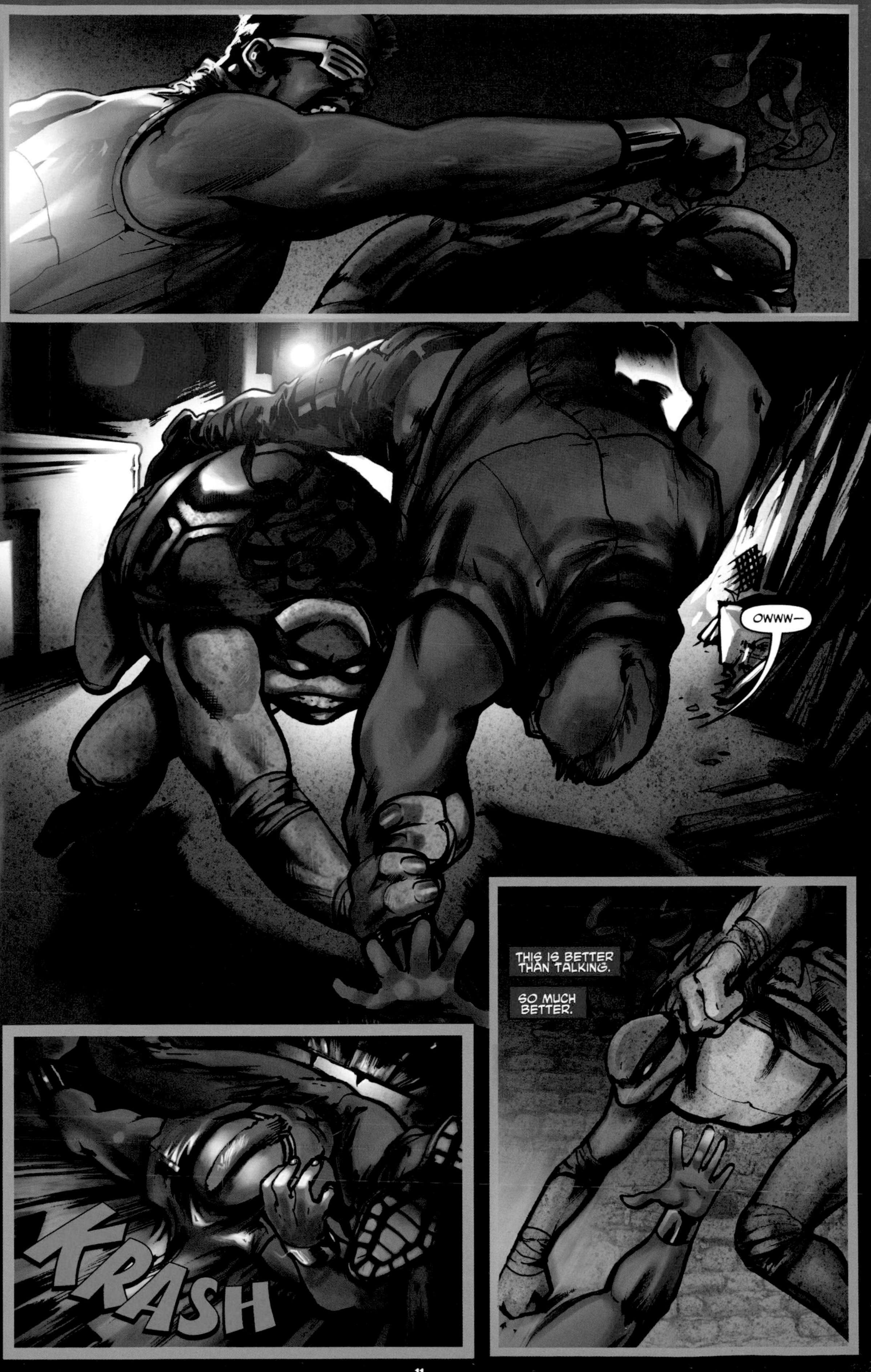
OWWW—
THIS IS BETTER THAN TALKING.
SO MUCH BETTER.
KRASH

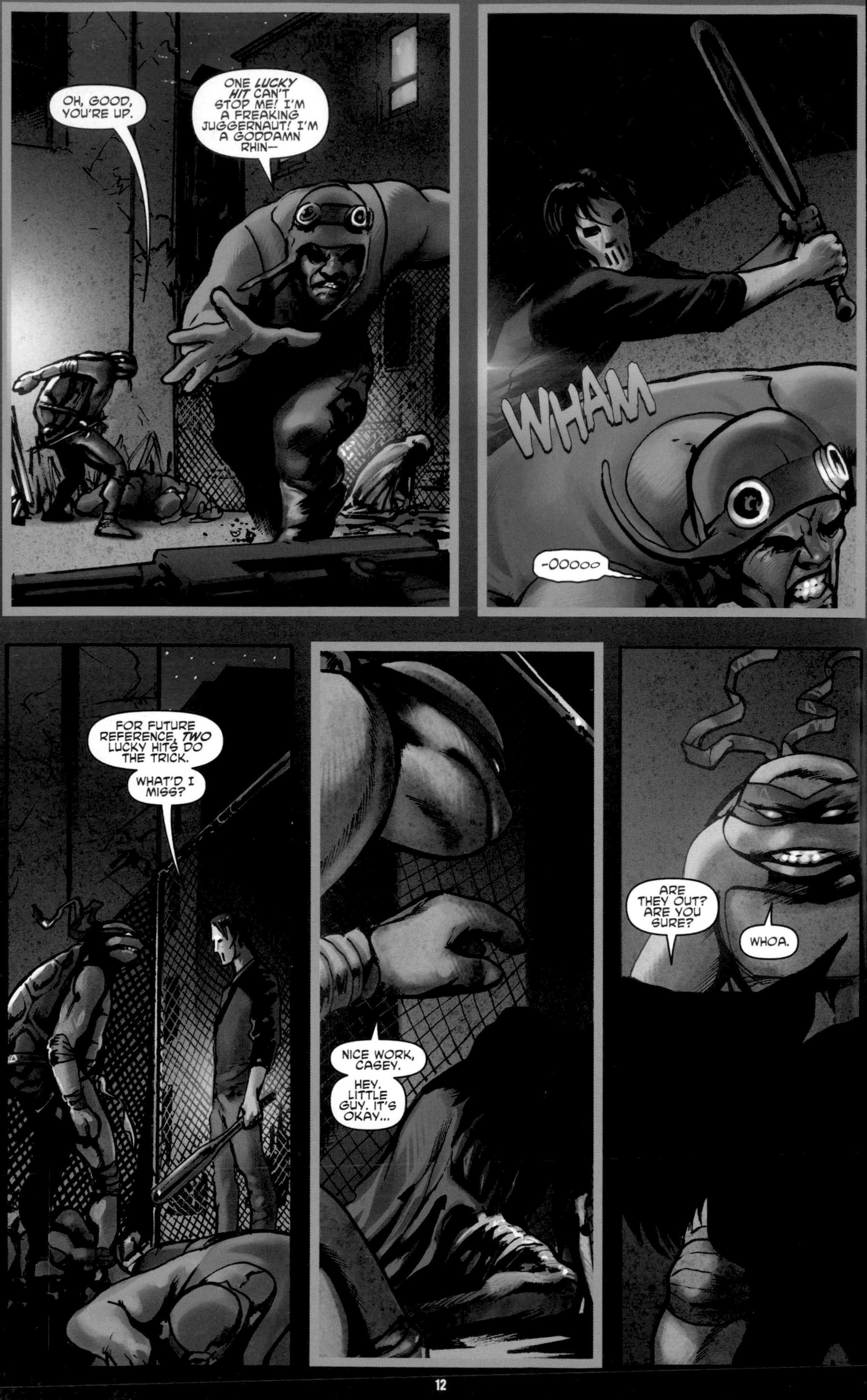
OH, GOOD, YOU'RE UP.
ONE LUCKY HIT CAN'T STOP ME! I'M A FREAKING JUGGERNAUT! I'M A GODDAMN RHIN—
WHAM
-OOOOO
FOR FUTURE REFERENCE, TWO LUCKY HITS DO THE TRICK.
WHAT'D I MISS?
NICE WORK, CASEY.
HEY. LITTLE GUY. IT'S OKAY...
ARE THEY OUT? ARE YOU SURE?
WHOA.

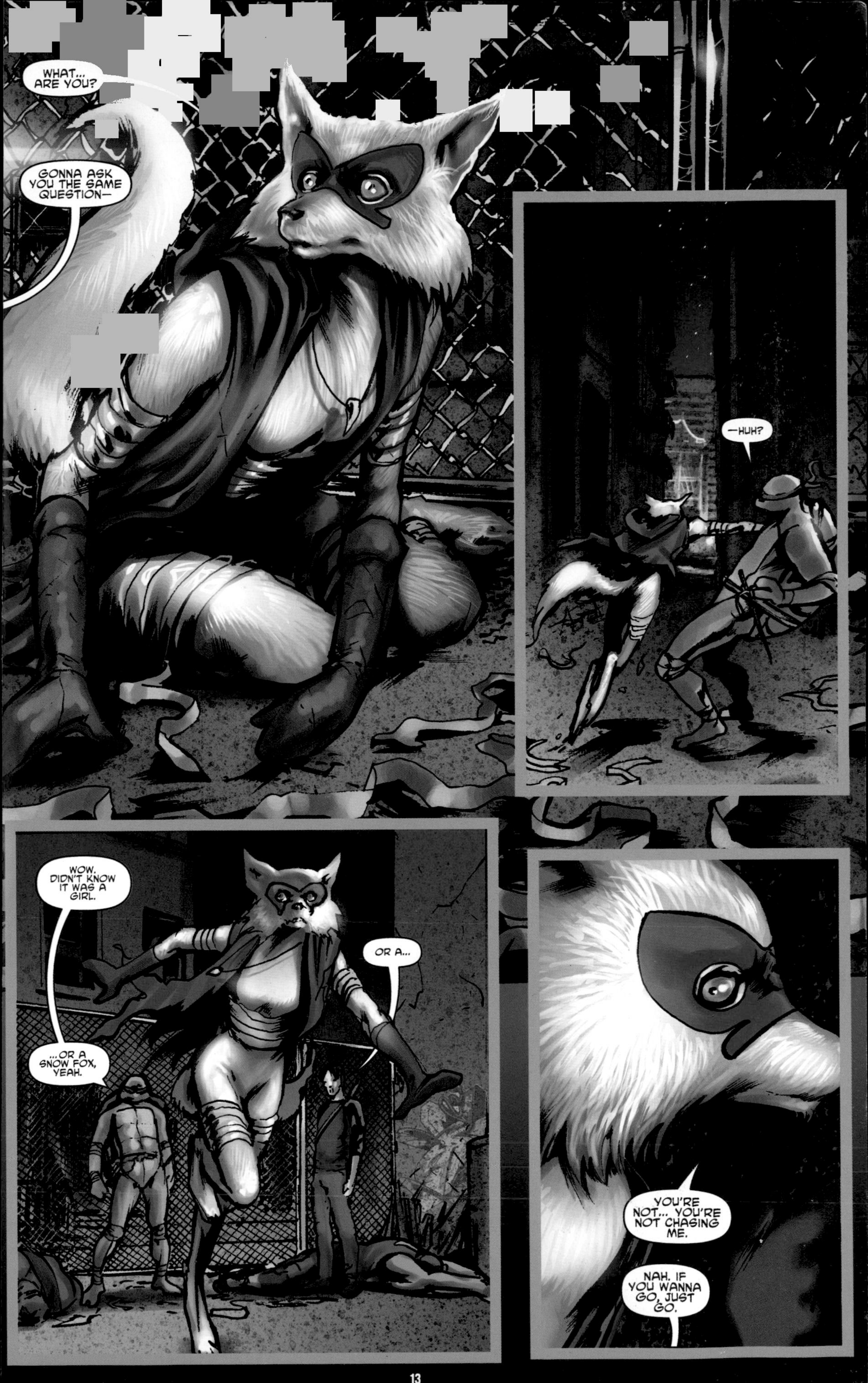

WHAT... ARE YOU?
GONNA ASK YOU THE SAME QUESTION—
—HUH?
WOW. DIDN'T KNOW IT WAS A GIRL.
OR A...
...OR A SNOW FOX, YEAH.
YOU'RE NOT... YOU'RE NOT CHASING ME.
NAH. IF YOU WANNA GO, JUST GO.

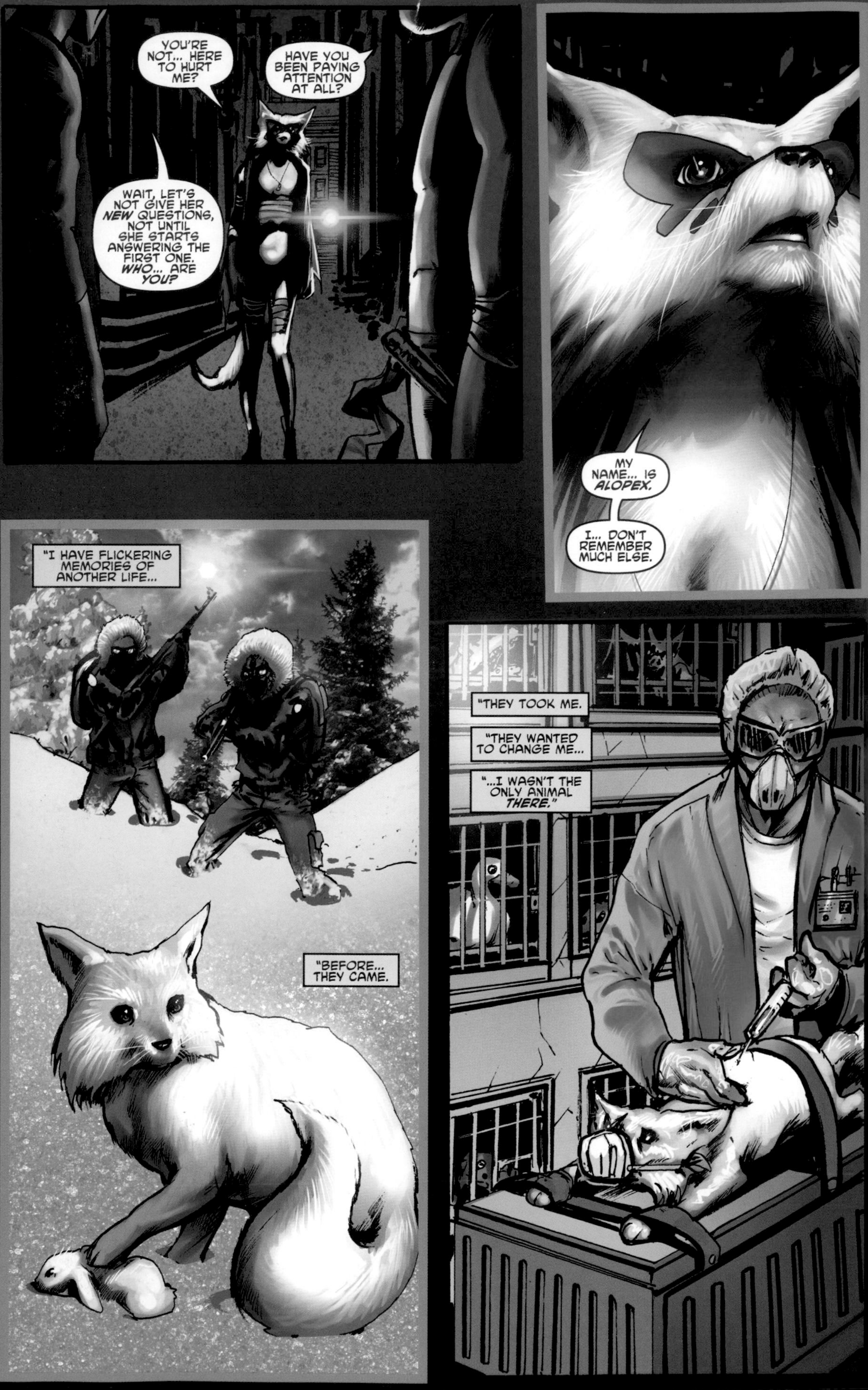
YOU'RE NOT... HERE TO HURT ME?
HAVE YOU BEEN PAYING ATTENTION AT ALL?
WAIT, LET'S NOT GIVE HER *NEW* QUESTIONS, NOT UNTIL SHE STARTS ANSWERING THE FIRST ONE. *WHO*... ARE *YOU*?
MY NAME... IS *ALOPEX.*
I... DON'T REMEMBER MUCH ELSE.
"I HAVE FLICKERING MEMORIES OF ANOTHER LIFE...
"BEFORE... THEY CAME.
"THEY TOOK ME.
"THEY WANTED TO CHANGE ME...
"...I WASN'T THE ONLY ANIMAL *THERE.*"

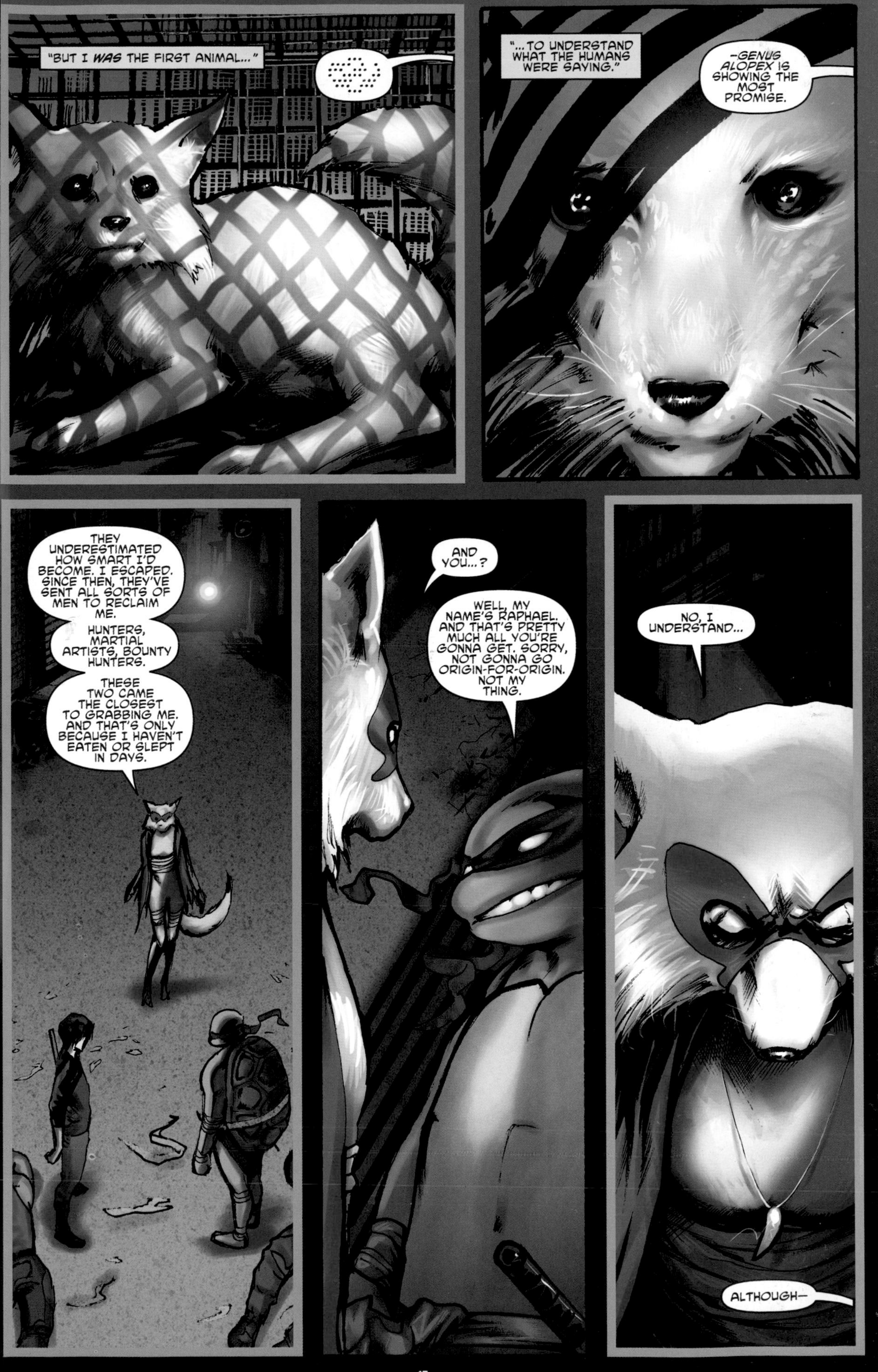

"BUT I *WAS* THE FIRST ANIMAL..."
"...TO UNDERSTAND WHAT THE HUMANS WERE SAYING."
–GENUS *ALOPEX* IS SHOWING THE MOST PROMISE.
THEY UNDERESTIMATED HOW SMART I'D BECOME. I ESCAPED. SINCE THEN, THEY'VE SENT ALL SORTS OF MEN TO RECLAIM ME.
HUNTERS, MARTIAL ARTISTS, BOUNTY HUNTERS.
THESE TWO CAME THE CLOSEST TO GRABBING ME. AND THAT'S ONLY BECAUSE I HAVEN'T EATEN OR SLEPT IN DAYS.
AND YOU...?
WELL, MY NAME'S RAPHAEL. AND THAT'S PRETTY MUCH ALL YOU'RE GONNA GET. SORRY, NOT GONNA GO ORIGIN-FOR-ORIGIN. NOT MY THING.
NO, I UNDERSTAND...
ALTHOUGH–

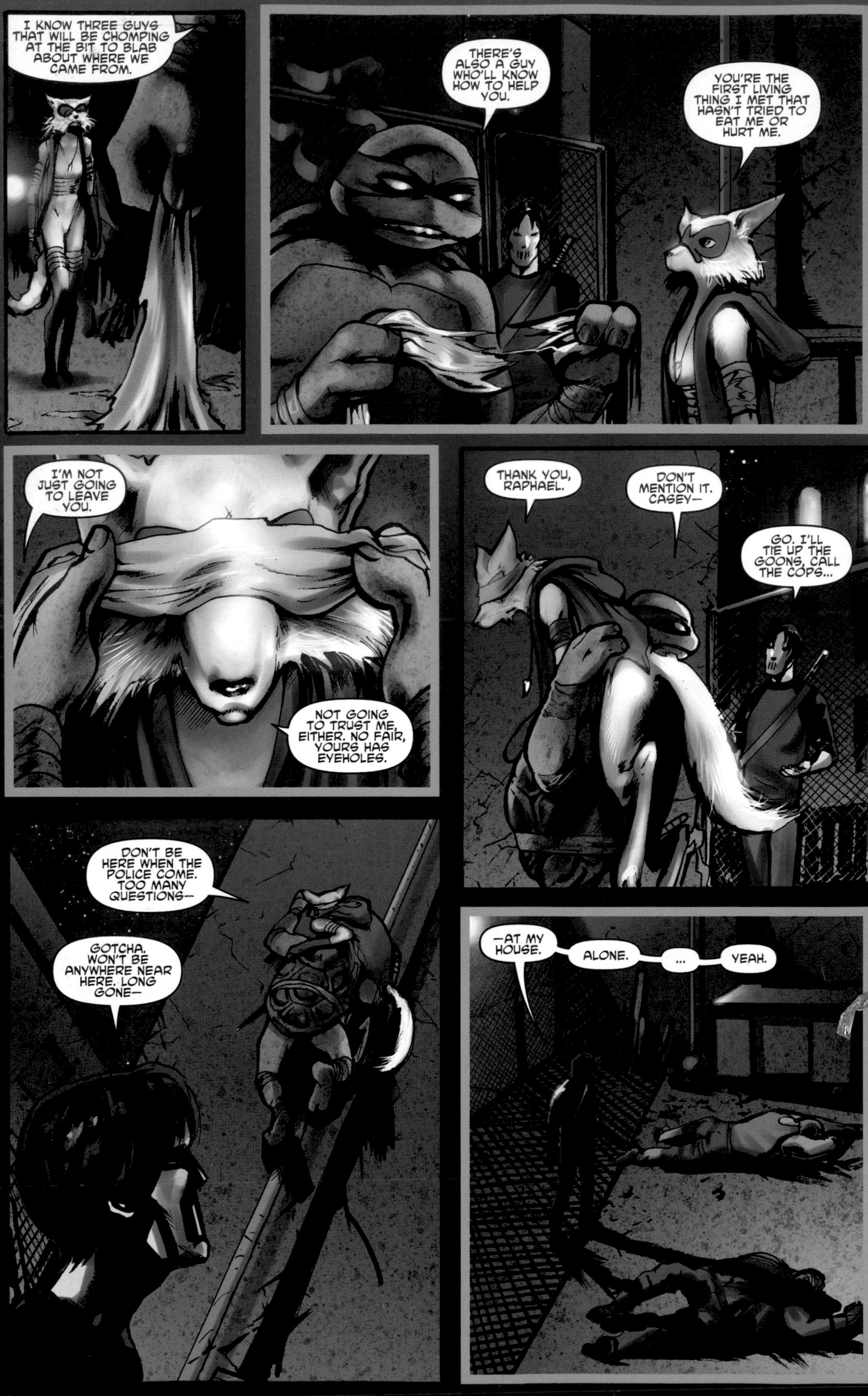
I KNOW THREE GUYS THAT WILL BE CHOMPING AT THE BIT TO BLAB ABOUT WHERE WE CAME FROM.
THERE'S ALSO A GUY WHO'LL KNOW HOW TO HELP YOU.
YOU'RE THE FIRST LIVING THING I MET THAT HASN'T TRIED TO EAT ME OR HURT ME.
I'M NOT JUST GOING TO LEAVE YOU.
NOT GOING TO TRUST ME, EITHER. NO FAIR, YOURS HAS EYEHOLES.
THANK YOU, RAPHAEL.
DON'T MENTION IT. CASEY—
GO. I'LL TIE UP THE GOONS, CALL THE COPS...
DON'T BE HERE WHEN THE POLICE COME. TOO MANY QUESTIONS—
GOTCHA. WON'T BE ANYWHERE NEAR HERE. LONG GONE—
—AT MY HOUSE.
ALONE.
...
YEAH.

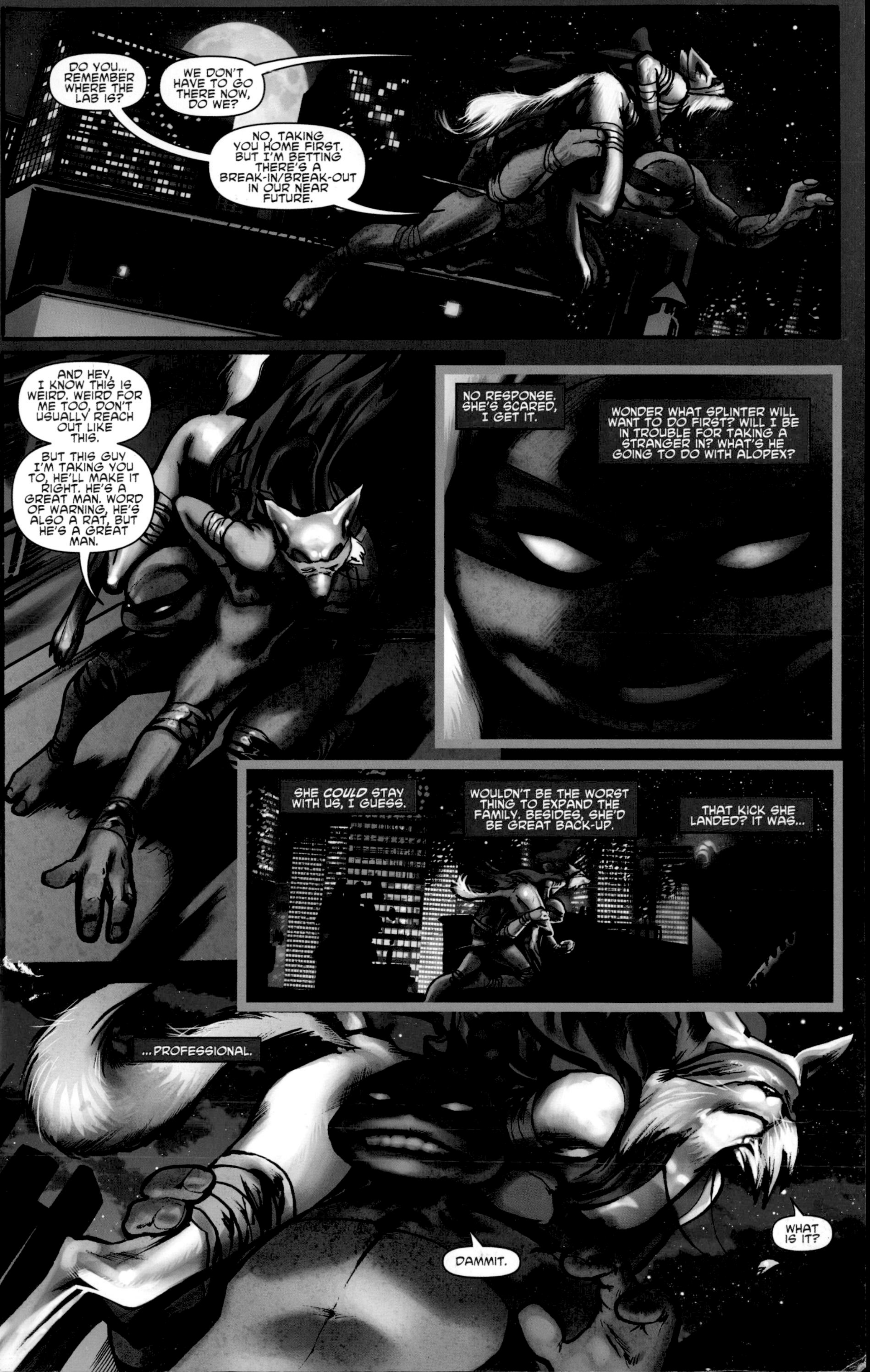
DO YOU... REMEMBER WHERE THE LAB IS?
WE DON'T HAVE TO GO THERE NOW, DO WE?
NO, TAKING YOU HOME FIRST. BUT I'M BETTING THERE'S A BREAK-IN/BREAK-OUT IN OUR NEAR FUTURE.
AND HEY, I KNOW THIS IS WEIRD. WEIRD FOR ME TOO, DON'T USUALLY REACH OUT LIKE THIS.
BUT THIS GUY I'M TAKING YOU TO, HE'LL MAKE IT RIGHT. HE'S A GREAT MAN. WORD OF WARNING, HE'S ALSO A RAT, BUT HE'S A GREAT MAN.
NO RESPONSE. SHE'S SCARED, I GET IT.
WONDER WHAT SPLINTER WILL WANT TO DO FIRST? WILL I BE IN TROUBLE FOR TAKING A STRANGER IN? WHAT'S HE GOING TO DO WITH ALOPEX?
SHE *COULD* STAY WITH US, I GUESS.
WOULDN'T BE THE WORST THING TO EXPAND THE FAMILY. BESIDES, SHE'D BE GREAT BACK-UP.
THAT KICK SHE LANDED? IT WAS...
...PROFESSIONAL.
DAMMIT.
WHAT IS IT?

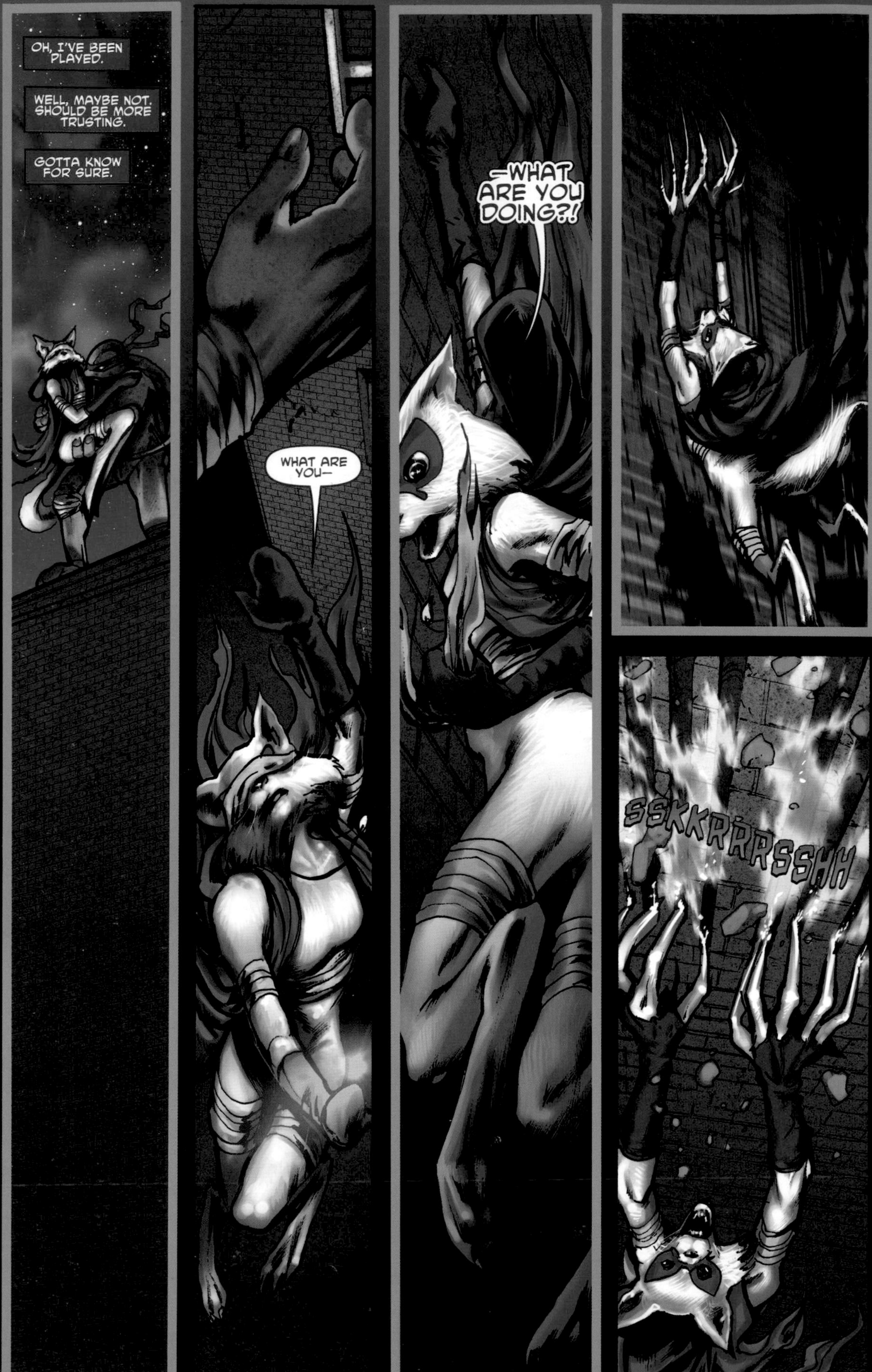
OH, I'VE BEEN PLAYED.
WELL, MAYBE NOT. SHOULD BE MORE TRUSTING.
GOTTA KNOW FOR SURE.
WHAT ARE YOU—
—WHAT ARE YOU DOING?!
SSKKRRRSSHH

YOU SAVED ME SO YOU COULD *DROP ME?!* WHAT ARE YOU—?

I WOULDA CAUGHT YOU IF YOU NEEDED IT.

BUT YOU DIDN'T, DID YOU?

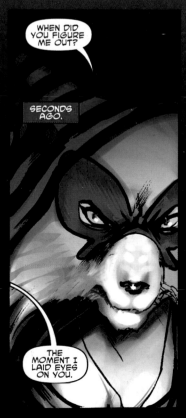

WHEN DID YOU FIGURE ME OUT?

SECONDS AGO.

THE MOMENT I LAID EYES ON YOU.

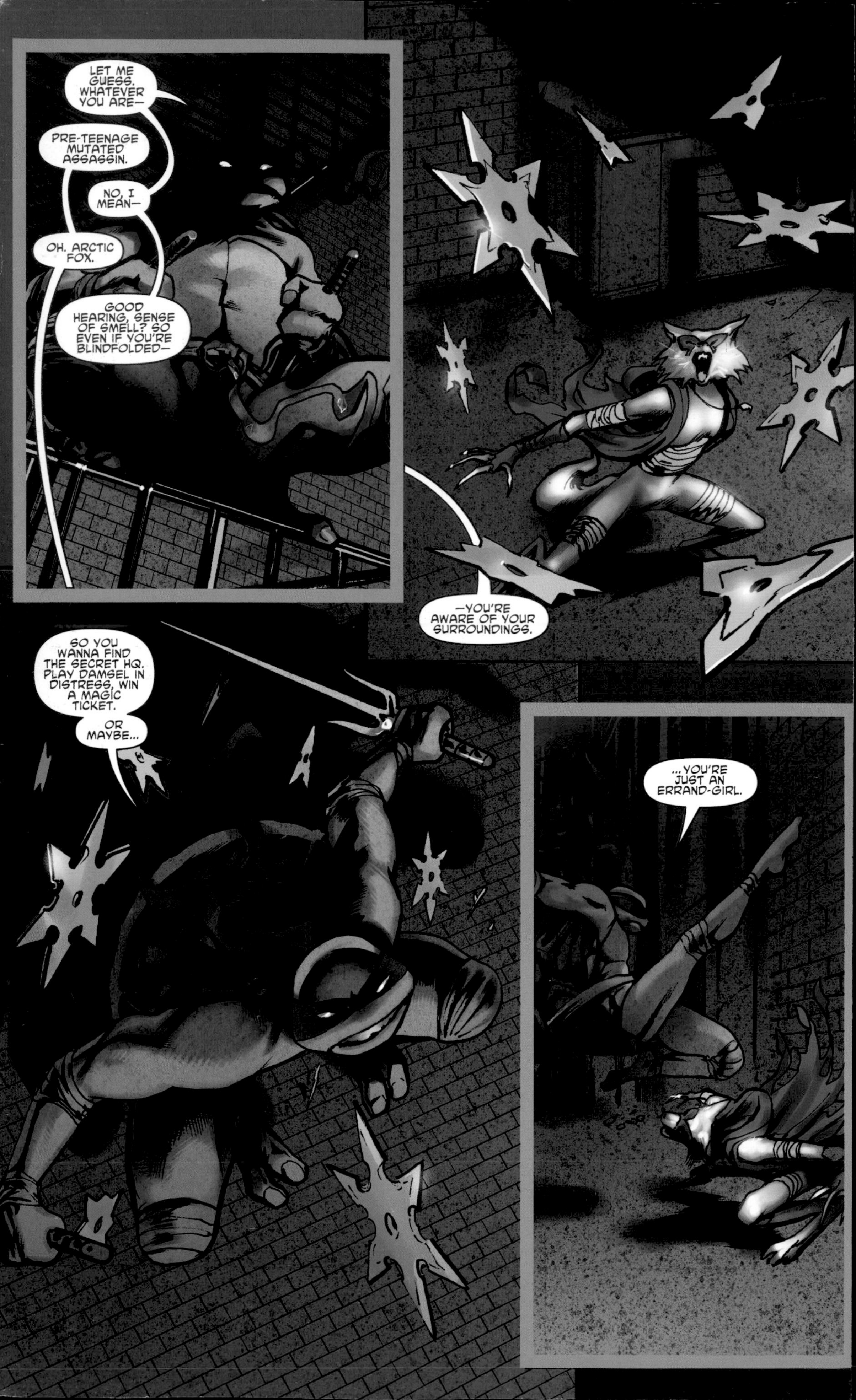
LET ME GUESS. WHATEVER YOU ARE—
PRE-TEENAGE MUTATED ASSASSIN.
NO, I MEAN—
OH. ARCTIC FOX.
GOOD HEARING, SENSE OF SMELL? SO EVEN IF YOU'RE BLINDFOLDED—
—YOU'RE AWARE OF YOUR SURROUNDINGS.
SO YOU WANNA FIND THE SECRET HQ. PLAY DAMSEL IN DISTRESS, WIN A MAGIC TICKET.
OR MAYBE...
...YOU'RE JUST AN ERRAND-GIRL.

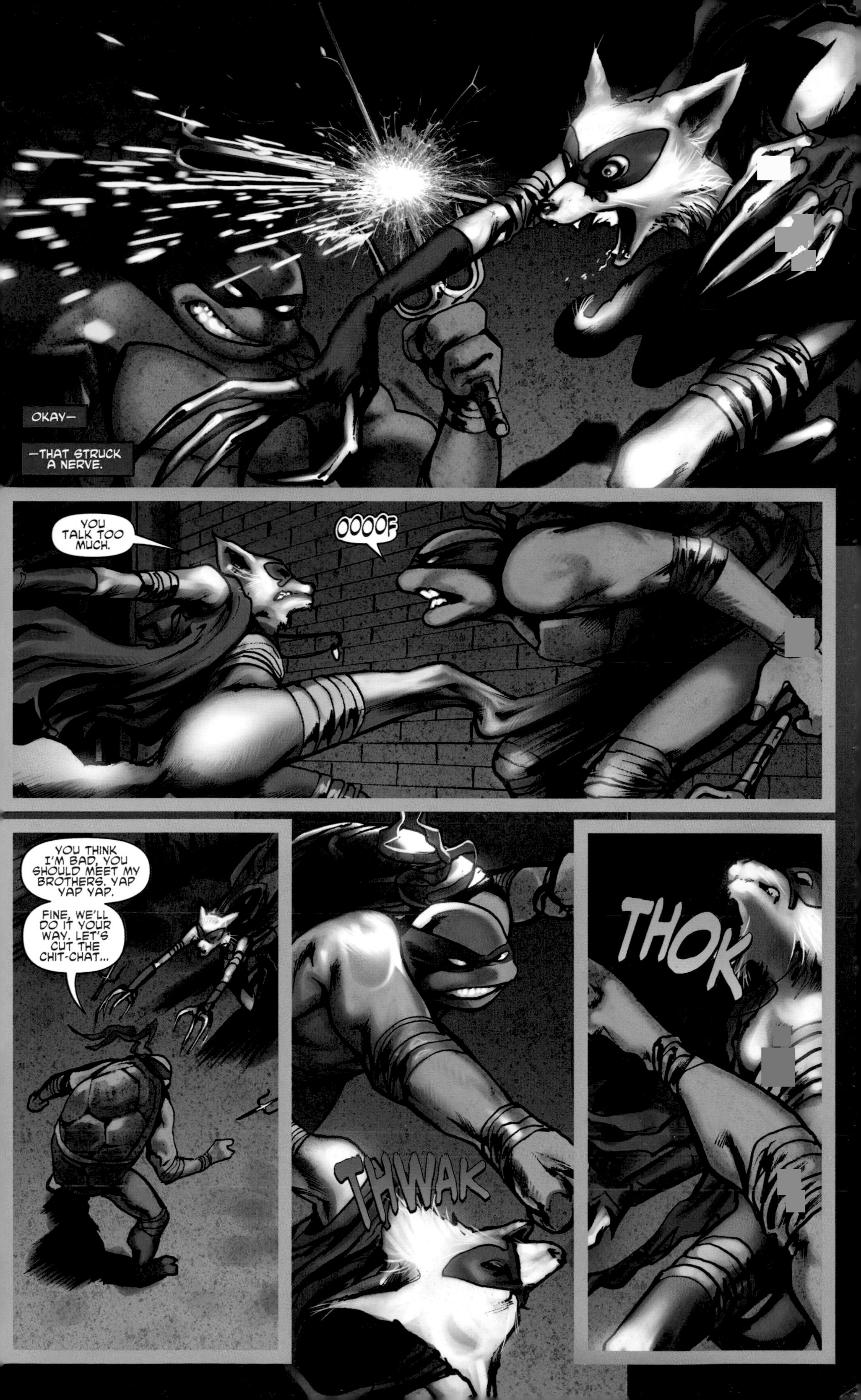
OKAY—
—THAT STRUCK A NERVE.
YOU TALK TOO MUCH.
OOOOF
YOU THINK I'M BAD, YOU SHOULD MEET MY BROTHERS. YAP YAP YAP.
FINE, WE'LL DO IT YOUR WAY. LET'S CUT THE CHIT-CHAT...
THWAK
THOK

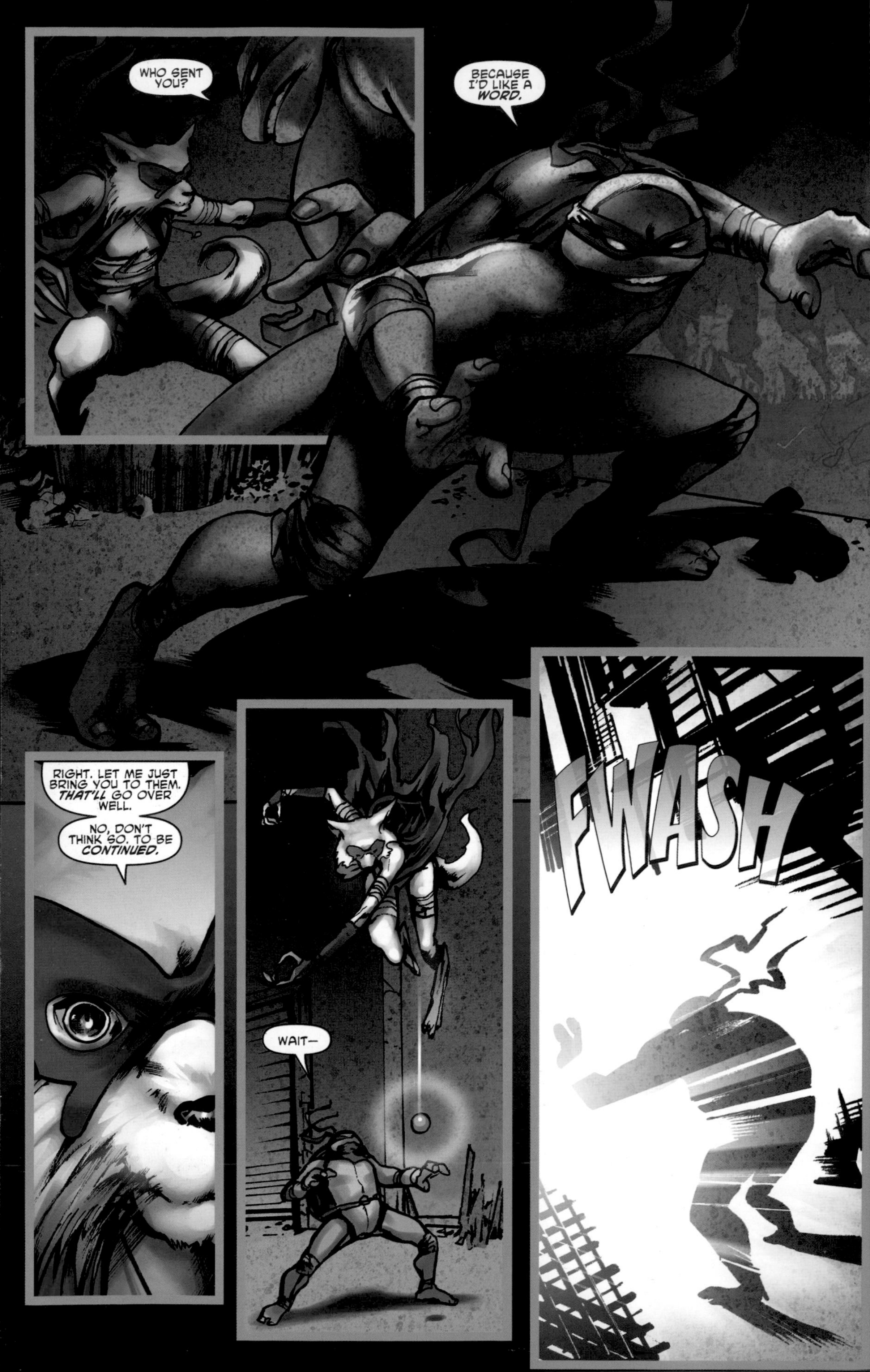
WHO SENT YOU?
BECAUSE I'D LIKE A *WORD.*
RIGHT. LET ME JUST BRING YOU TO THEM. *THAT'LL* GO OVER WELL.
NO, DON'T THINK SO. TO BE *CONTINUED.*
WAIT—
FWASH

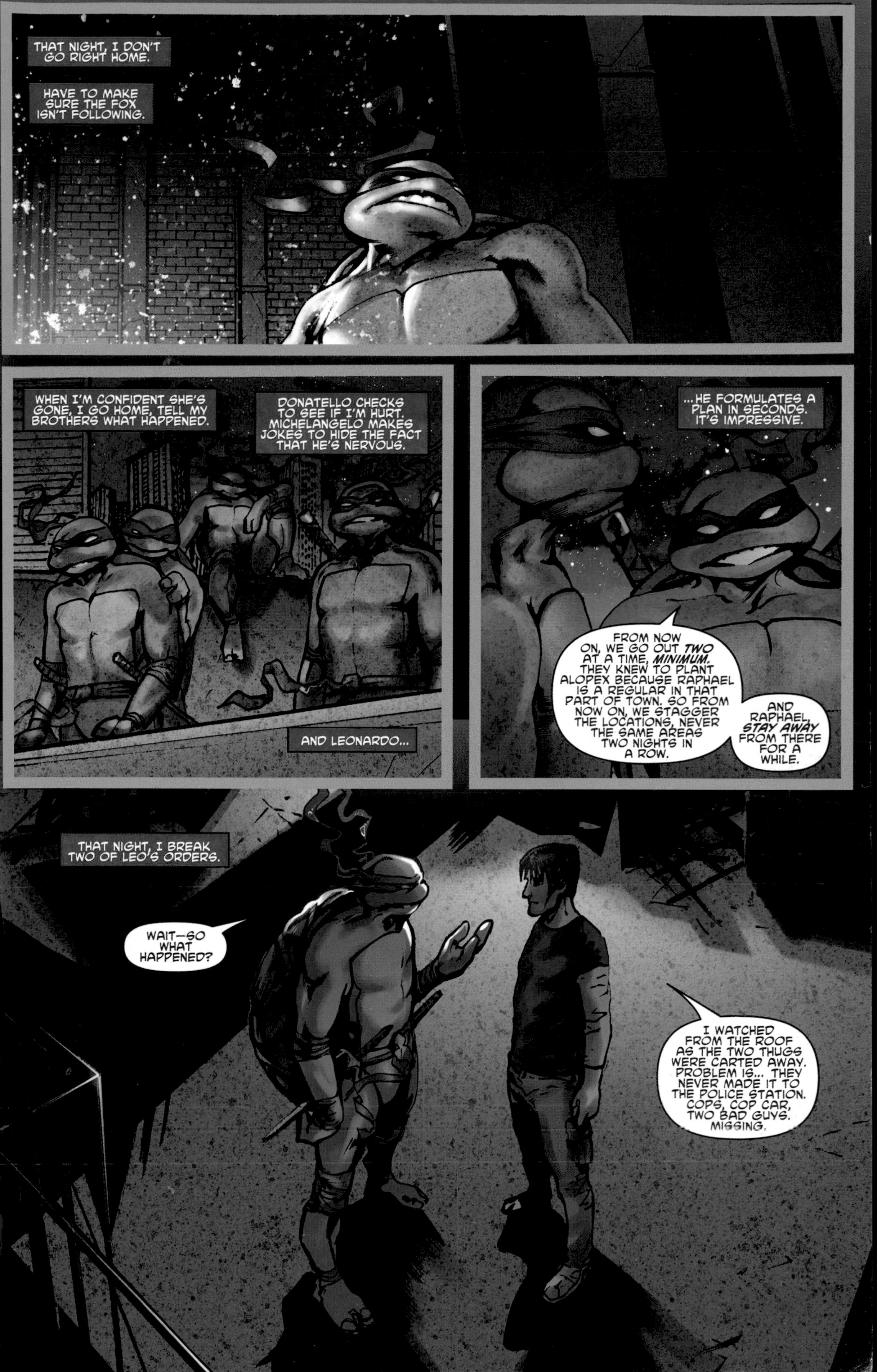

THAT NIGHT, I DON'T GO RIGHT HOME.
HAVE TO MAKE SURE THE FOX ISN'T FOLLOWING.
WHEN I'M CONFIDENT SHE'S GONE, I GO HOME, TELL MY BROTHERS WHAT HAPPENED.
DONATELLO CHECKS TO SEE IF I'M HURT. MICHELANGELO MAKES JOKES TO HIDE THE FACT THAT HE'S NERVOUS.
AND LEONARDO...
...HE FORMULATES A PLAN IN SECONDS. IT'S IMPRESSIVE.
FROM NOW ON, WE GO OUT TWO AT A TIME, MINIMUM. THEY KNEW TO PLANT ALOPEX BECAUSE RAPHAEL IS A REGULAR IN THAT PART OF TOWN. SO FROM NOW ON, WE STAGGER THE LOCATIONS, NEVER THE SAME AREAS TWO NIGHTS IN A ROW.
AND RAPHAEL, STAY AWAY FROM THERE FOR A WHILE.
THAT NIGHT, I BREAK TWO OF LEO'S ORDERS.
WAIT—SO WHAT HAPPENED?
I WATCHED FROM THE ROOF AS THE TWO THUGS WERE CARTED AWAY. PROBLEM IS... THEY NEVER MADE IT TO THE POLICE STATION. COPS, COP CAR, TWO BAD GUYS. MISSING.

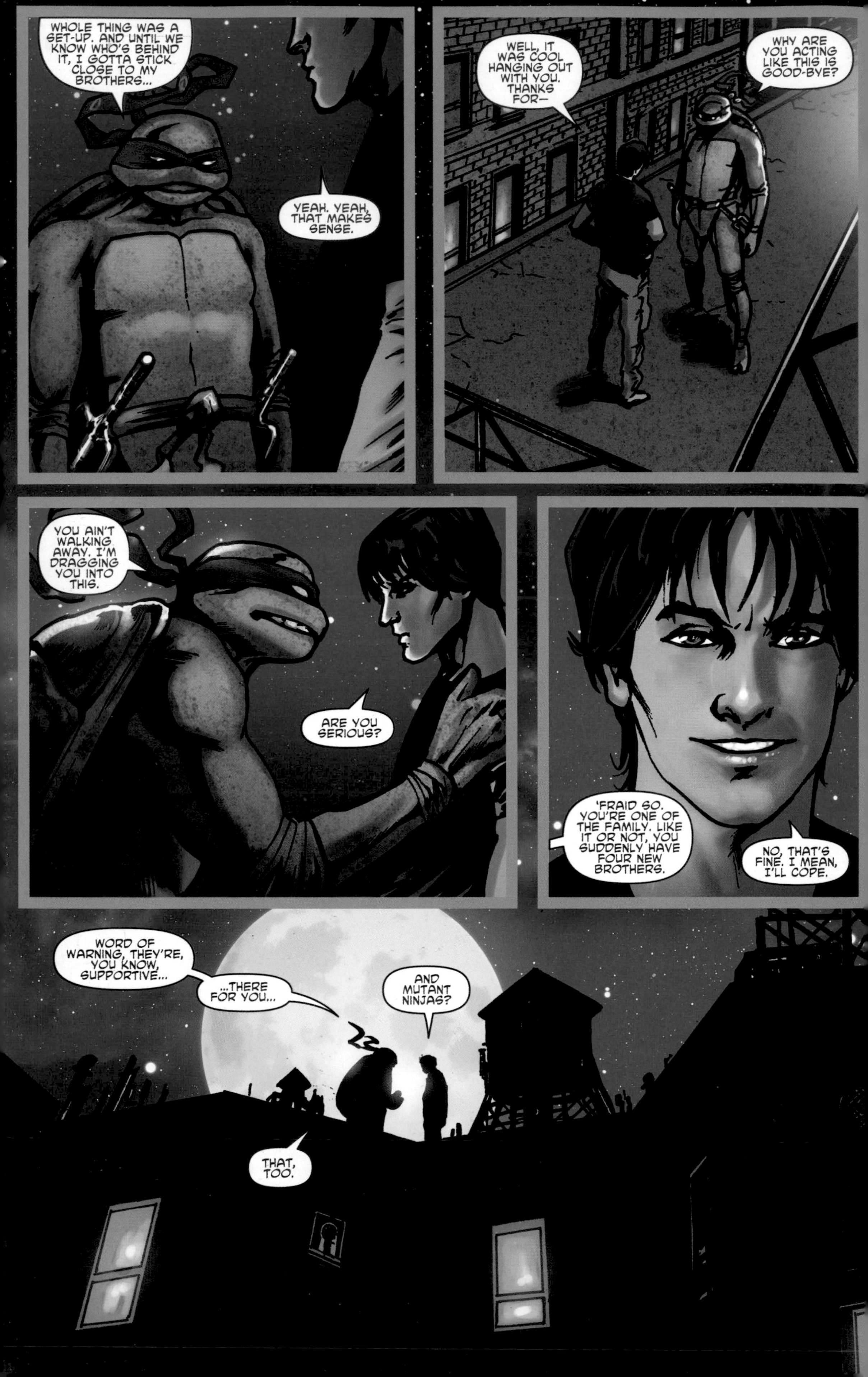
WHOLE THING WAS A SET-UP. AND UNTIL WE KNOW WHO'S BEHIND IT, I GOTTA STICK CLOSE TO MY BROTHERS...
YEAH. YEAH, THAT MAKES SENSE.
WELL, IT WAS COOL HANGING OUT WITH YOU. THANKS FOR—
WHY ARE YOU ACTING LIKE THIS IS GOOD-BYE?
YOU AIN'T WALKING AWAY. I'M DRAGGING YOU INTO THIS.
ARE YOU SERIOUS?
'FRAID SO. YOU'RE ONE OF THE FAMILY. LIKE IT OR NOT, YOU SUDDENLY HAVE FOUR NEW BROTHERS.
NO, THAT'S FINE. I MEAN, I'LL COPE.
WORD OF WARNING, THEY'RE, YOU KNOW, SUPPORTIVE...
...THERE FOR YOU...
AND MUTANT NINJAS?
THAT, TOO.

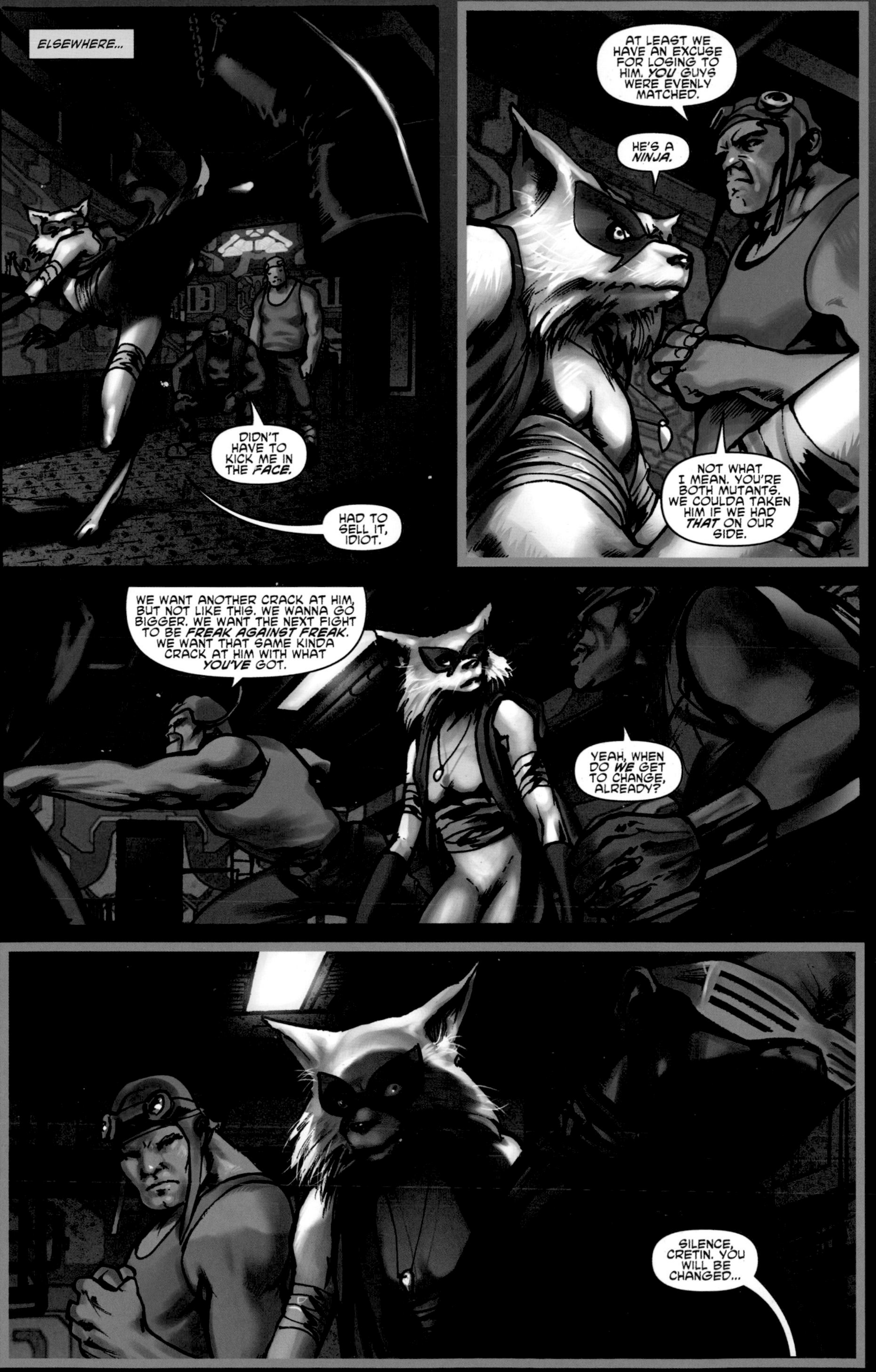
ELSEWHERE...
DIDN'T HAVE TO KICK ME IN THE *FACE.*
HAD TO SELL IT, IDIOT.
AT LEAST WE HAVE AN EXCUSE FOR LOSING TO HIM. *YOU* GUYS WERE EVENLY MATCHED.
HE'S A *NINJA.*
NOT WHAT I MEAN. YOU'RE BOTH MUTANTS. WE COULDA TAKEN HIM IF WE HAD *THAT* ON OUR SIDE.
WE WANT ANOTHER CRACK AT HIM, BUT NOT LIKE THIS. WE WANNA GO BIGGER. WE WANT THE NEXT FIGHT TO BE *FREAK AGAINST FREAK.* WE WANT THAT SAME KINDA CRACK AT HIM WITH WHAT *YOU'VE* GOT.
YEAH, WHEN DO *WE* GET TO CHANGE, ALREADY?
SILENCE, CRETIN. YOU WILL BE CHANGED...

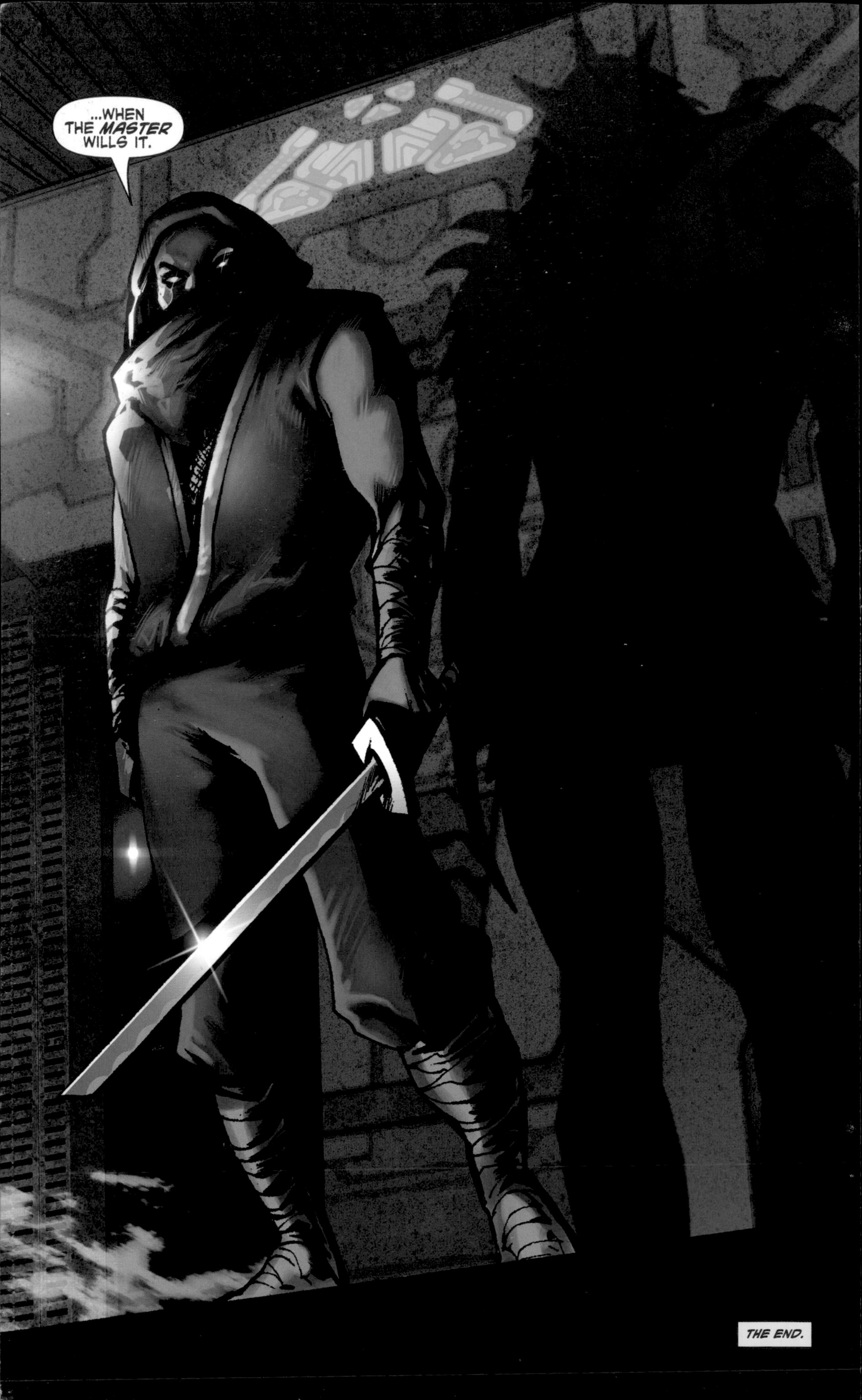

...WHEN THE *MASTER* WILLS IT.
THE END.

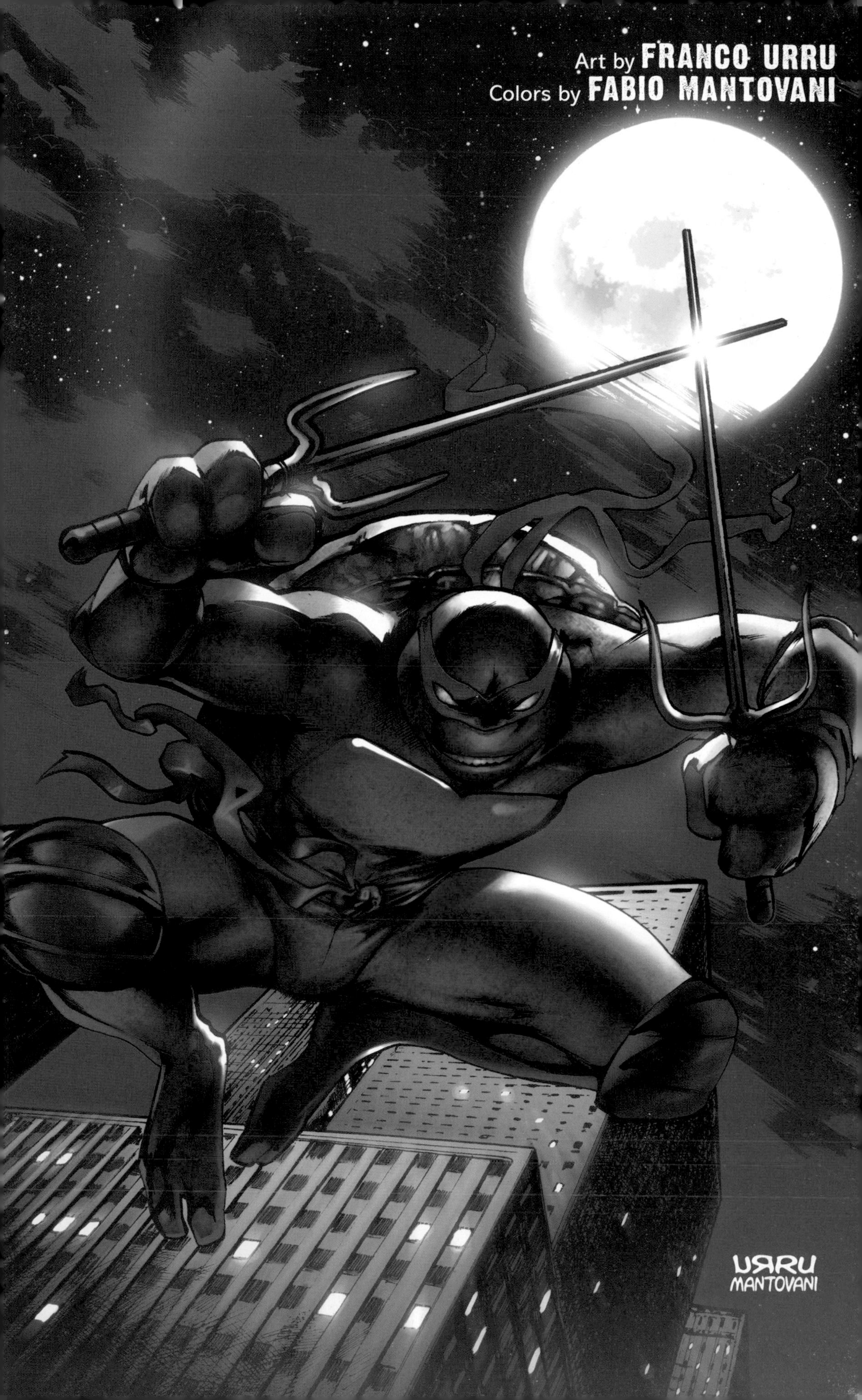
Art by FRANCO URRU
Colors by FABIO MANTOVANI
URRU
MANTOVANI

Art by **DAVID PETERSEN**

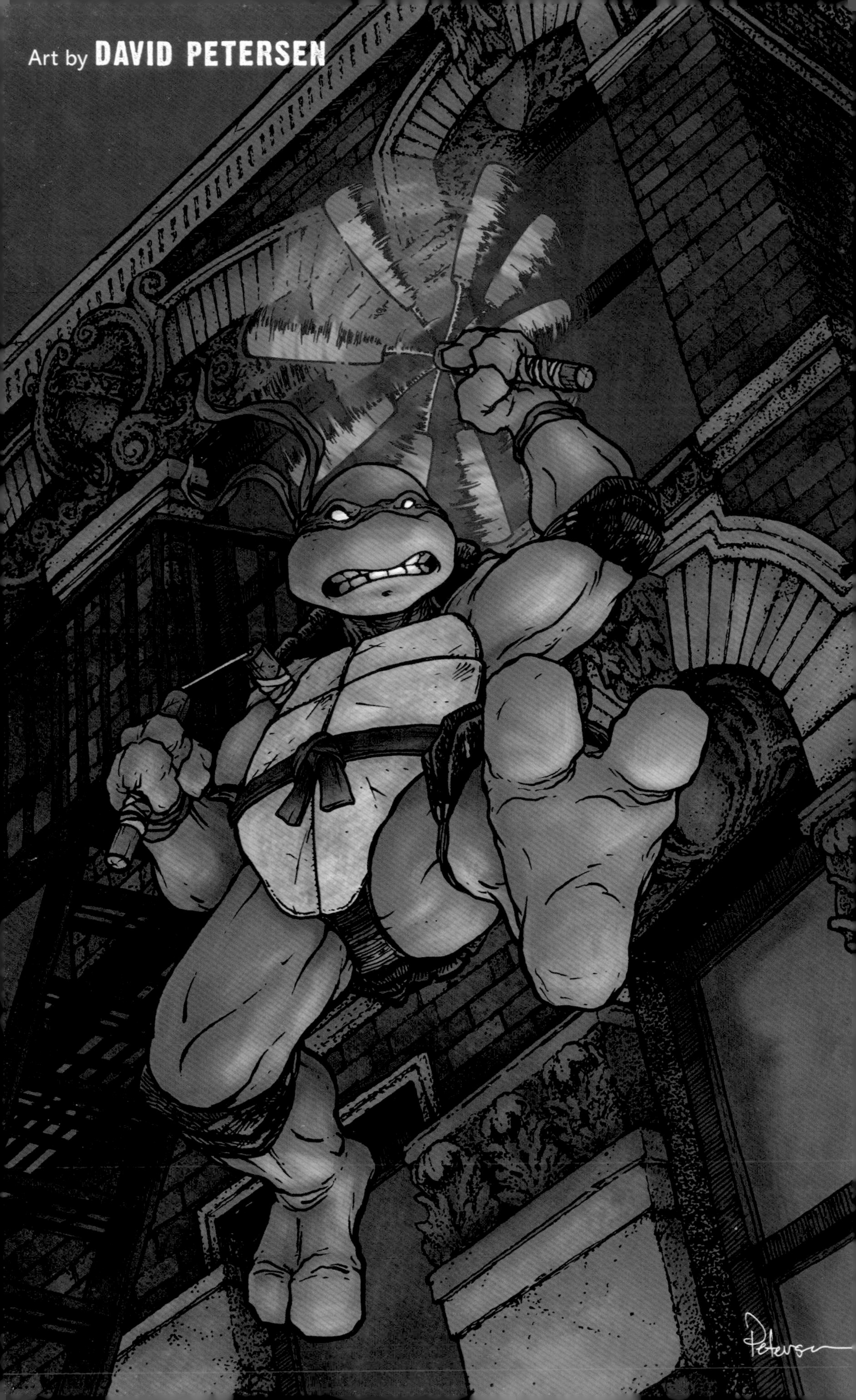
Petersen

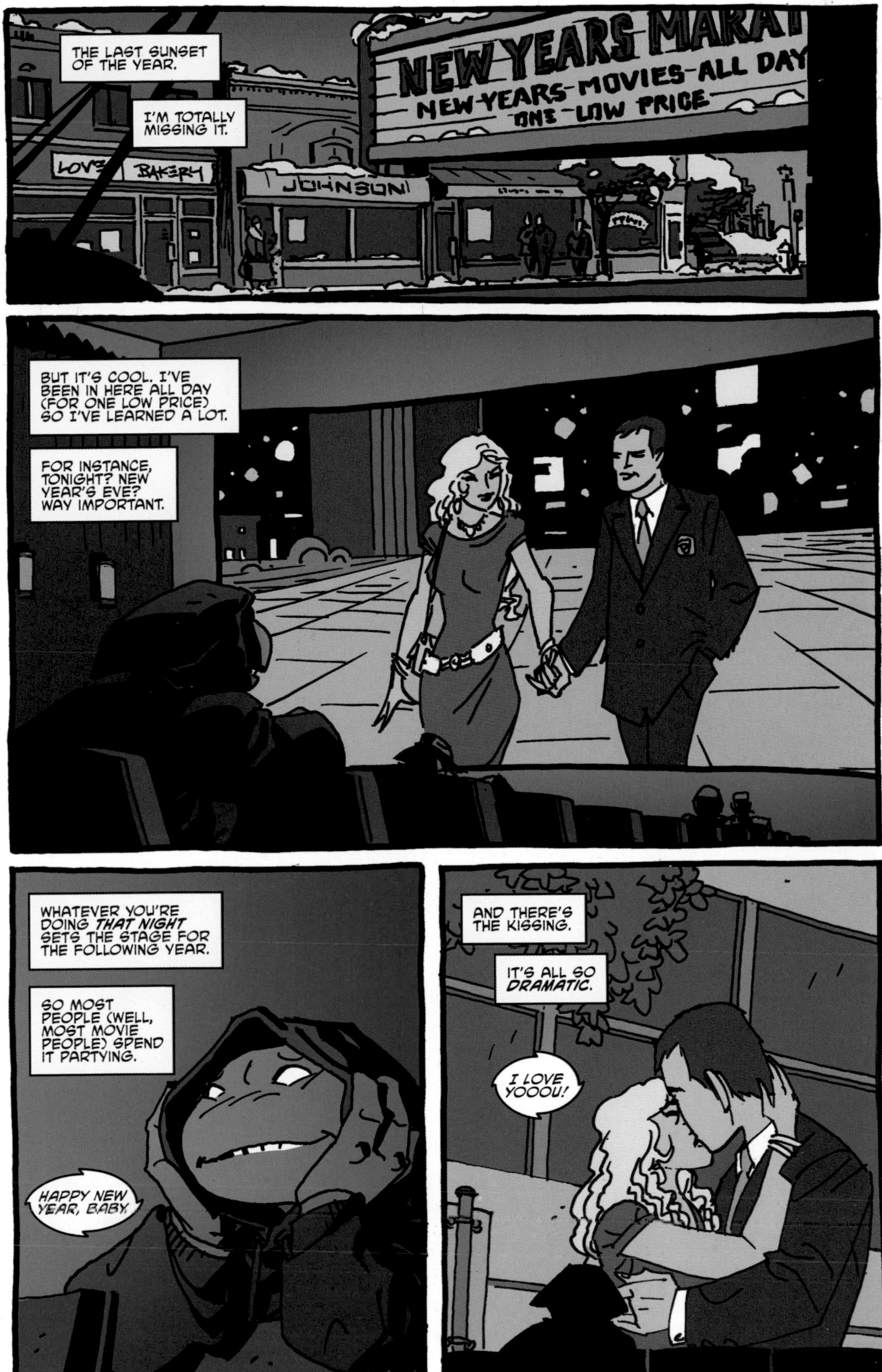
NEW YEARS MOVIES ALL DAY
ONE LOW PRICE
BAKERY
JOHNSON
THE LAST SUNSET OF THE YEAR.
I'M TOTALLY MISSING IT.
BUT IT'S COOL. I'VE BEEN IN HERE ALL DAY (FOR ONE LOW PRICE) SO I'VE LEARNED A LOT.
FOR INSTANCE, TONIGHT? NEW YEAR'S EVE? WAY IMPORTANT.
WHATEVER YOU'RE DOING *THAT NIGHT* SETS THE STAGE FOR THE FOLLOWING YEAR.
SO MOST PEOPLE (WELL, MOST MOVIE PEOPLE) SPEND IT PARTYING.
HAPPY NEW YEAR, BABY.
AND THERE'S THE KISSING.
IT'S ALL SO *DRAMATIC*.
I LOVE YOOOU!

EXIT
AND NOW...
...NOW I FEEL PRESSURE, TO, YOU KNOW, *DO SOMETHING* TONIGHT.
TIME'S RUNNING OUT! IT'S ALMOST MIDNIGHT AND I HAVE NO PLANS! NONE AT ALL! JUST ONCE, I WANT TO TAKE A BREAK FROM BEING...
MICHELANGELO
TEENAGE MUTANT NINJA TURTLE
I WANNA BE MICHELANGELO... *PARTY DUDE*.
HAPPY NEW YEAR

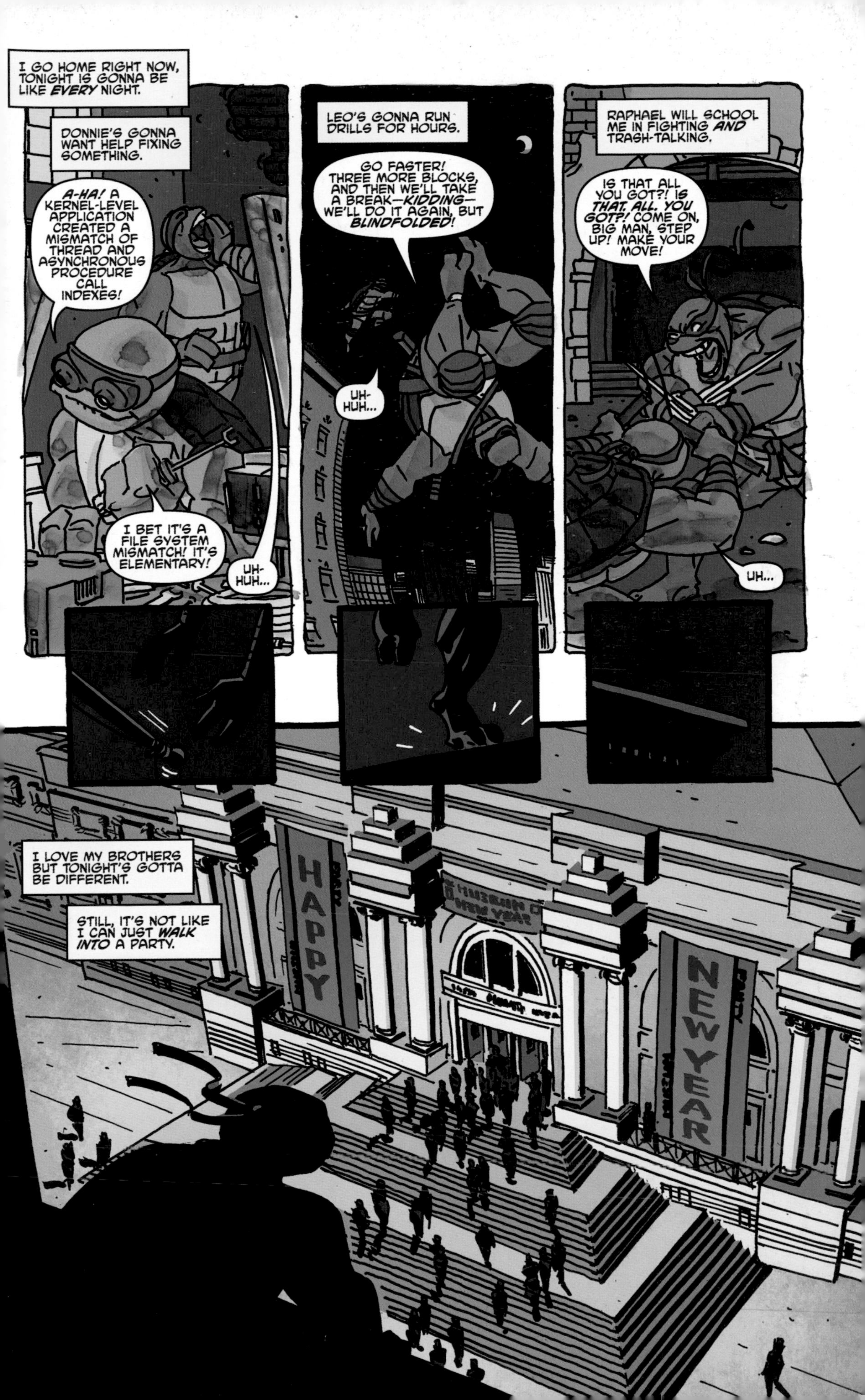

I GO HOME RIGHT NOW, TONIGHT IS GONNA BE LIKE *EVERY* NIGHT.
DONNIE'S GONNA WANT HELP FIXING SOMETHING.
A-HA! A KERNEL-LEVEL APPLICATION CREATED A MISMATCH OF THREAD AND ASYNCHRONOUS PROCEDURE CALL INDEXES!
I BET IT'S A FILE SYSTEM MISMATCH! IT'S ELEMENTARY!
UH-HUH...
LEO'S GONNA RUN DRILLS FOR HOURS.
GO FASTER! THREE MORE BLOCKS, AND THEN WE'LL TAKE A BREAK—*KIDDING*—WE'LL DO IT AGAIN, BUT *BLINDFOLDED*!
UH-HUH...
RAPHAEL WILL SCHOOL ME IN FIGHTING *AND* TRASH-TALKING.
IS THAT ALL YOU GOT?! IS *THAT. ALL. YOU GOT?!* COME ON, BIG MAN, STEP UP! MAKE YOUR MOVE!
UH...
I LOVE MY BROTHERS BUT TONIGHT'S GOTTA BE DIFFERENT.
STILL, IT'S NOT LIKE I CAN JUST *WALK INTO* A PARTY.
HAPPY
NEW YEAR

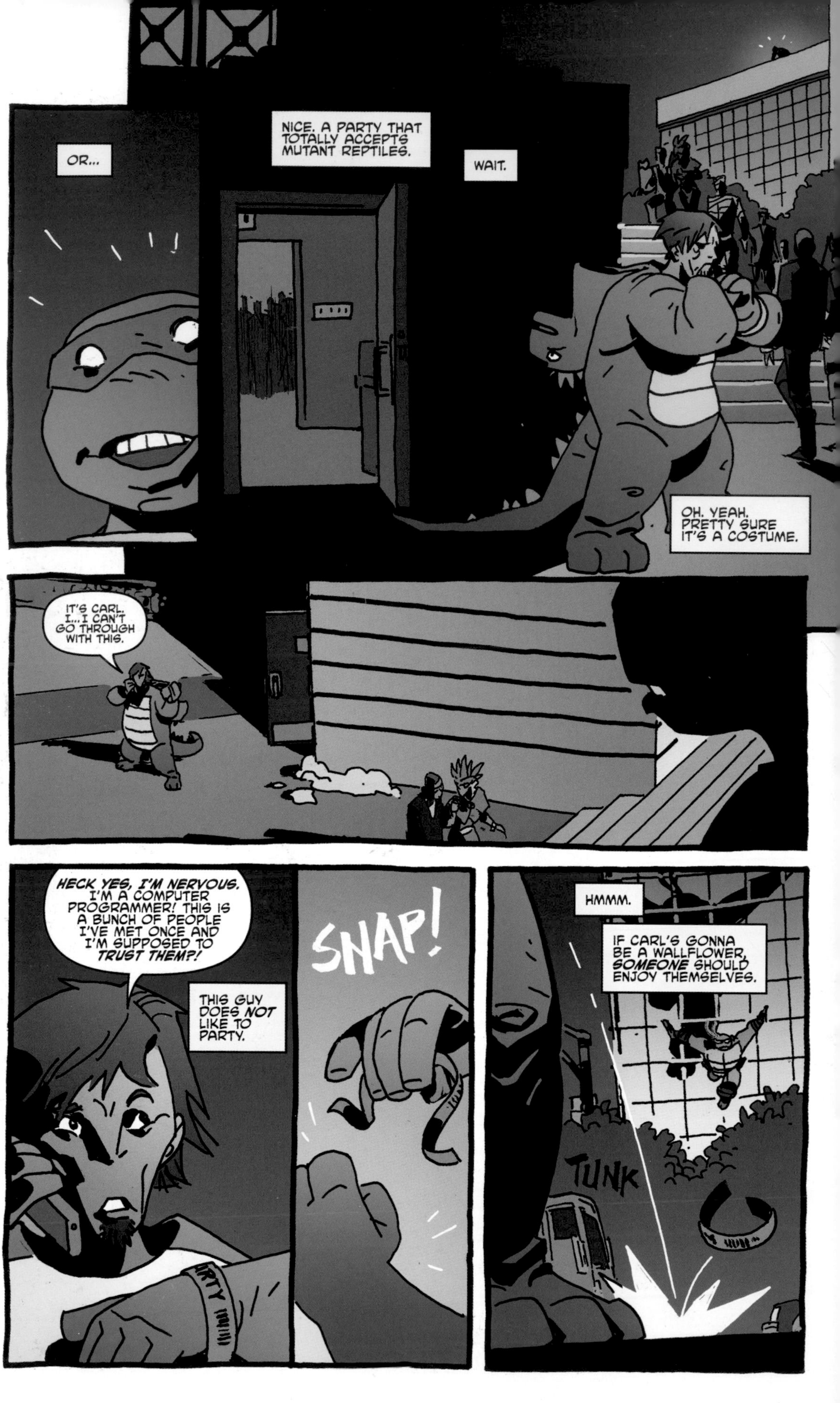
OR...
NICE. A PARTY THAT TOTALLY ACCEPTS MUTANT REPTILES.
WAIT.
OH. YEAH. PRETTY SURE IT'S A COSTUME.
IT'S CARL. I...I CAN'T GO THROUGH WITH THIS.
HECK YES, I'M NERVOUS. I'M A COMPUTER PROGRAMMER! THIS IS A BUNCH OF PEOPLE I'VE MET ONCE AND I'M SUPPOSED TO TRUST THEM?!
THIS GUY DOES NOT LIKE TO PARTY.
SNAP!
HMMM.
IF CARL'S GONNA BE A WALLFLOWER, SOMEONE SHOULD ENJOY THEMSELVES.
TUNK

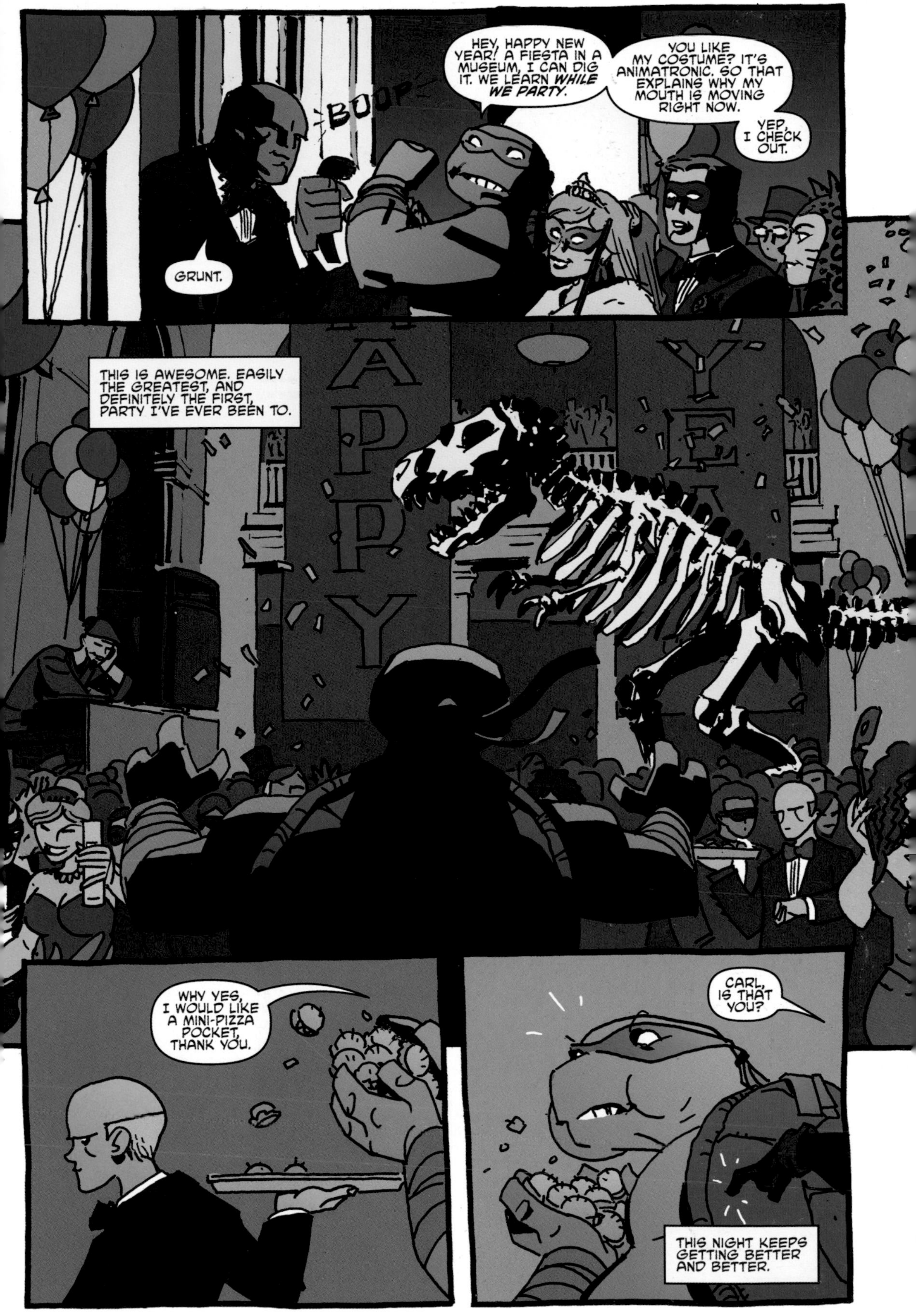
BOOP
HEY, HAPPY NEW YEAR! A FIESTA IN A MUSEUM, I CAN DIG IT. WE LEARN *WHILE WE PARTY*.
YOU LIKE MY COSTUME? IT'S ANIMATRONIC. SO THAT EXPLAINS WHY MY MOUTH IS MOVING RIGHT NOW.
YEP, I CHECK OUT.
GRUNT.
THIS IS AWESOME. EASILY THE GREATEST, AND DEFINITELY THE FIRST, PARTY I'VE EVER BEEN TO.
HAPPY
YE
WHY YES, I WOULD LIKE A MINI-PIZZA POCKET, THANK YOU.
CARL, IS THAT YOU?
THIS NIGHT KEEPS GETTING BETTER AND BETTER.

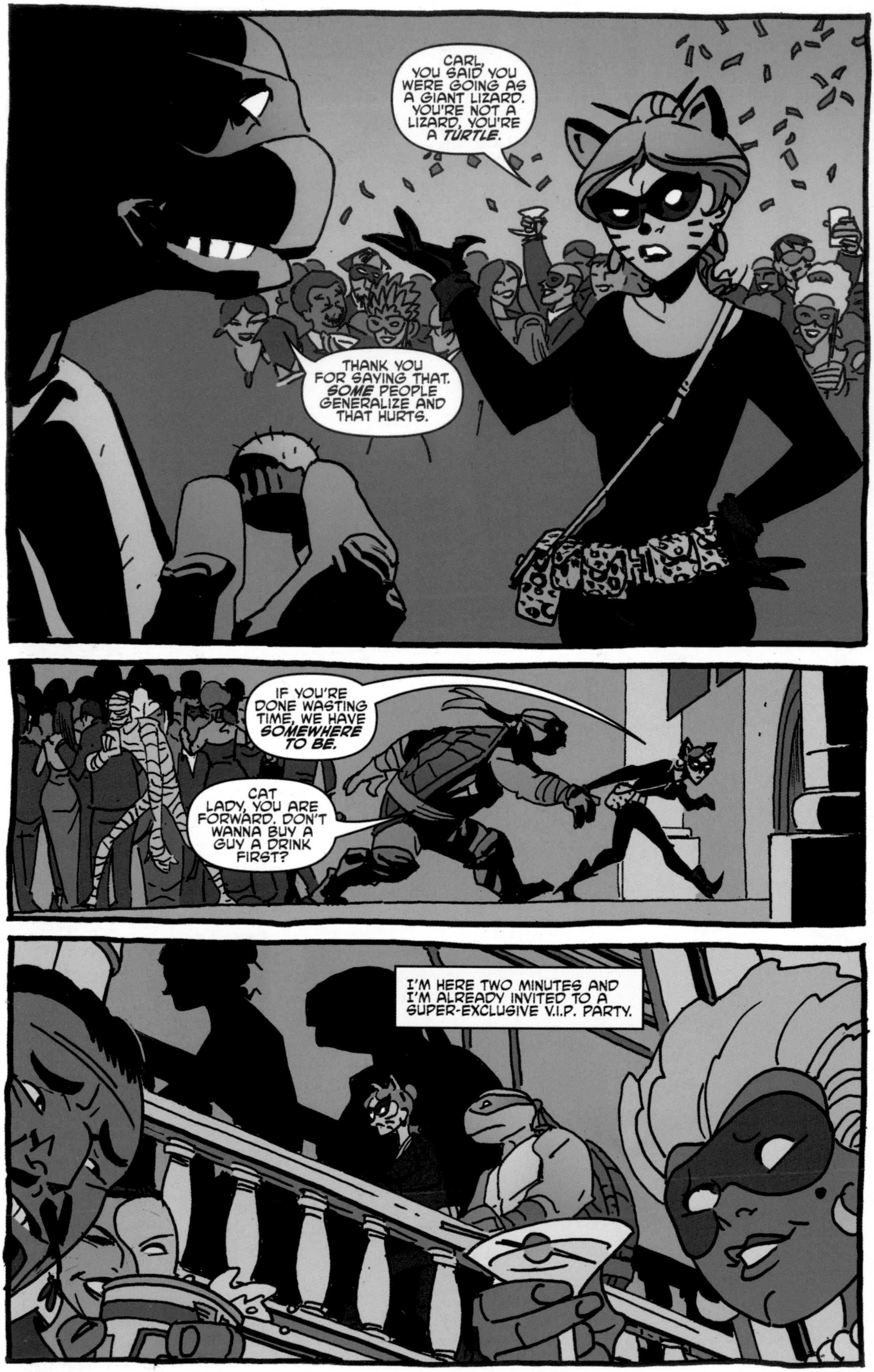
CARL, YOU SAID YOU WERE GOING AS A GIANT LIZARD. YOU'RE NOT A LIZARD, YOU'RE A *TURTLE*.
THANK YOU FOR SAYING THAT. *SOME* PEOPLE GENERALIZE AND THAT HURTS.
IF YOU'RE DONE WASTING TIME, WE HAVE *SOMEWHERE TO BE.*
CAT LADY, YOU ARE FORWARD. DON'T WANNA BUY A GUY A DRINK FIRST?
I'M HERE TWO MINUTES AND I'M ALREADY INVITED TO A SUPER-EXCLUSIVE V.I.P. PARTY.

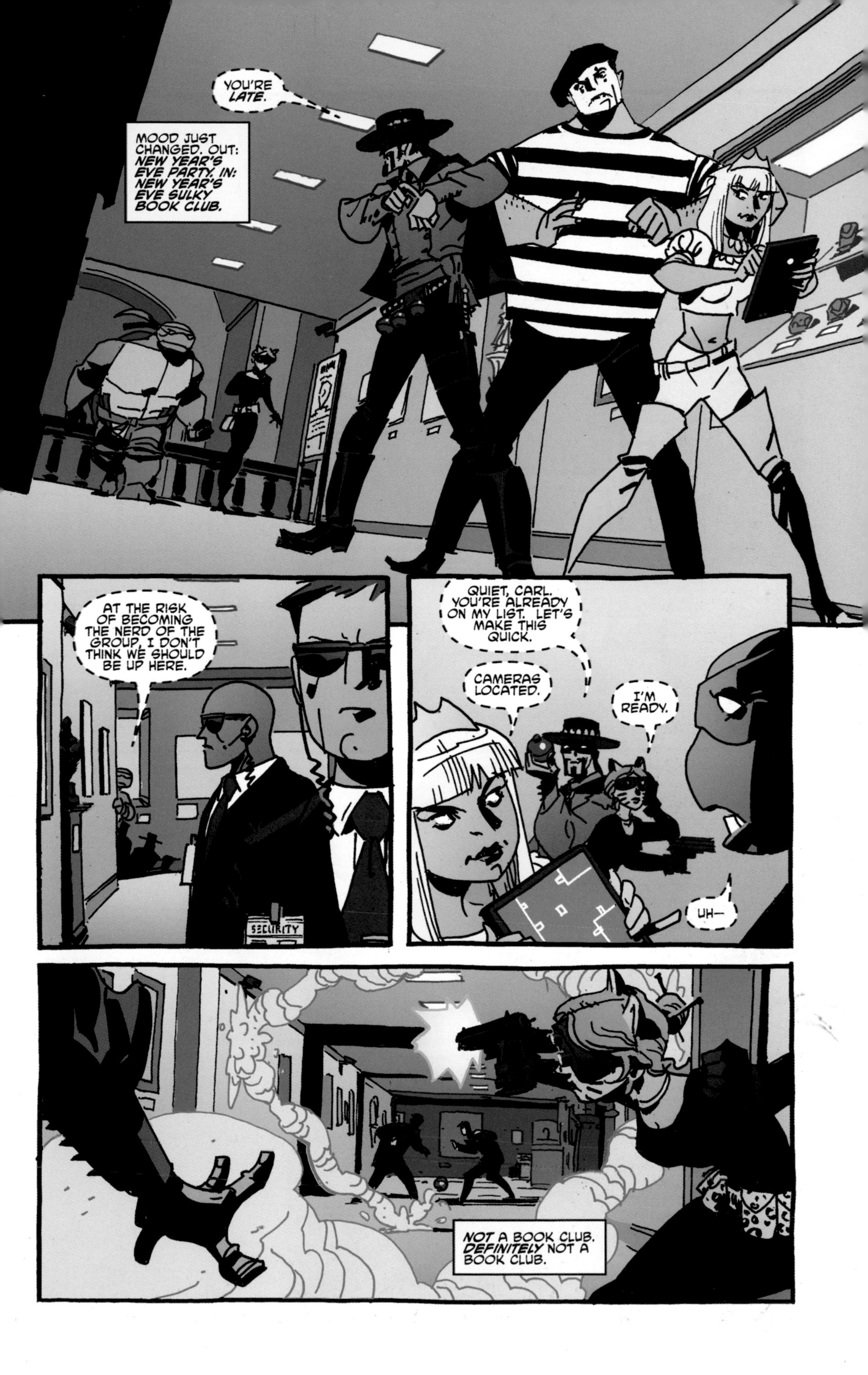
YOU'RE *LATE*.
MOOD JUST CHANGED. OUT: ***NEW YEAR'S EVE PARTY.*** IN: ***NEW YEAR'S EVE SULKY BOOK CLUB.***
AT THE RISK OF BECOMING THE NERD OF THE GROUP, I DON'T THINK WE SHOULD BE UP HERE.
SECURITY
QUIET, CARL. YOU'RE ALREADY ON MY LIST. LET'S MAKE THIS QUICK.
CAMERAS LOCATED.
I'M READY.
UH—
NOT A BOOK CLUB. ***DEFINITELY*** NOT A BOOK CLUB.

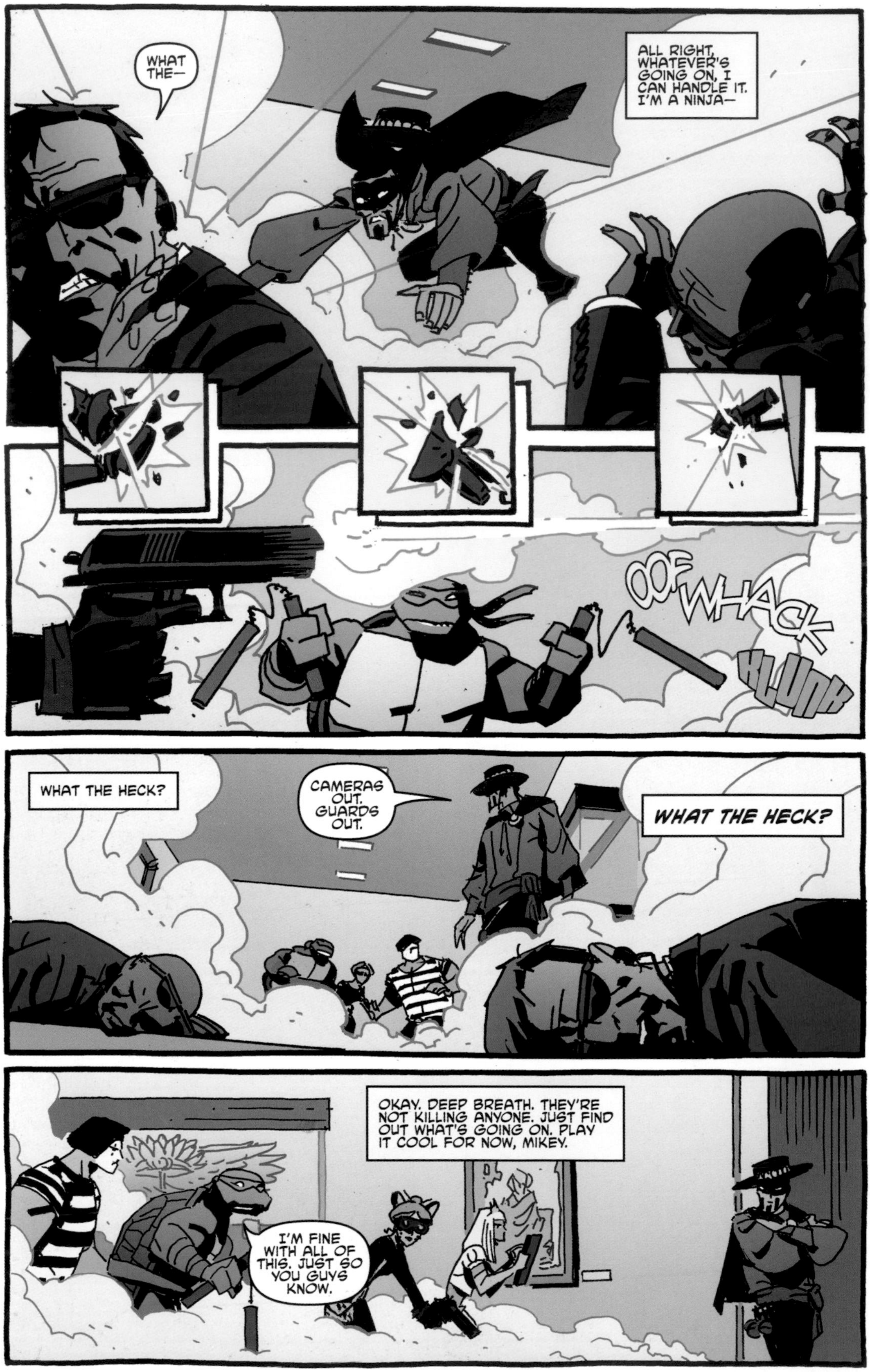

WHAT THE—
ALL RIGHT, WHATEVER'S GOING ON, I CAN HANDLE IT. I'M A NINJA—
OOF
WHACK
KLUNK
WHAT THE HECK?
CAMERAS OUT. GUARDS OUT.
WHAT THE HECK?
OKAY. DEEP BREATH. THEY'RE NOT KILLING ANYONE. JUST FIND OUT WHAT'S GOING ON. PLAY IT COOL FOR NOW, MIKEY.
I'M FINE WITH ALL OF THIS. JUST SO YOU GUYS KNOW.

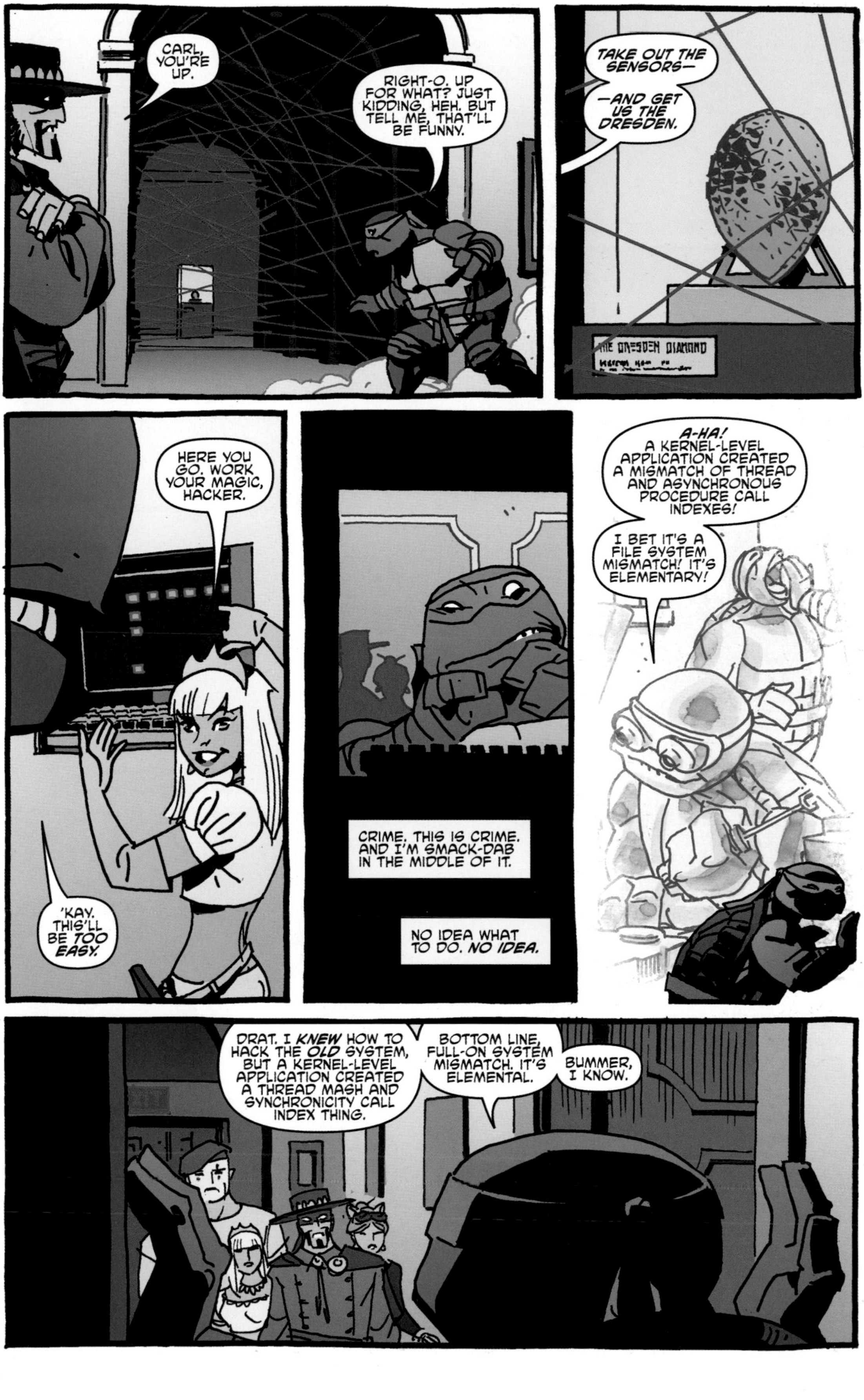
CARL, YOU'RE UP.
RIGHT-O. UP FOR WHAT? JUST KIDDING, HEH. BUT TELL ME, THAT'LL BE FUNNY.
TAKE OUT THE SENSORS—
—AND GET US THE DRESDEN.
THE DRESDEN DIAMOND
HERE YOU GO. WORK YOUR MAGIC, HACKER.
'KAY. THIS'LL BE TOO EASY.
CRIME. THIS IS CRIME. AND I'M SMACK-DAB IN THE MIDDLE OF IT.
NO IDEA WHAT TO DO. NO IDEA.
A-HA! A KERNEL-LEVEL APPLICATION CREATED A MISMATCH OF THREAD AND ASYNCHRONOUS PROCEDURE CALL INDEXES!
I BET IT'S A FILE SYSTEM MISMATCH! IT'S ELEMENTARY!
DRAT. I KNEW HOW TO HACK THE OLD SYSTEM, BUT A KERNEL-LEVEL APPLICATION CREATED A THREAD MASH AND SYNCHRONICITY CALL INDEX THING.
BOTTOM LINE, FULL-ON SYSTEM MISMATCH. IT'S ELEMENTAL.
BUMMER, I KNOW.

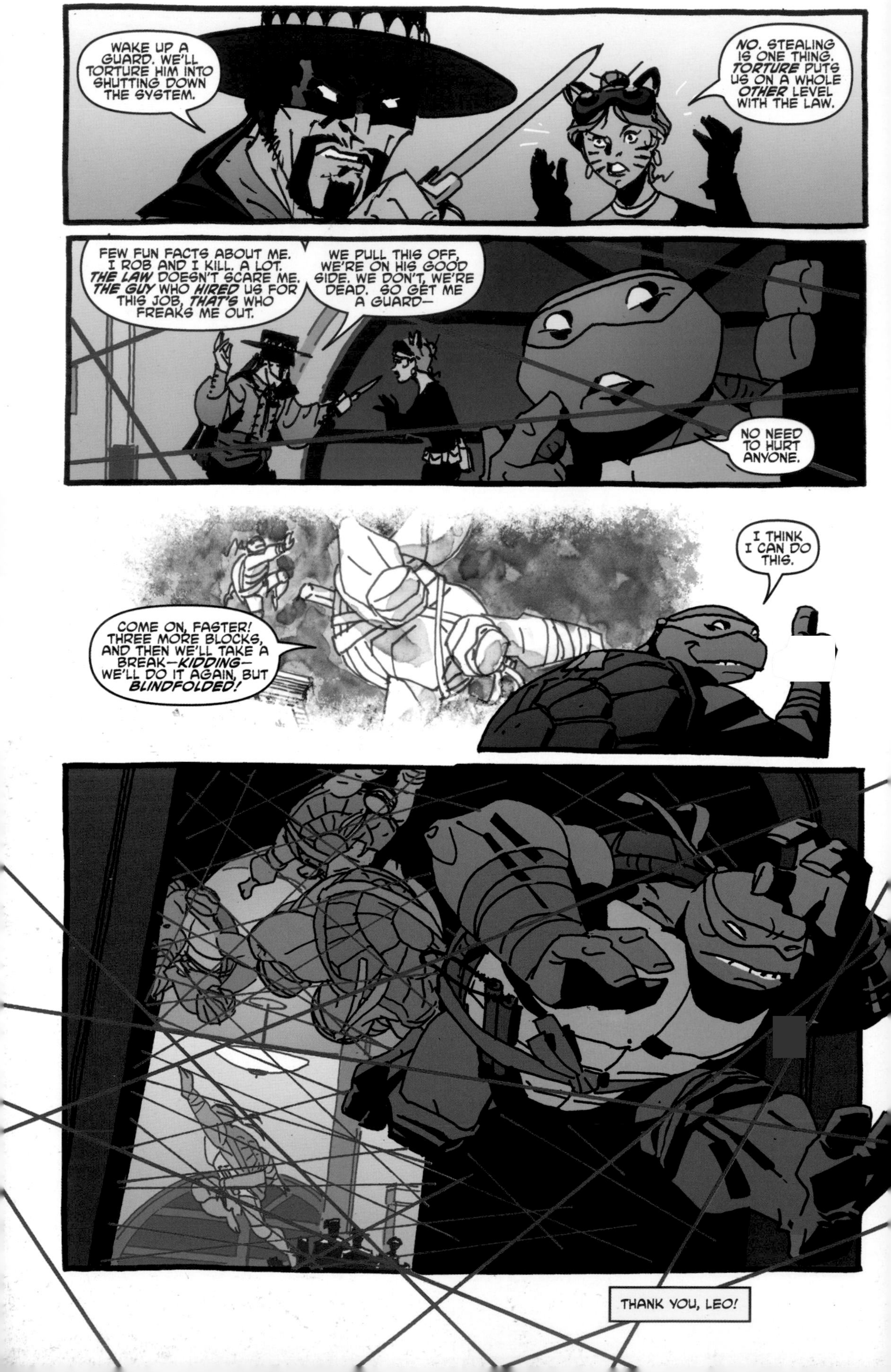
WAKE UP A GUARD. WE'LL TORTURE HIM INTO SHUTTING DOWN THE SYSTEM.
NO. STEALING IS ONE THING. TORTURE PUTS US ON A WHOLE OTHER LEVEL WITH THE LAW.
FEW FUN FACTS ABOUT ME. I ROB AND I KILL. A LOT. THE LAW DOESN'T SCARE ME. THE GUY WHO HIRED US FOR THIS JOB, THAT'S WHO FREAKS ME OUT.
WE PULL THIS OFF, WE'RE ON HIS GOOD SIDE. WE DON'T, WE'RE DEAD. SO GET ME A GUARD—
NO NEED TO HURT ANYONE.
I THINK I CAN DO THIS.
COME ON, FASTER! THREE MORE BLOCKS, AND THEN WE'LL TAKE A BREAK—KIDDING—WE'LL DO IT AGAIN, BUT BLINDFOLDED!
THANK YOU, LEO!

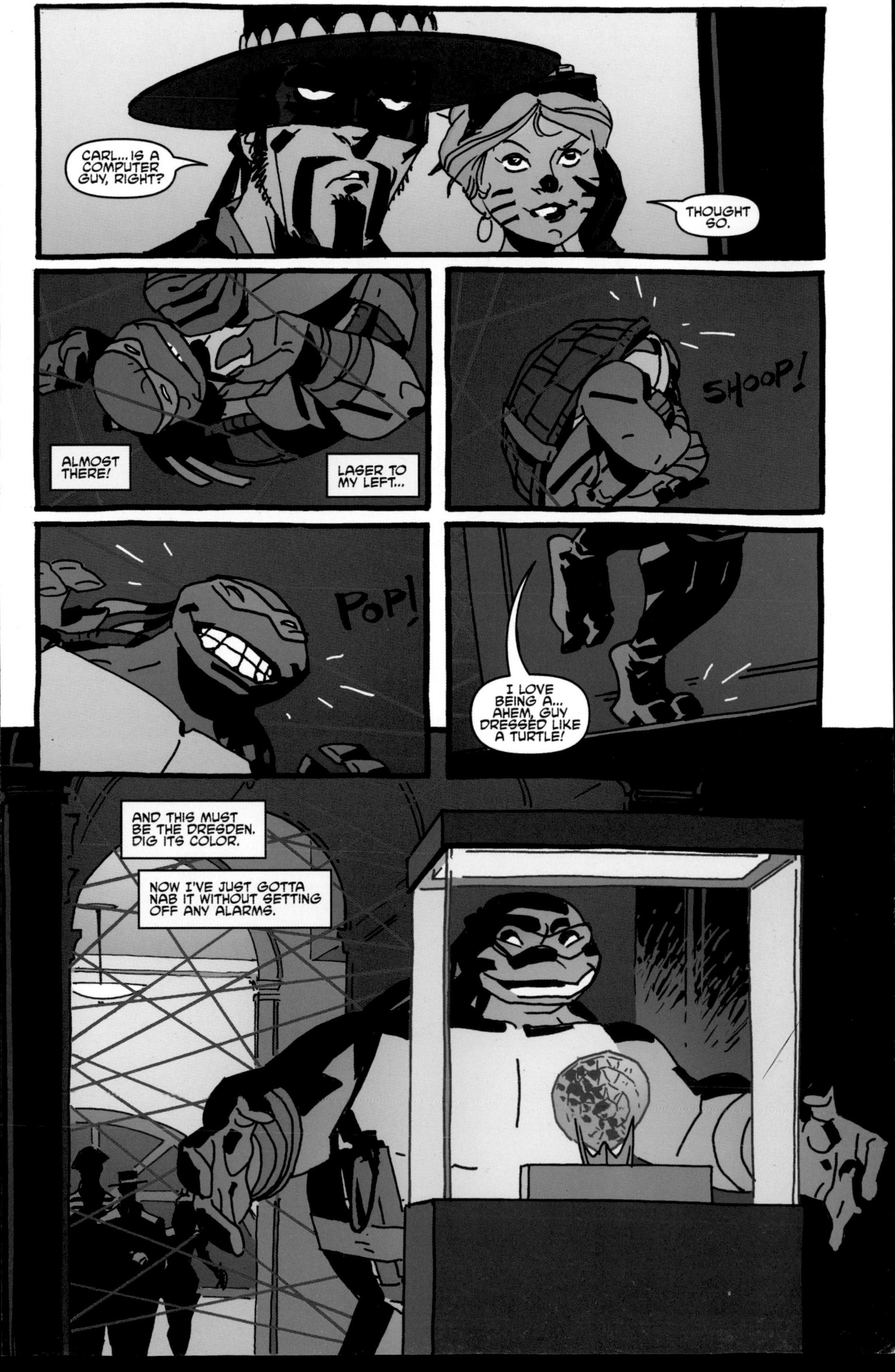
CARL... IS A COMPUTER GUY, RIGHT?
THOUGHT SO.
ALMOST THERE!
LASER TO MY LEFT...
SHOOP!
POP!
I LOVE BEING A... AHEM, GUY DRESSED LIKE A TURTLE!
AND THIS MUST BE THE DRESDEN. DIG ITS COLOR.
NOW I'VE JUST GOTTA NAB IT WITHOUT SETTING OFF ANY ALARMS.

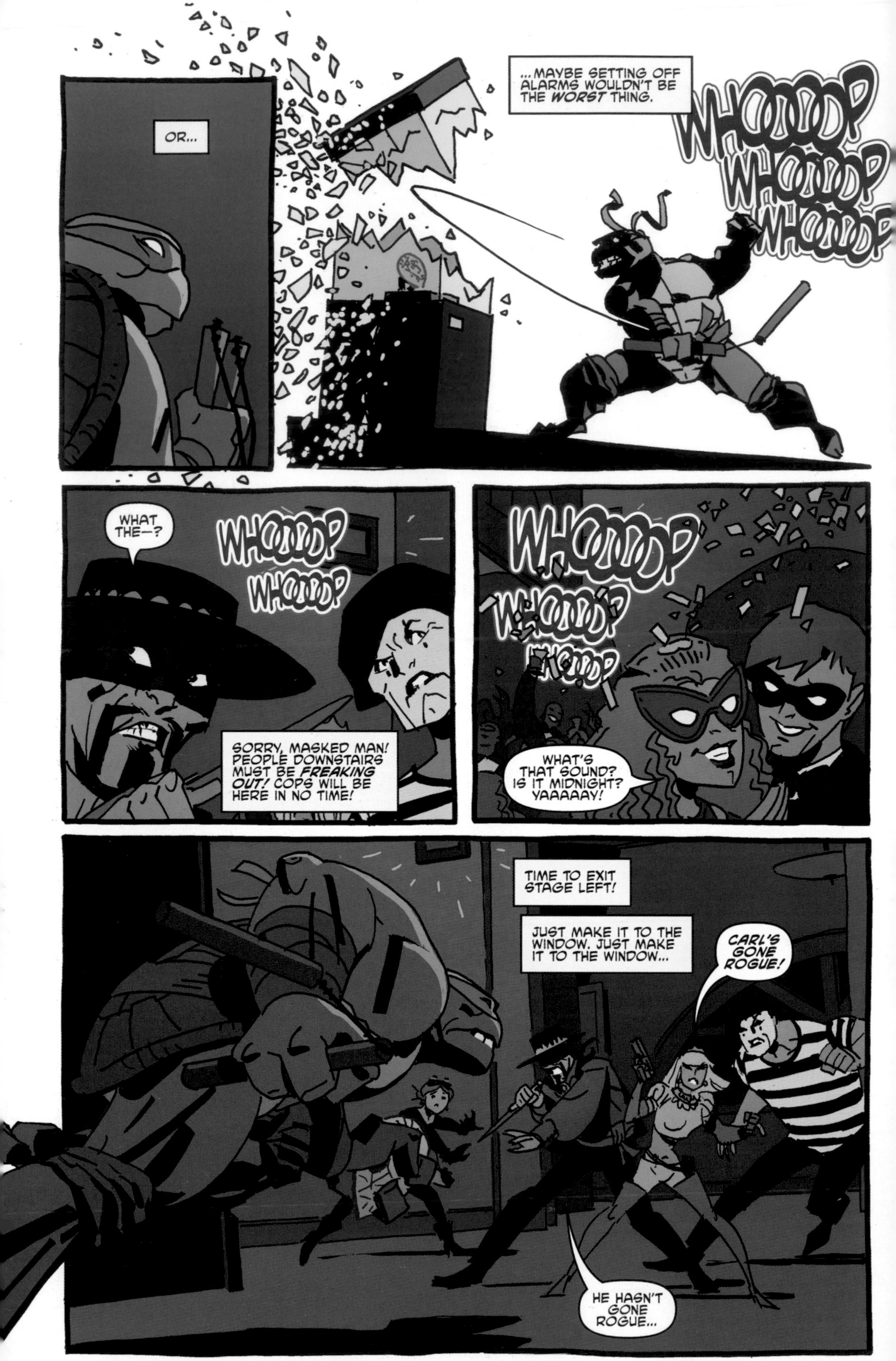

OR...
...MAYBE SETTING OFF ALARMS WOULDN'T BE THE *WORST* THING.
WHOOOOP WHOOOOP WHOOOOP
WHAT THE--?
WHOOOOP WHOOOOP
SORRY, MASKED MAN! PEOPLE DOWNSTAIRS MUST BE *FREAKING OUT!* COPS WILL BE HERE IN NO TIME!
WHOOOOP WHOOOOP WHOOOP
WHAT'S THAT SOUND? IS IT MIDNIGHT? YAAAAAY!
TIME TO EXIT STAGE LEFT!
JUST MAKE IT TO THE WINDOW. JUST MAKE IT TO THE WINDOW...
CARL'S GONE ROGUE!
HE HASN'T GONE ROGUE...

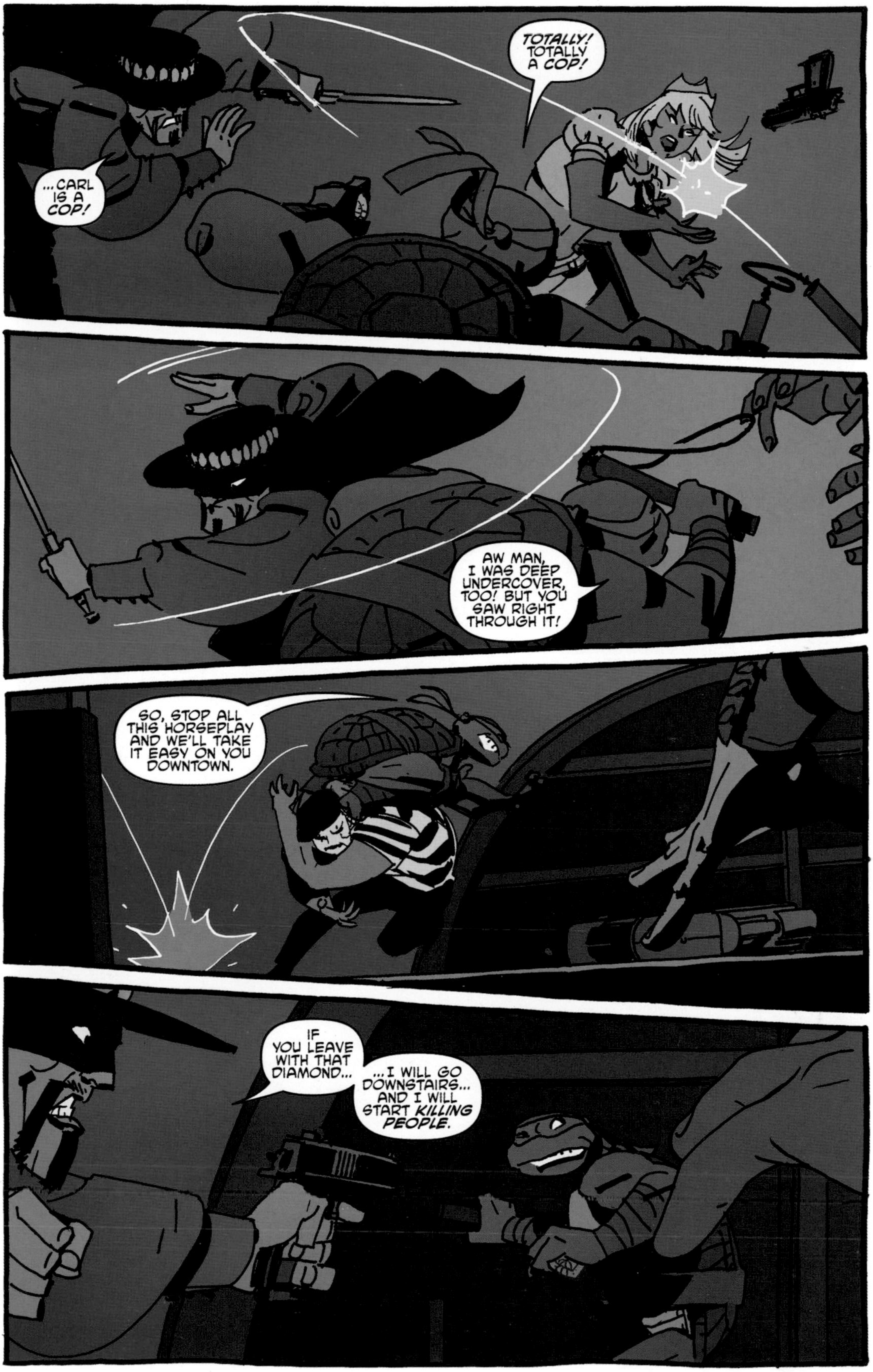
TOTALLY! TOTALLY A COP!
...CARL IS A COP!
AW MAN, I WAS DEEP UNDERCOVER, TOO! BUT YOU SAW RIGHT THROUGH IT!
SO, STOP ALL THIS HORSEPLAY AND WE'LL TAKE IT EASY ON YOU DOWNTOWN.
IF YOU LEAVE WITH THAT DIAMOND...
...I WILL GO DOWNSTAIRS... AND I WILL START KILLING PEOPLE.

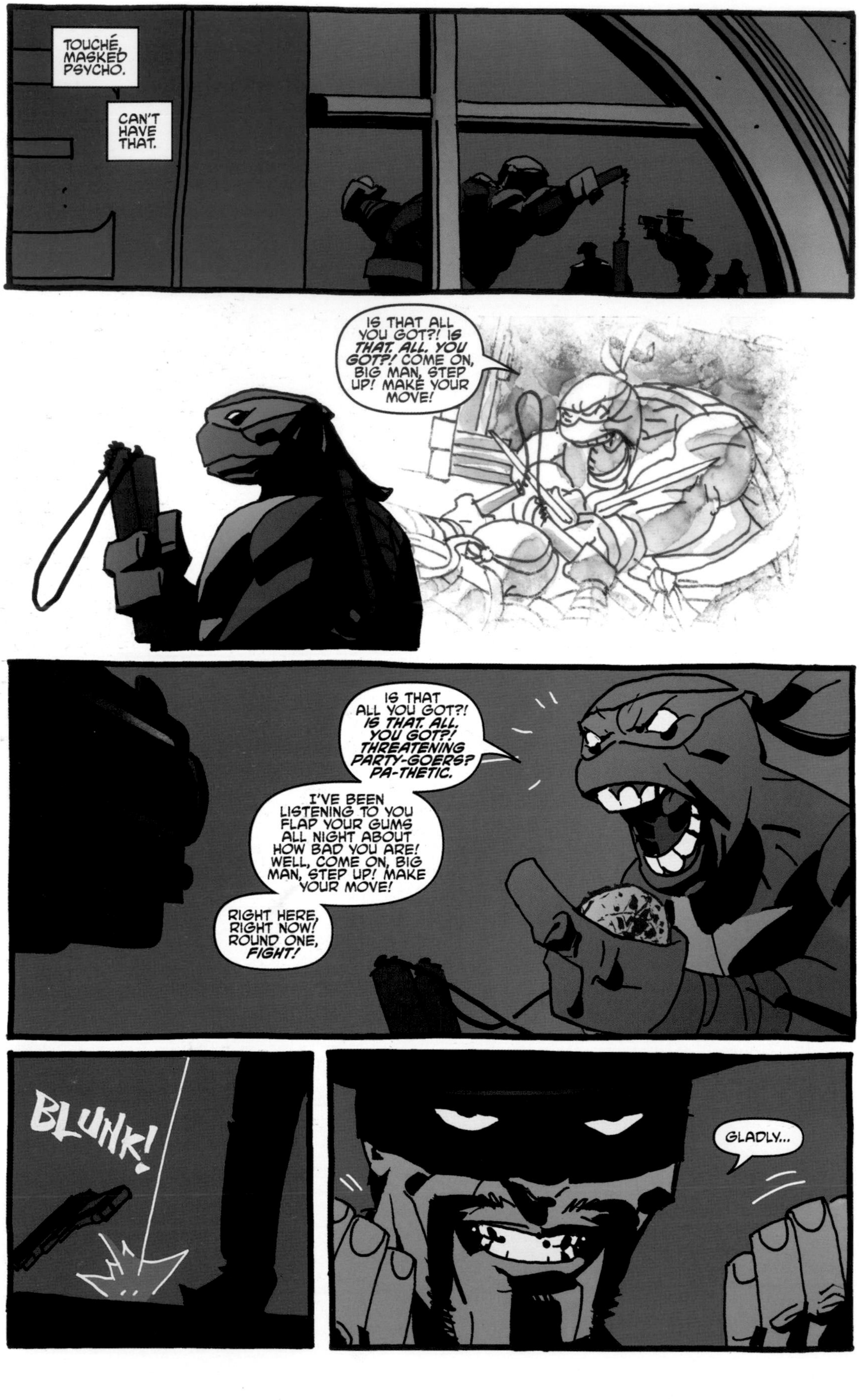
TOUCHÉ, MASKED PSYCHO.
CAN'T HAVE THAT.
IS THAT ALL YOU GOT?! IS *THAT. ALL. YOU GOT?!* COME ON, BIG MAN, STEP UP! MAKE YOUR MOVE!
IS THAT ALL YOU GOT?! *IS THAT. ALL. YOU GOT?! THREATENING PARTY-GOERS? PA-THETIC.*
I'VE BEEN LISTENING TO YOU FLAP YOUR GUMS ALL NIGHT ABOUT HOW BAD YOU ARE! WELL, COME ON, BIG MAN, STEP UP! MAKE YOUR MOVE!
RIGHT HERE, RIGHT NOW! ROUND ONE, *FIGHT!*
BLUNK!
GLADLY...

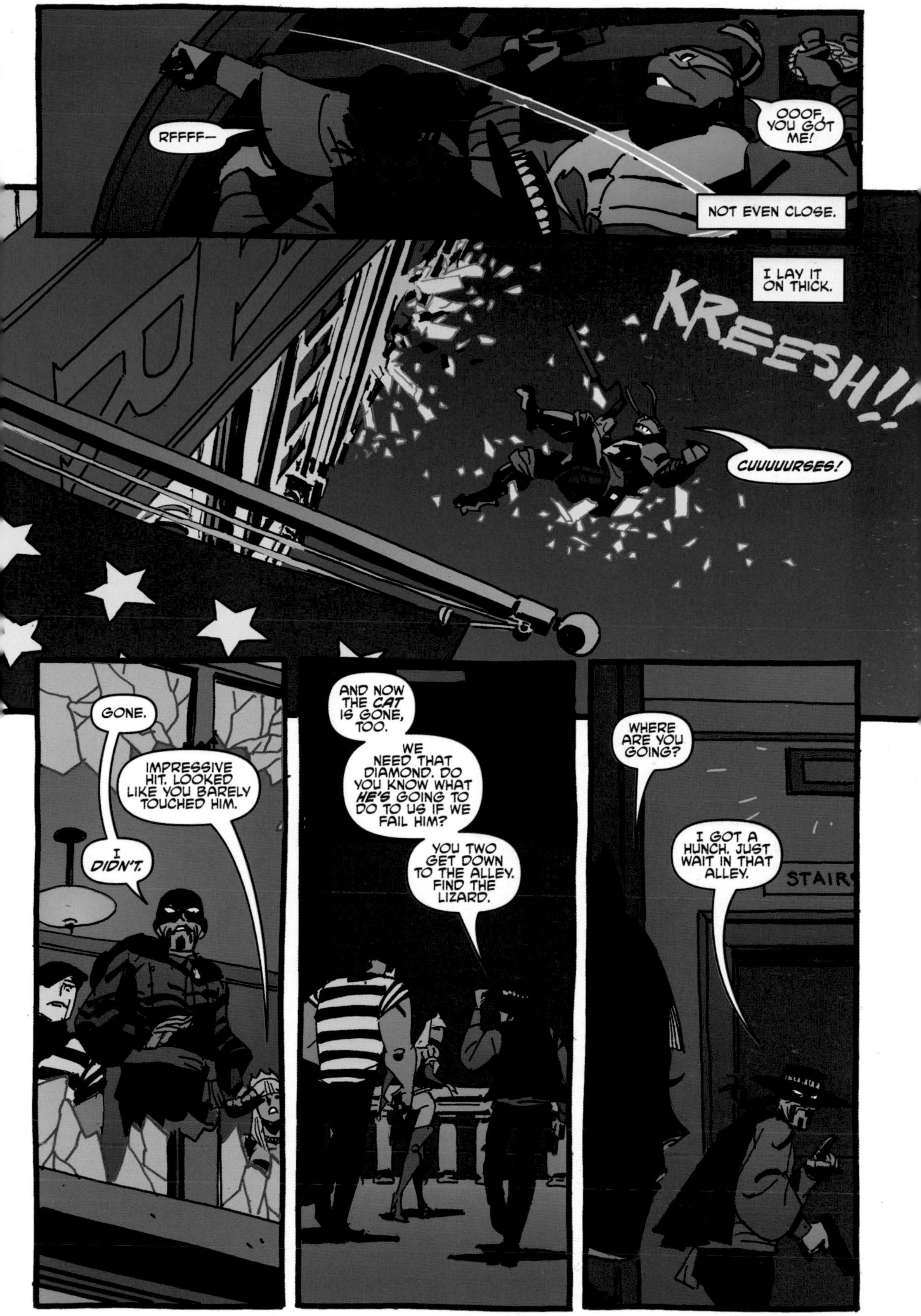
RFFFF—
OOOF, YOU GOT ME!
NOT EVEN CLOSE.
I LAY IT ON THICK.
KREESH!!
CUUUUURSES!
GONE.
IMPRESSIVE HIT. LOOKED LIKE YOU BARELY TOUCHED HIM.
I DIDN'T.
AND NOW THE CAT IS GONE, TOO.
WE NEED THAT DIAMOND. DO YOU KNOW WHAT HE'S GOING TO DO TO US IF WE FAIL HIM?
YOU TWO GET DOWN TO THE ALLEY. FIND THE LIZARD.
WHERE ARE YOU GOING?
I GOT A HUNCH. JUST WAIT IN THAT ALLEY.

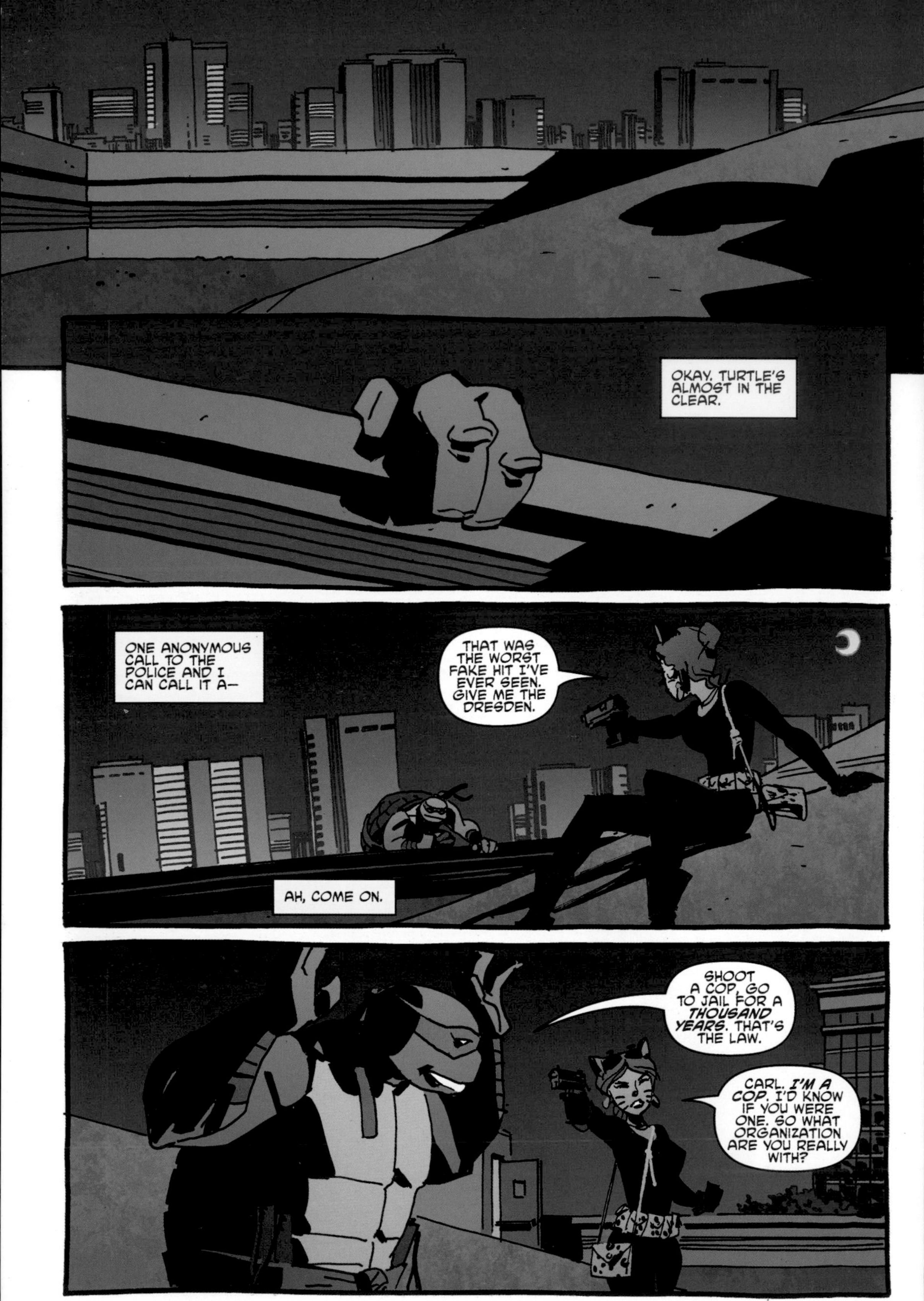
OKAY. TURTLE'S ALMOST IN THE CLEAR.
ONE ANONYMOUS CALL TO THE POLICE AND I CAN CALL IT A—
THAT WAS THE WORST FAKE HIT I'VE EVER SEEN. GIVE ME THE DRESDEN.
AH, COME ON.
SHOOT A COP, GO TO JAIL FOR A THOUSAND YEARS. THAT'S THE LAW.
CARL. I'M A COP. I'D KNOW IF YOU WERE ONE. SO WHAT ORGANIZATION ARE YOU REALLY WITH?

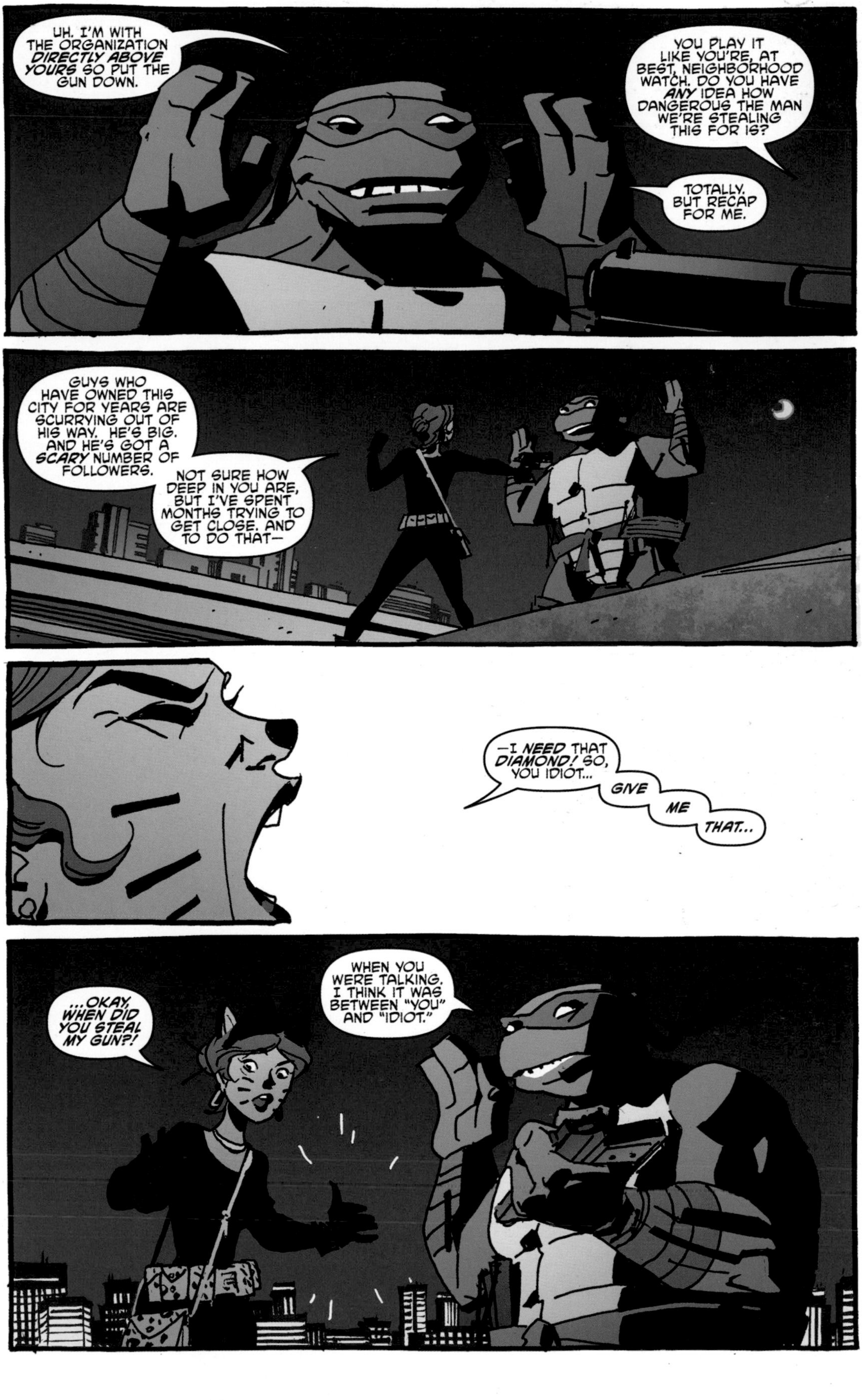
UH. I'M WITH THE ORGANIZATION *DIRECTLY ABOVE YOURS* SO PUT THE GUN DOWN.
YOU PLAY IT LIKE YOU'RE, AT BEST, NEIGHBORHOOD WATCH. DO YOU HAVE *ANY* IDEA HOW DANGEROUS THE MAN WE'RE STEALING THIS FOR IS?
TOTALLY. BUT RECAP FOR ME.
GUYS WHO HAVE OWNED THIS CITY FOR YEARS ARE SCURRYING OUT OF HIS WAY. HE'S BIG. AND HE'S GOT A *SCARY* NUMBER OF FOLLOWERS.
NOT SURE HOW DEEP IN YOU ARE, BUT I'VE SPENT MONTHS TRYING TO GET CLOSE. AND TO DO THAT—
—I *NEED* THAT *DIAMOND!* SO, YOU IDIOT...
GIVE
ME
THAT...
...OKAY, WHEN DID YOU STEAL MY GUN?!
WHEN YOU WERE TALKING. I THINK IT WAS BETWEEN "YOU" AND "IDIOT."

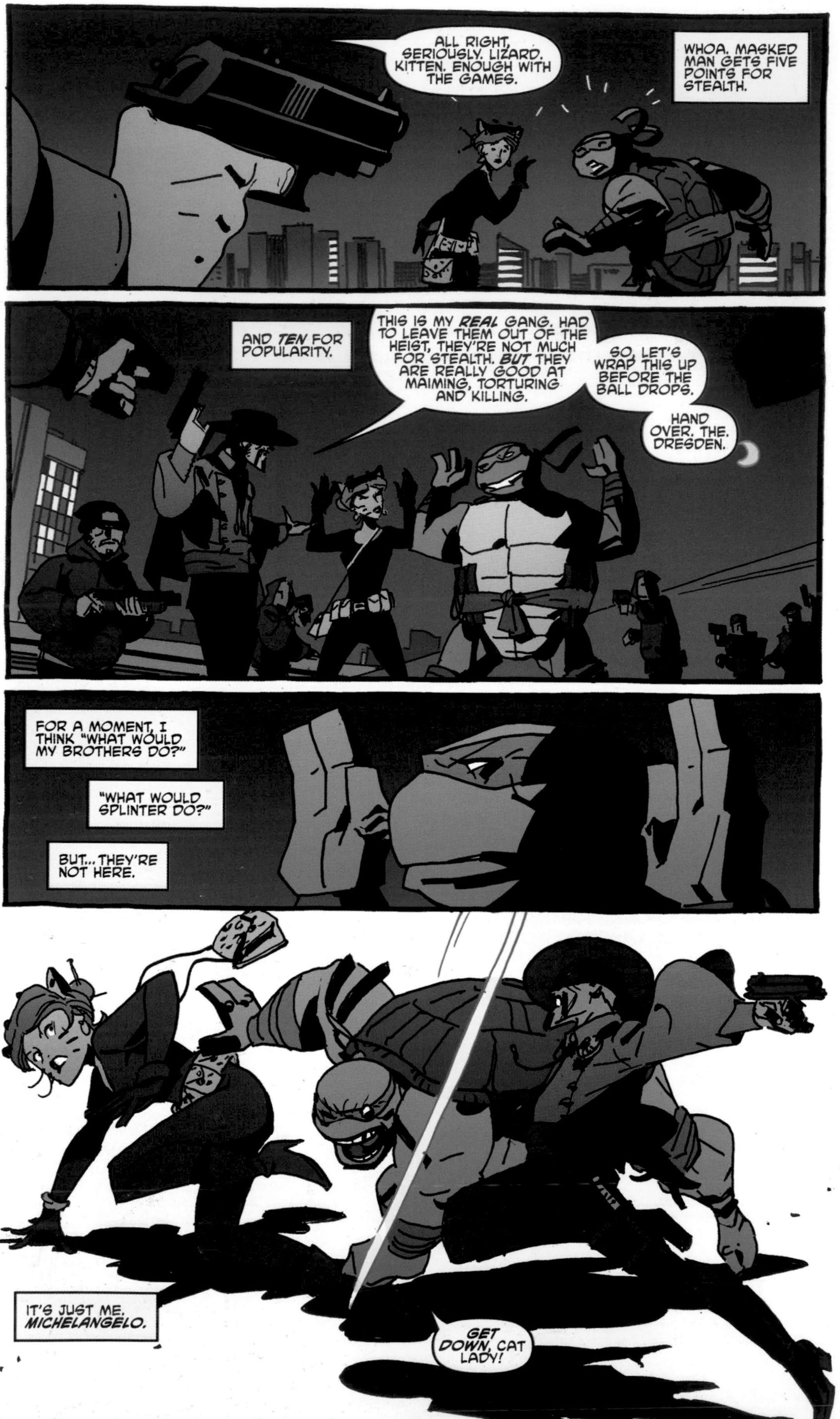
ALL RIGHT, SERIOUSLY. LIZARD. KITTEN. ENOUGH WITH THE GAMES.
WHOA. MASKED MAN GETS FIVE POINTS FOR STEALTH.
AND *TEN* FOR POPULARITY.
THIS IS MY *REAL* GANG. HAD TO LEAVE THEM OUT OF THE HEIST, THEY'RE NOT MUCH FOR STEALTH. *BUT* THEY ARE REALLY GOOD AT MAIMING, TORTURING AND KILLING.
SO, LET'S WRAP THIS UP BEFORE THE BALL DROPS.
HAND OVER. THE. DRESDEN.
FOR A MOMENT, I THINK "WHAT WOULD MY BROTHERS DO?"
"WHAT WOULD SPLINTER DO?"
BUT... THEY'RE NOT HERE.
IT'S JUST ME. *MICHELANGELO.*
GET DOWN, CAT LADY!

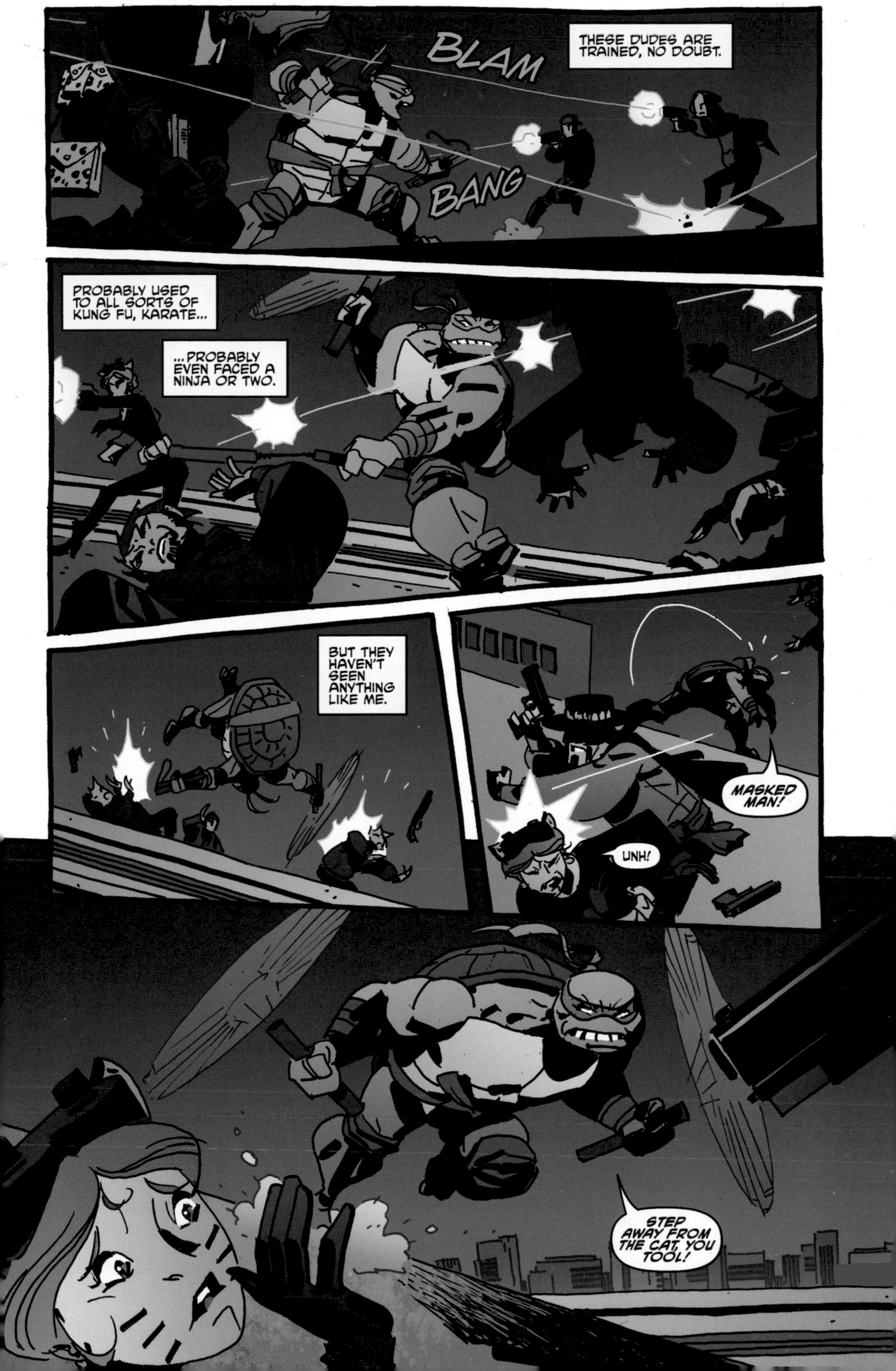
BLAM
THESE DUDES ARE TRAINED, NO DOUBT.
BANG
PROBABLY USED TO ALL SORTS OF KUNG FU, KARATE...
...PROBABLY EVEN FACED A NINJA OR TWO.
BUT THEY HAVEN'T SEEN ANYTHING LIKE ME.
MASKED MAN!
UNH!
STEP AWAY FROM THE CAT, YOU TOOL!

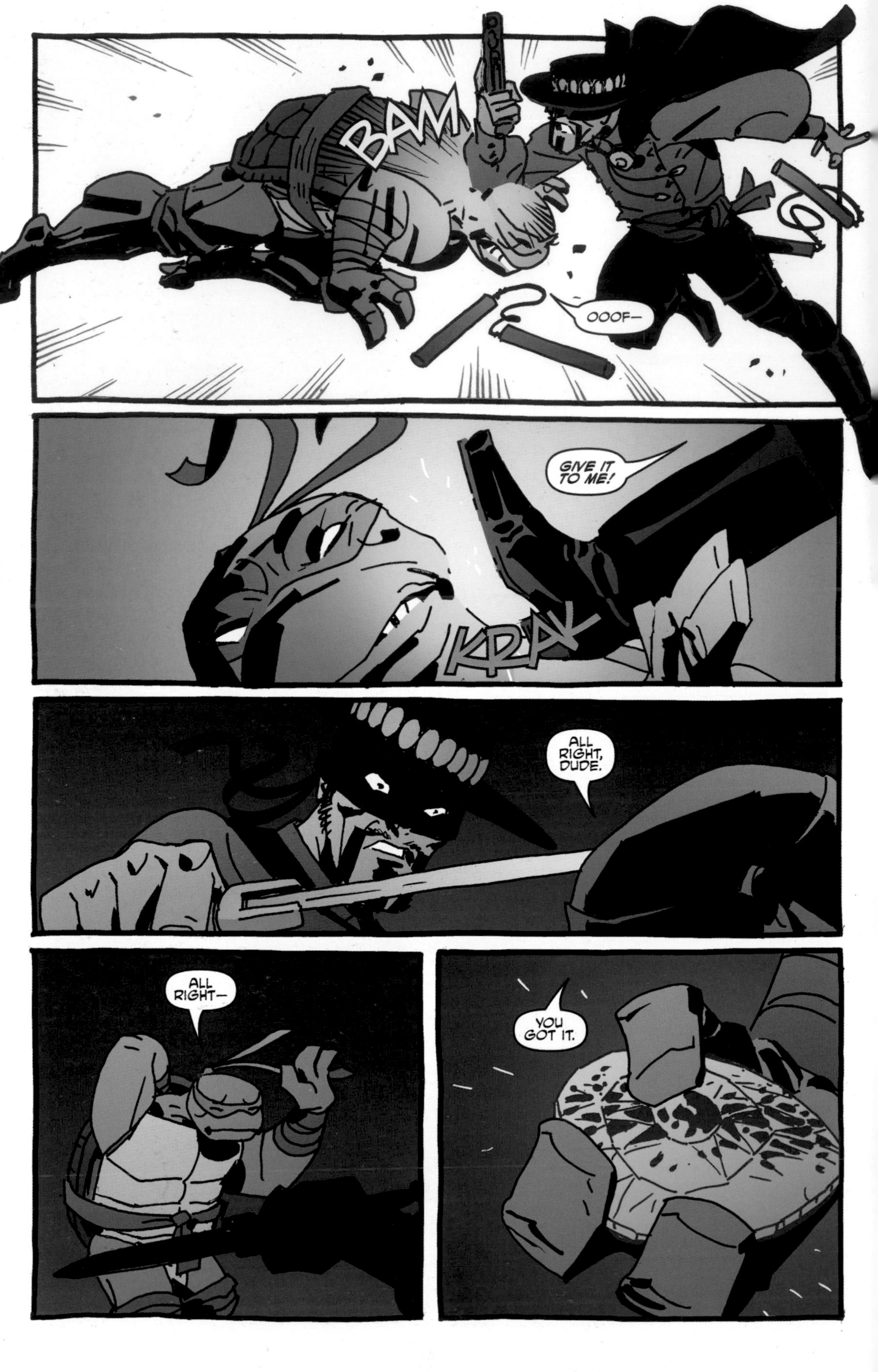
BAM
OOOF—
GIVE IT TO ME!
KRAK
ALL RIGHT, DUDE.
ALL RIGHT—
YOU GOT IT.

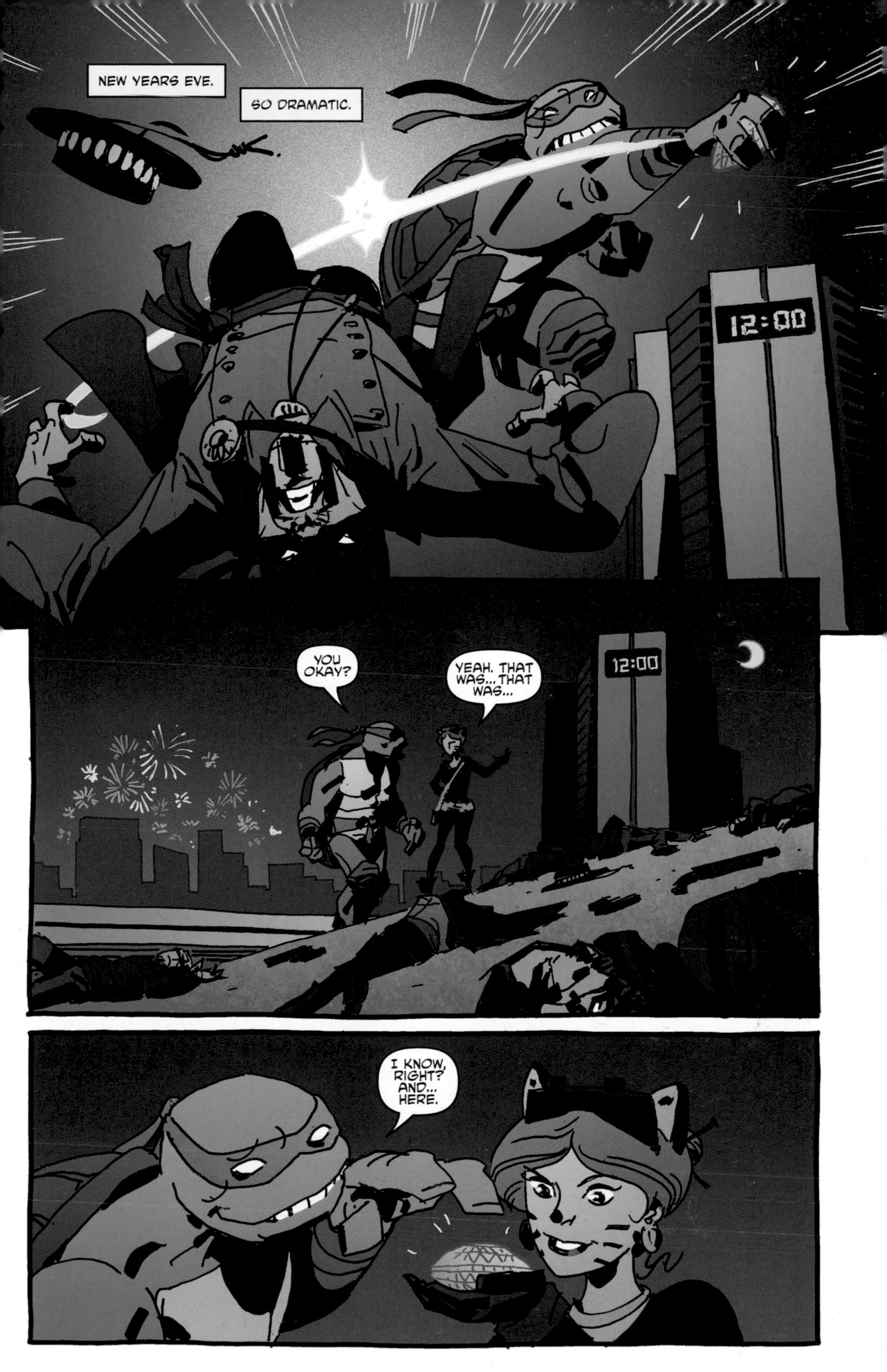

NEW YEARS EVE.
SO DRAMATIC.
12:00
12:00
YOU OKAY?
YEAH. THAT WAS... THAT WAS...
I KNOW, RIGHT? AND... HERE.

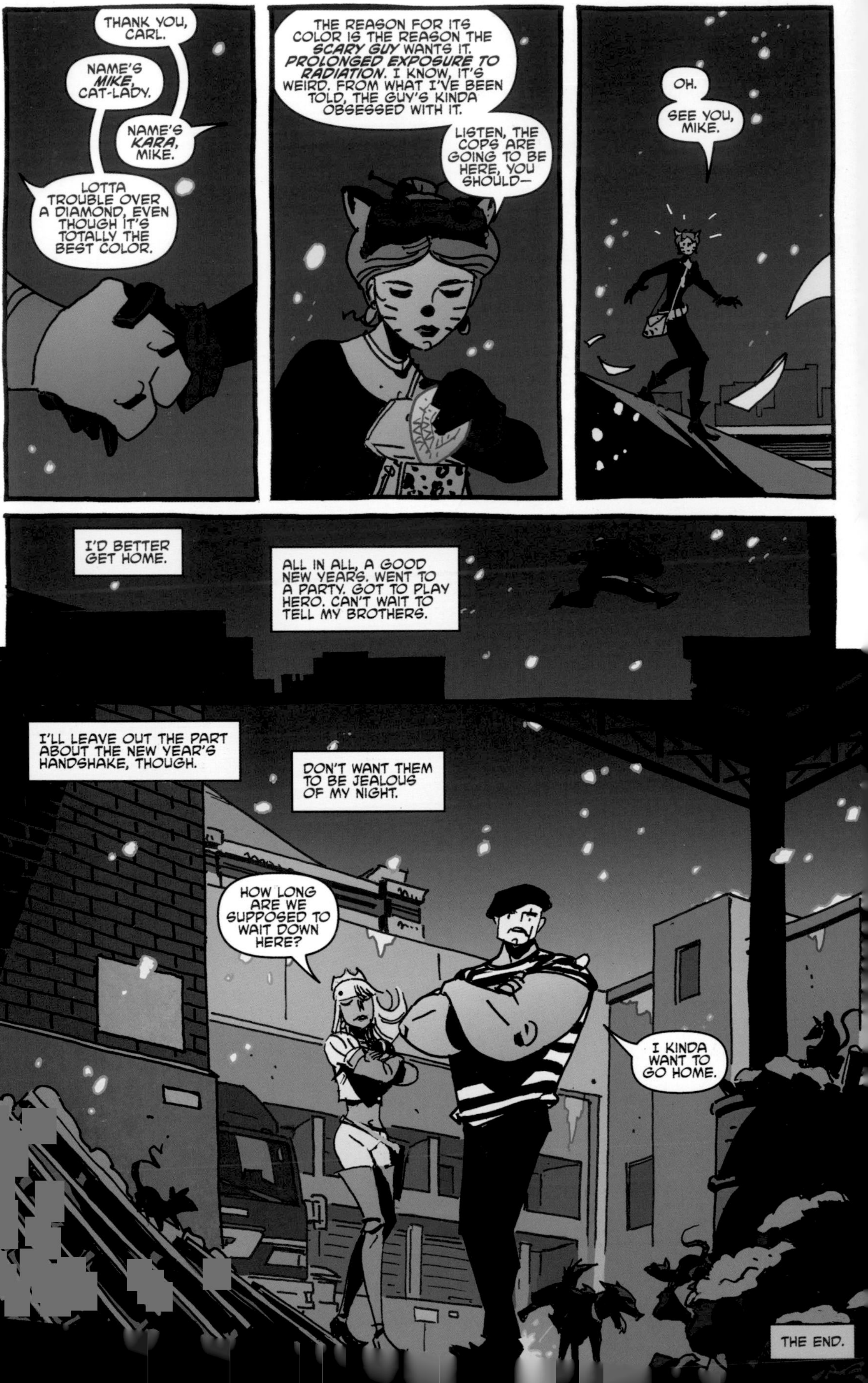
THANK YOU, CARL.
NAME'S MIKE, CAT-LADY.
NAME'S KARA, MIKE.
LOTTA TROUBLE OVER A DIAMOND, EVEN THOUGH IT'S TOTALLY THE BEST COLOR.
THE REASON FOR ITS COLOR IS THE REASON THE SCARY GUY WANTS IT. PROLONGED EXPOSURE TO RADIATION. I KNOW, IT'S WEIRD. FROM WHAT I'VE BEEN TOLD, THE GUY'S KINDA OBSESSED WITH IT.
LISTEN, THE COPS ARE GOING TO BE HERE, YOU SHOULD—
OH.
SEE YOU, MIKE.
I'D BETTER GET HOME.
ALL IN ALL, A GOOD NEW YEARS. WENT TO A PARTY. GOT TO PLAY HERO. CAN'T WAIT TO TELL MY BROTHERS.
I'LL LEAVE OUT THE PART ABOUT THE NEW YEAR'S HANDSHAKE, THOUGH.
DON'T WANT THEM TO BE JEALOUS OF MY NIGHT.
HOW LONG ARE WE SUPPOSED TO WAIT DOWN HERE?
I KINDA WANT TO GO HOME.
THE END.

Art by **ANDY KUHN**
Colors by **BILL CRABTREE**

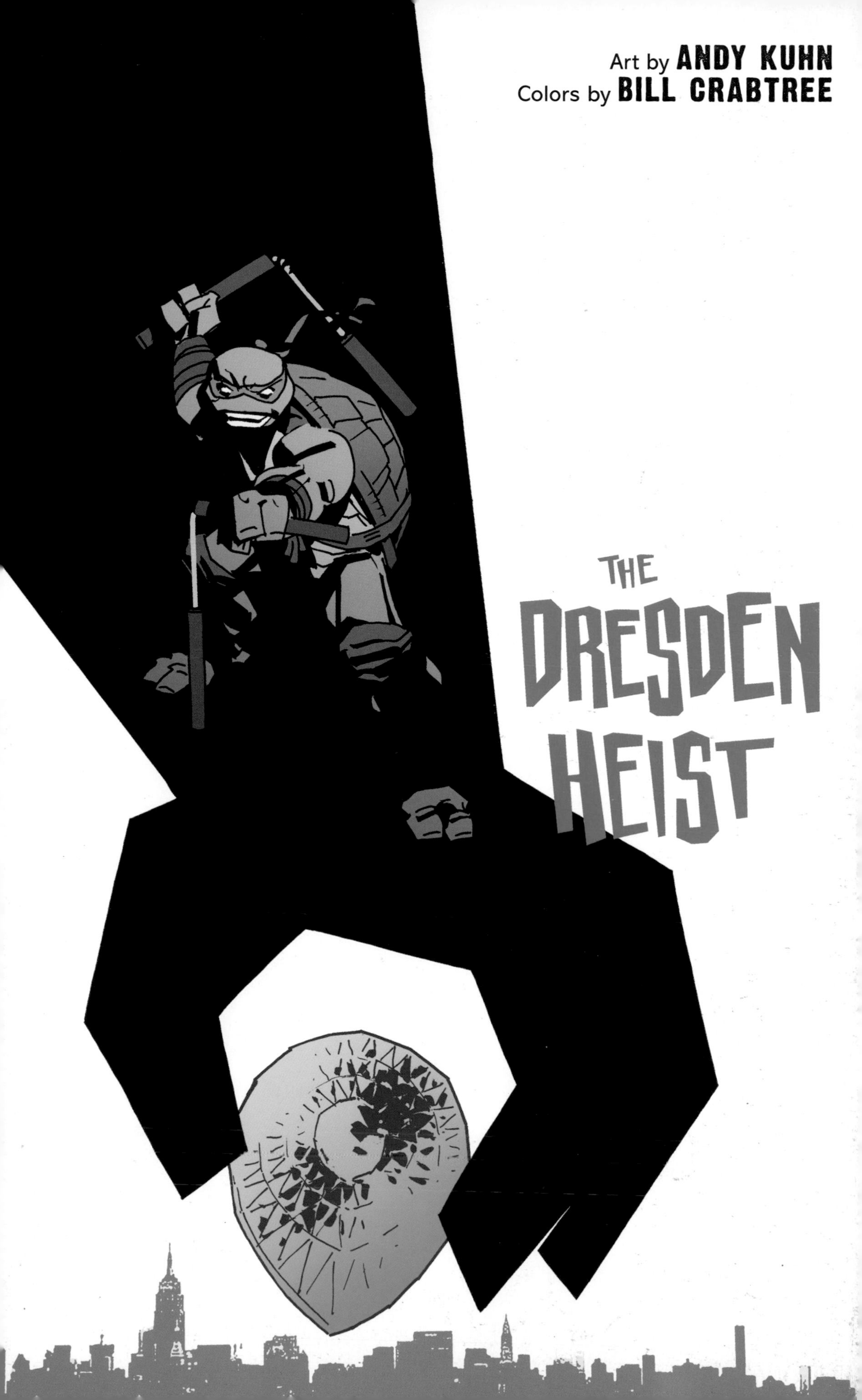

THE DRESDEN HEIST

Art by **DAVID PETERSEN**

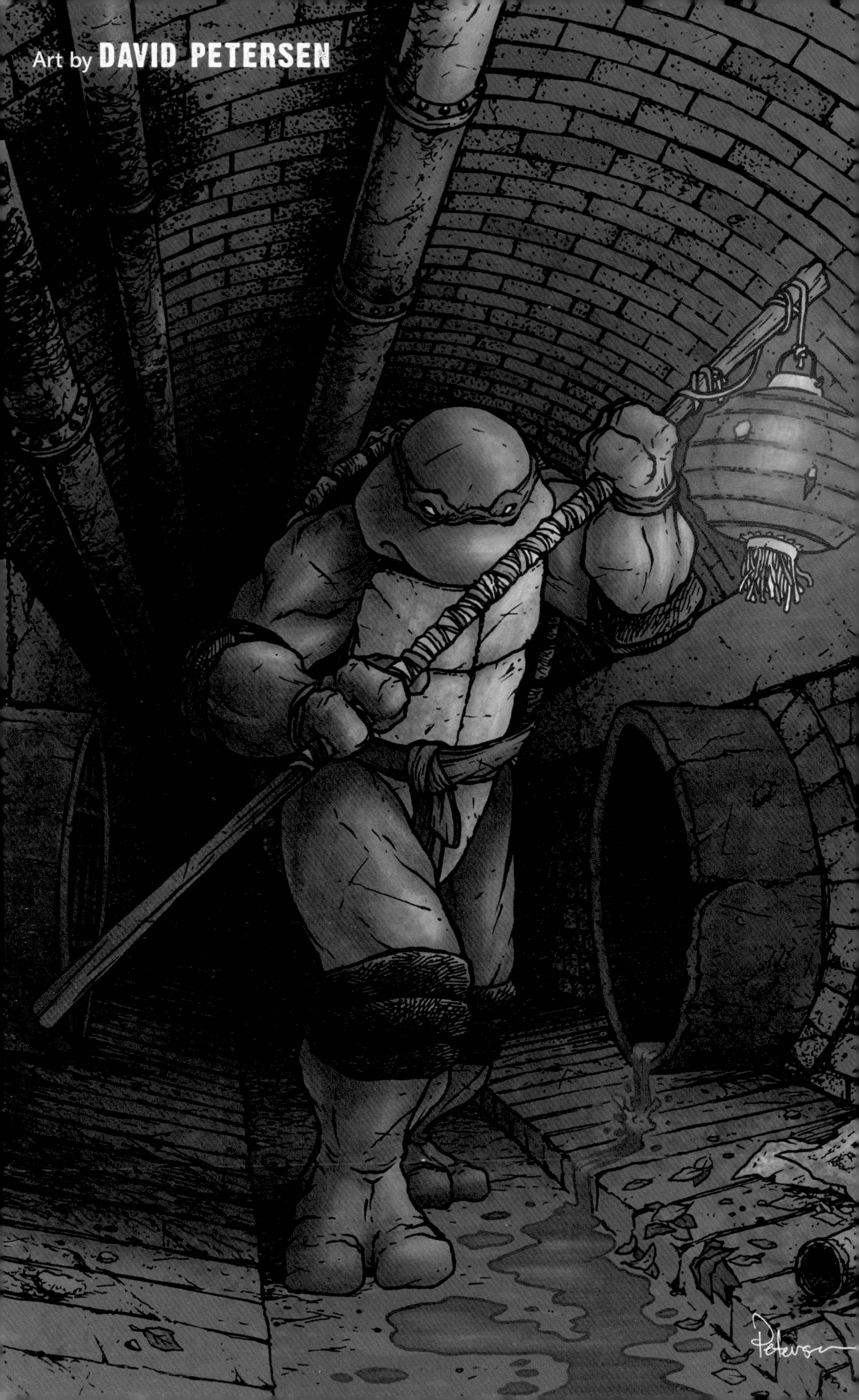
Petersen

I'M DONATELLO TEENAGE MUTANT NINJA TURTLE

IN THE HEAT OF BATTLE, MY BROTHERS AND I ARE A SIGHT TO BEHOLD.
FOUR DISTINCT STYLES, UNITING AS ONE. WHEN FACED WITH A COMMON ENEMY, WE'RE A WELL-OILED MACHINE.
OFF-DUTY, THOUGH? OIL AND WATER.
MIKEY, I REALLY NEED TO GET ONLINE.
ONE SEC, BRO—I GOTTA SEE HOW THIS VIDEO ENDS.
THIS KID'S WARNING HIS BROTHER NOT TO BITE HIM, BUT THAT LITTLE DUDE'S GOT THAT LOOK IN HIS EYES...
I LOVE COMPUTERS. USING THEM, FIXING THEM, BUILDING THEM. MY BROTHERS, NOT SO MUCH...
RAPH, CAN I FINISH WORKING ON THAT COMPUTER TOWER?
SIXTY-FOUR... AFTER I'M DONE... SIXTY-FIVE... USING IT... SIXTY-SIX...
SOMETIMES, I JUST WANT TO GET AWAY. BUT IT'S NOT LIKE I CAN GO FOR A LEISURELY STROLL OUTSIDE WHENEVER I WANT.
SO I FIND OTHER WAYS TO ESCAPE.
THIS ONE'S CALLED STRANGENESS. IT'S A MMORPG. I CAN DOWNLOAD THE CORE RULEBOOK FOR YOU—
LEO TRIES TO BE INTERESTED, HE REALLY DOES.
IS THIS THE KINDA M-M-O... O... ER, GAME WHERE WE CAN ACTUALLY KICK AND PUNCH STUFF?
NO, THAT'S A WHOLE OTHER SYSTEM.
BUT IT'S NOT HIS THING.

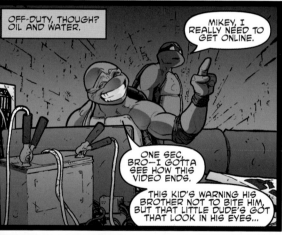

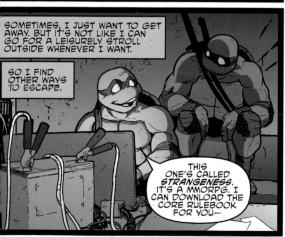

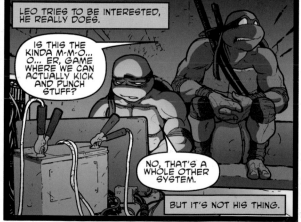

I GO ONLINE LATE AT NIGHT WHILE MY BROTHERS SLEEP.
AND NOT JUST VIDEO GAMES—I VISIT A VARIETY OF FORUMS.
AS DUZ_MACHINES_84, I TALK TO ALL SORTS OF INTERESTING PEOPLE!
FRC.forum
BETTA_GEORGE: What was it you do for a living again?
DUZ_MACHINES_84: Karate Instructor
DUZ_MACHINES_84: Need tech advice. Computer fan is busted. Bro used laptop as pizza plate
BETTA_GEORGE: Pizza plate? LOL! Email me specifics
AND THEN THERE'S KIRBY_FAN01. HE'S A TOOL. CONSTANTLY CUTTING ME DOWN. CONSTANTLY MISUSING WORDS.
FRC.forum
KIRBYFAN_01: Duz_Machines, your st00pid opinions are so obstruse.
DUZ_MACHINES_84: That's not even a WORD.
KIRBYFAN_01: Meh.
WAIT. WHAT'S THIS?
FRC.forum
PROF_J_PERRY: Are U going 2 New World Expo? Click this LINK.
DUZ_MACHINES_84: ??
SOUNDS COOL, BUT I CAN'T REALLY GO ANYWHERE UNLESS IT'S NIGHT. OR IN THE SEWER. OR ON A ROOFTOP.
STILL...
CLICK
New world expo.pdf - Adobe Reader
New world EXPO
The Universe's Most Brilliant Minds in 1 Place to Win 1 Grant that will fund their projects for 2 lifetimes!
NEW WORLD EXPO
To Compete: Invite Only
To Behold: 10 Dollars at Door
Countdown: 1 Day
WHOA! A SCIENCE FAIR FOR SUPER-GENIUSES. WISH I COULD CHECK IT OUT.
WAIT A MINUTE! I'M A NINJA. I CAN BLEND. ART OF INVISIBILITY AND ALL.
FRC.forum
DUZ_MACHINES_84: Maybe I'll see you there.
KIRBY_FAN01: Right, like you'll go. Don't be obstruse.
OH, SHUT UP, KIRBY_FAN01.

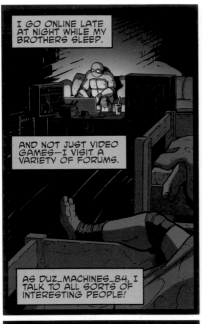

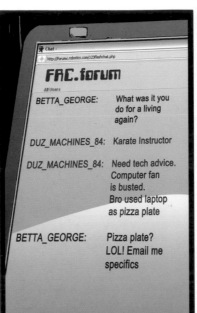

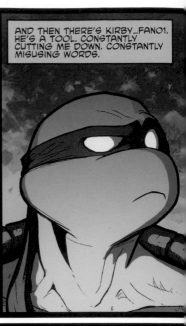

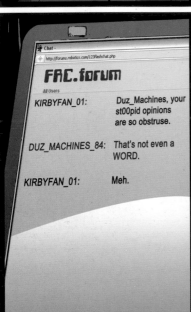

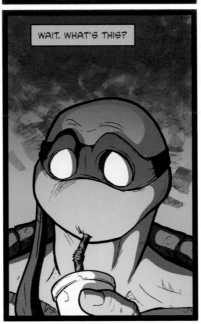

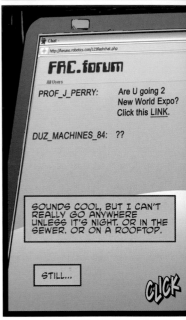

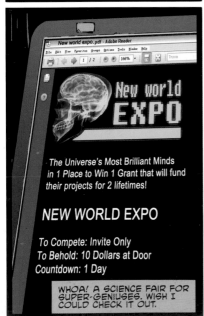

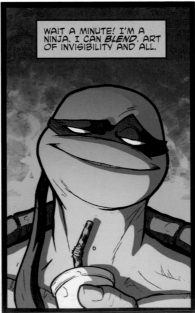

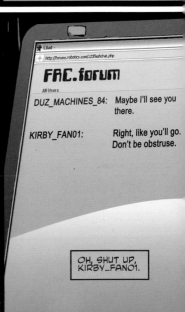

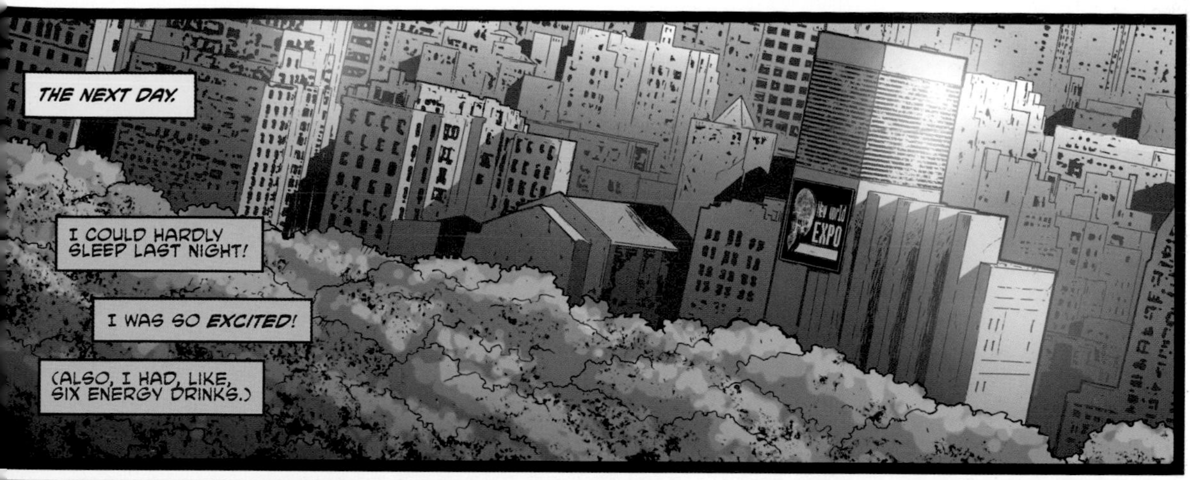
THE NEXT DAY.
New world EXPO
I COULD HARDLY SLEEP LAST NIGHT!
I WAS SO EXCITED!
(ALSO, I HAD, LIKE, SIX ENERGY DRINKS.)

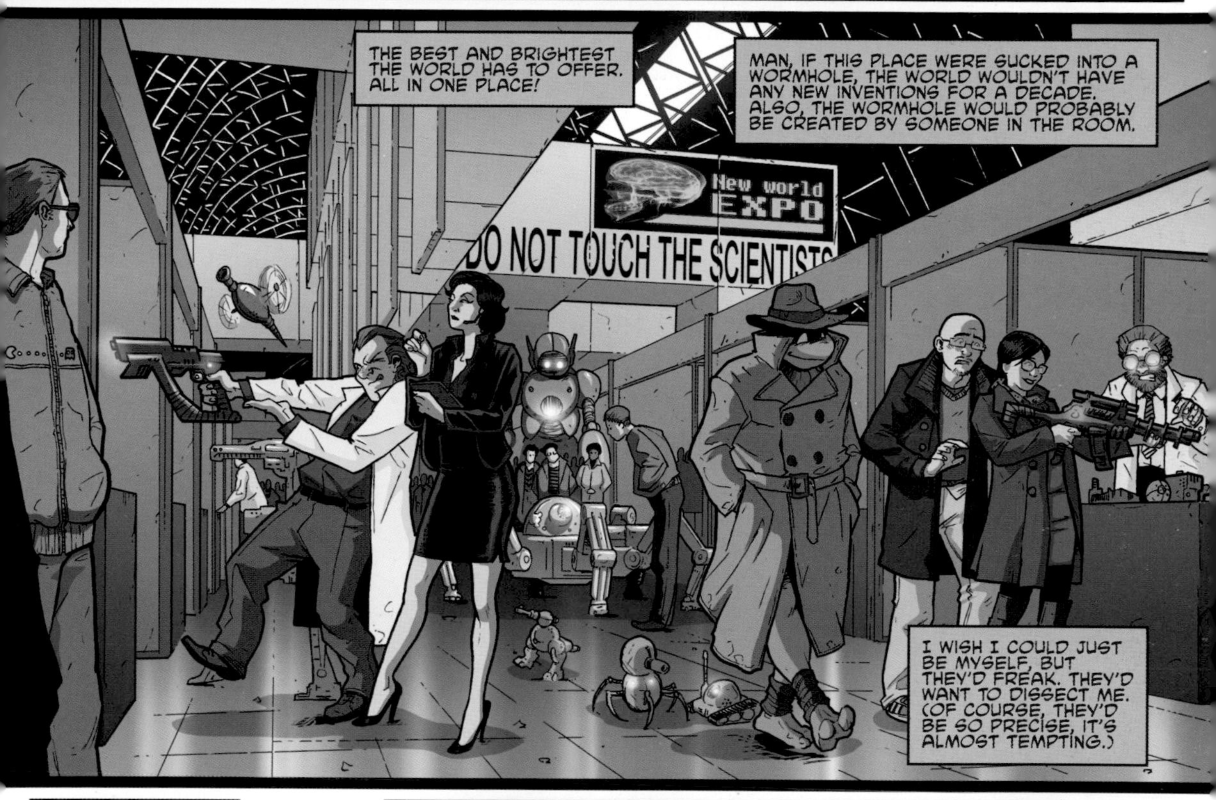
THE BEST AND BRIGHTEST THE WORLD HAS TO OFFER. ALL IN ONE PLACE!
MAN, IF THIS PLACE WERE SUCKED INTO A WORMHOLE, THE WORLD WOULDN'T HAVE ANY NEW INVENTIONS FOR A DECADE. ALSO, THE WORMHOLE WOULD PROBABLY BE CREATED BY SOMEONE IN THE ROOM.
New world EXPO
DO NOT TOUCH THE SCIENTISTS
I WISH I COULD JUST BE MYSELF, BUT THEY'D FREAK. THEY'D WANT TO DISSECT ME. (OF COURSE, THEY'D BE SO PRECISE, IT'S ALMOST TEMPTING.)

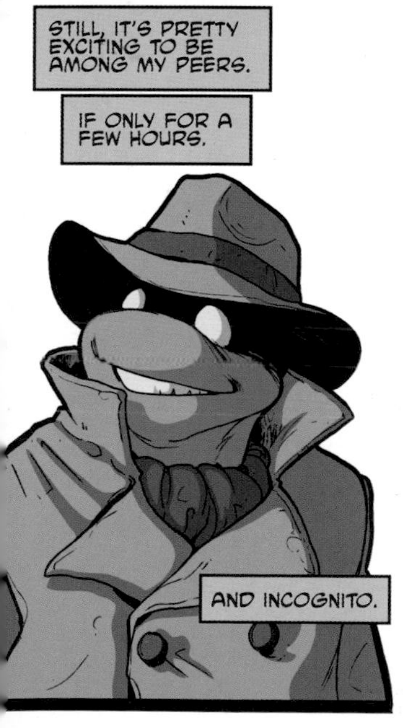
STILL, IT'S PRETTY EXCITING TO BE AMONG MY PEERS.
IF ONLY FOR A FEW HOURS.
AND INCOGNITO.

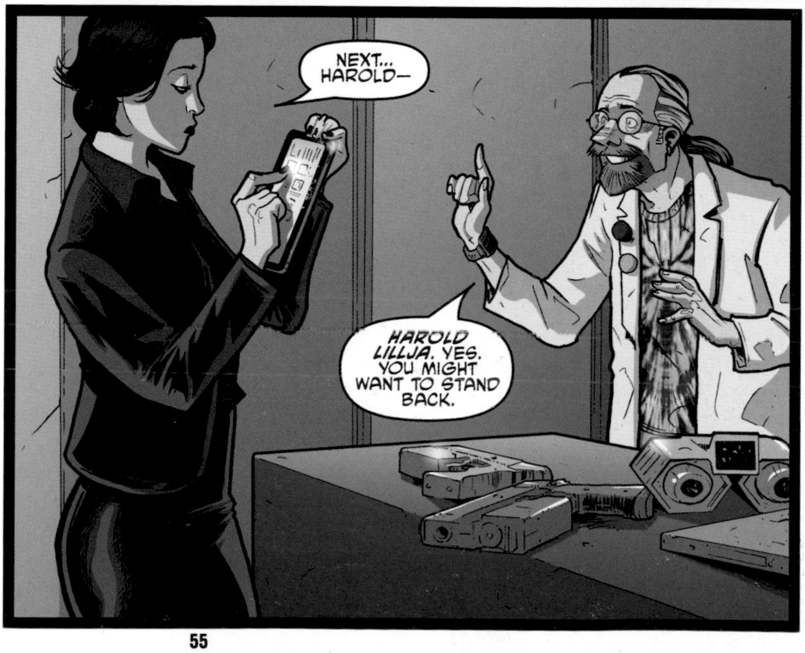
NEXT... HAROLD—
HAROLD LILLJA, YES. YOU MIGHT WANT TO STAND BACK.

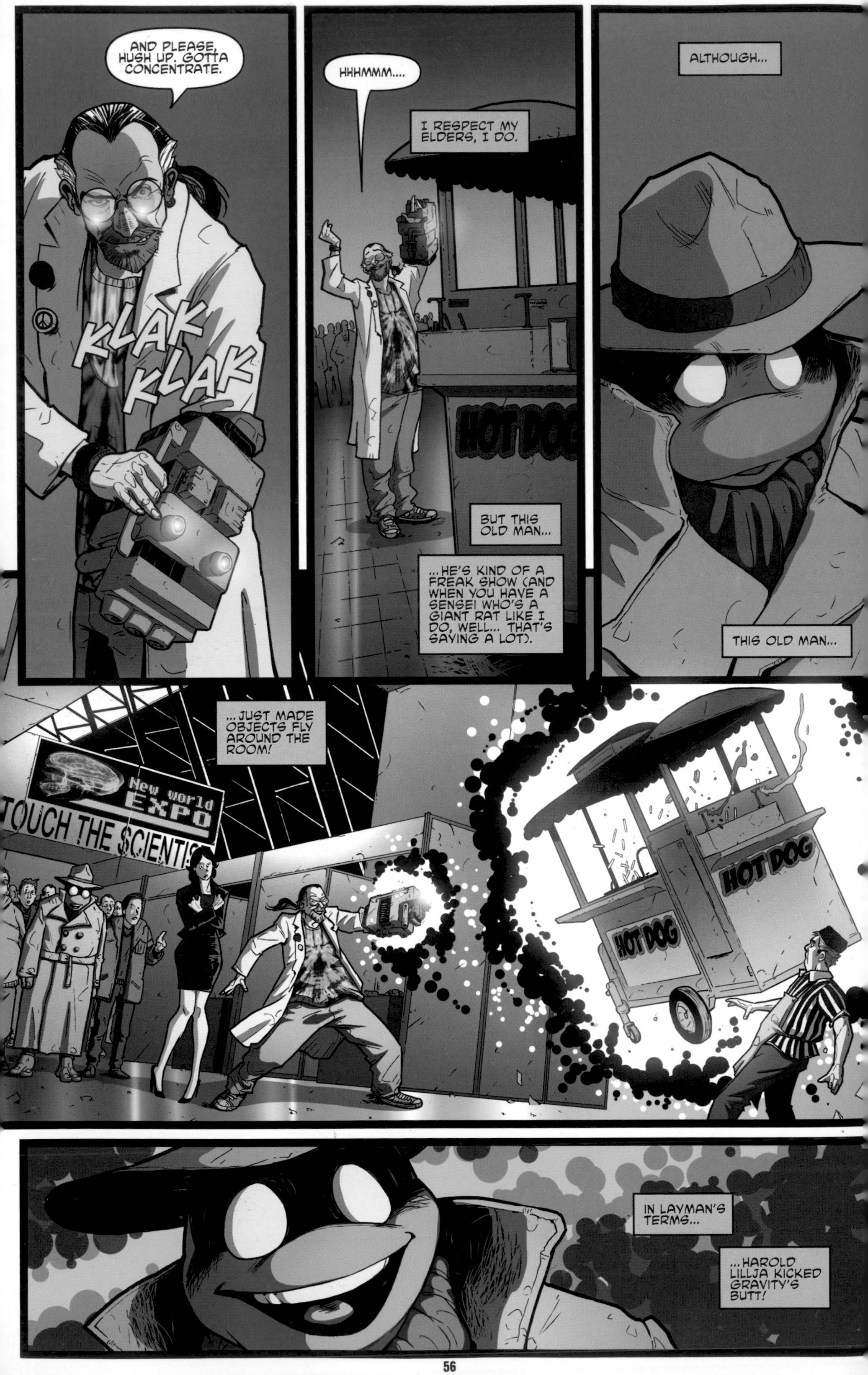
AND PLEASE, HUSH UP. GOTTA CONCENTRATE.
KLAK KLAK
HHHMMM....
I RESPECT MY ELDERS, I DO.
HOT DOG
BUT THIS OLD MAN...
...HE'S KIND OF A FREAK SHOW (AND WHEN YOU HAVE A SENSEI WHO'S A GIANT RAT LIKE I DO, WELL... THAT'S SAYING A LOT).
ALTHOUGH...
THIS OLD MAN...
...JUST MADE OBJECTS FLY AROUND THE ROOM!
New world EXPO
TOUCH THE SCIENTIS
HOT DOG
HOT DOG
IN LAYMAN'S TERMS...
...HAROLD LILLJA KICKED GRAVITY'S BUTT!

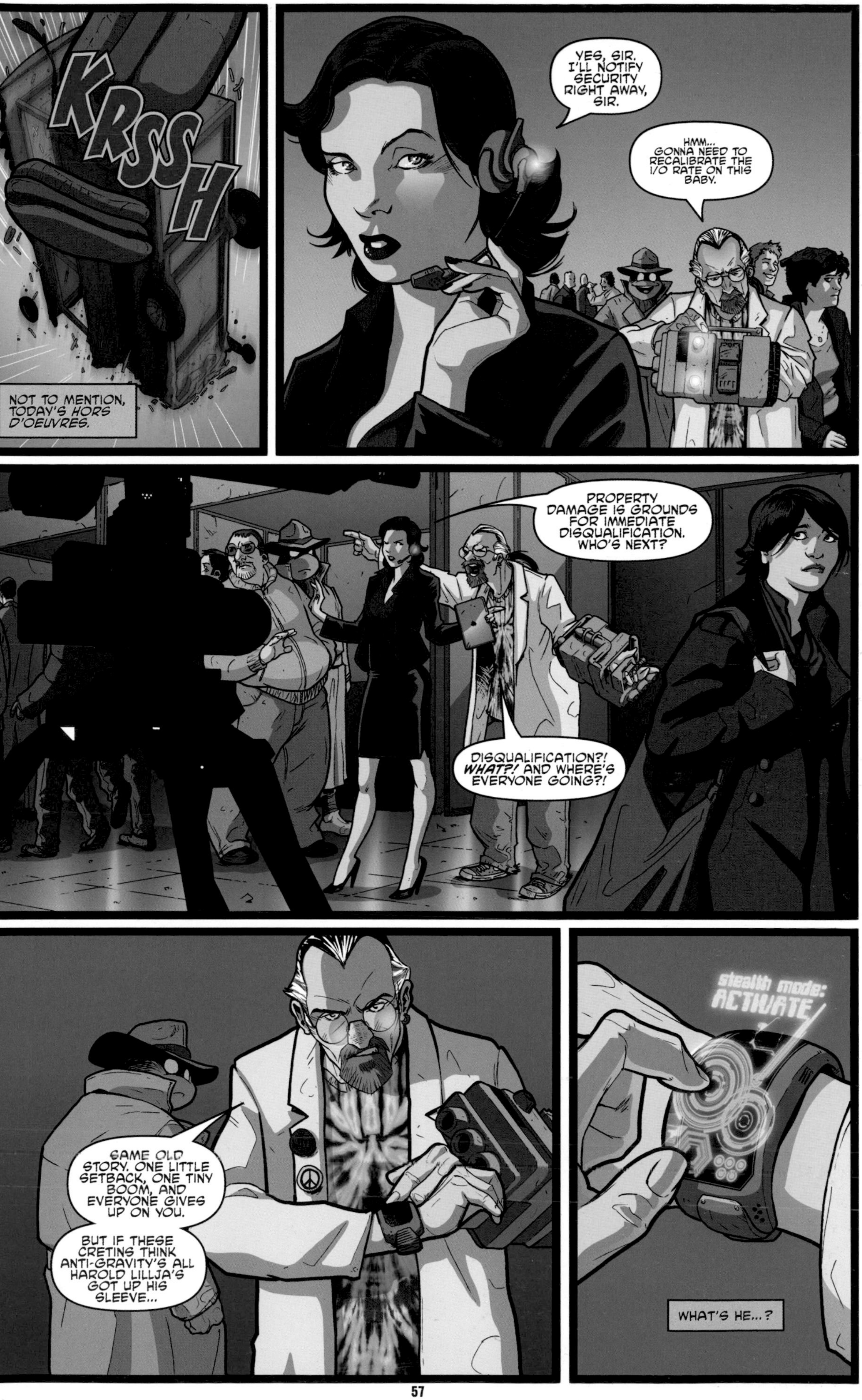
KRSSH
NOT TO MENTION, TODAY'S HORS D'OEUVRES.
YES, SIR. I'LL NOTIFY SECURITY RIGHT AWAY, SIR.
HMM... GONNA NEED TO RECALIBRATE THE I/O RATE ON THIS BABY.
PROPERTY DAMAGE IS GROUNDS FOR IMMEDIATE DISQUALIFICATION. WHO'S NEXT?
DISQUALIFICATION?! WHAT?! AND WHERE'S EVERYONE GOING?!
SAME OLD STORY. ONE LITTLE SETBACK, ONE TINY BOOM, AND EVERYONE GIVES UP ON YOU.
BUT IF THESE CRETINS THINK ANTI-GRAVITY'S ALL HAROLD LILLJA'S GOT UP HIS SLEEVE...
stealth mode: ACTIVATE
WHAT'S HE...?

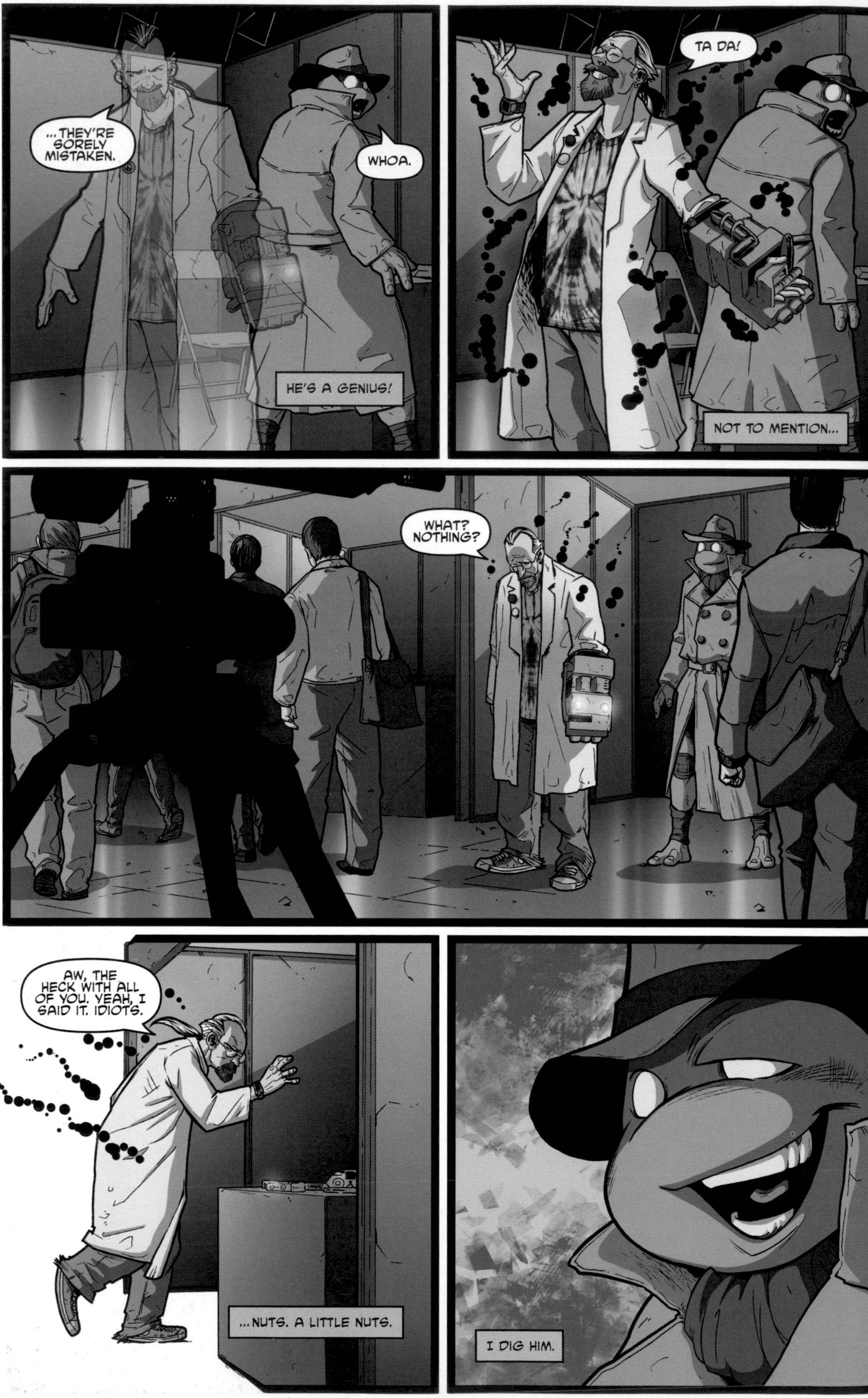
...THEY'RE SORELY MISTAKEN.
WHOA.
HE'S A GENIUS!
TA DA!
NOT TO MENTION...
WHAT? NOTHING?
AW, THE HECK WITH ALL OF YOU. YEAH, I SAID IT. IDIOTS.
...NUTS. A LITTLE NUTS.
I DIG HIM.

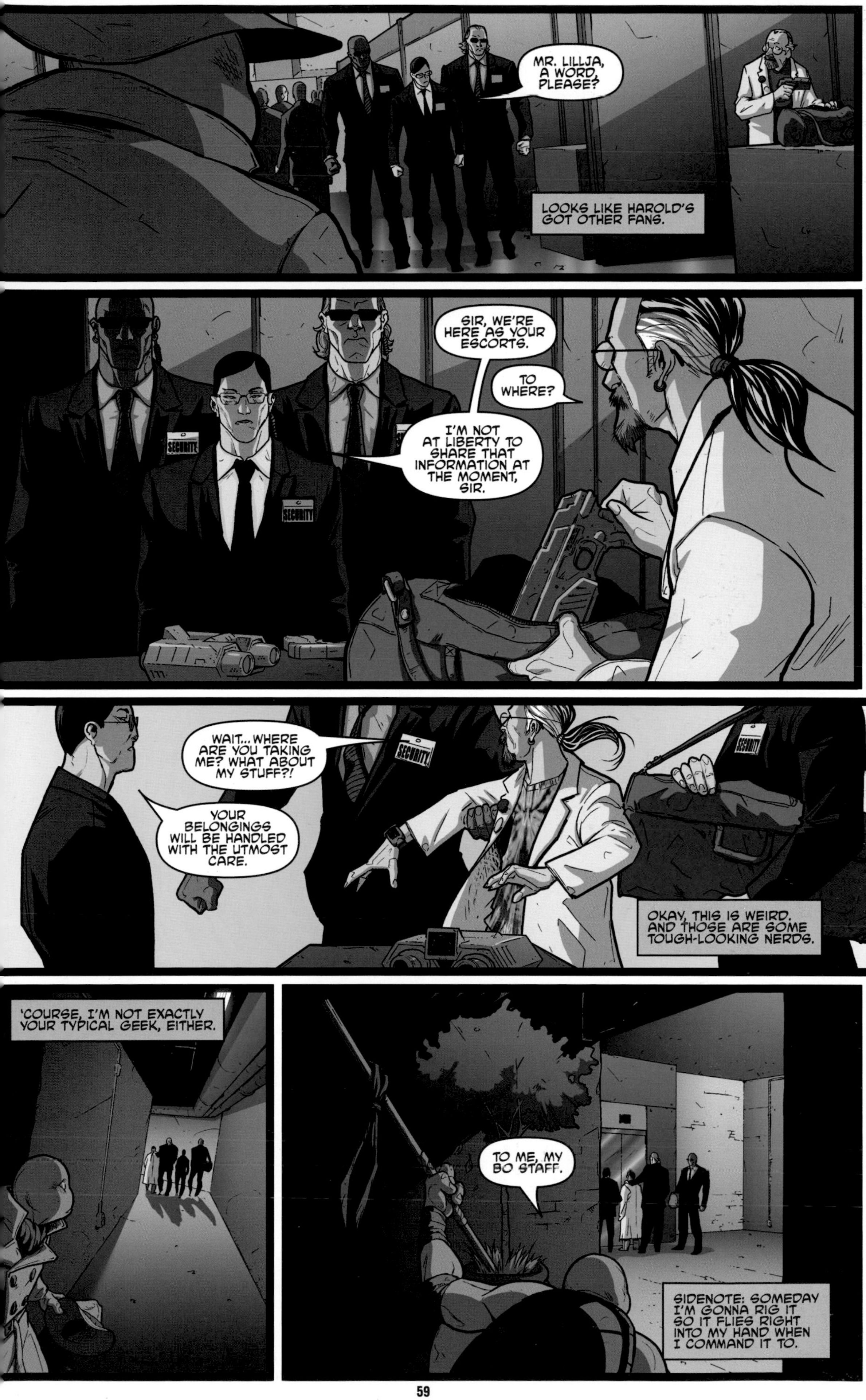
MR. LILLJA, A WORD, PLEASE?
LOOKS LIKE HAROLD'S GOT OTHER FANS.
SIR, WE'RE HERE AS YOUR ESCORTS.
TO WHERE?
I'M NOT AT LIBERTY TO SHARE THAT INFORMATION AT THE MOMENT, SIR.
SECURITY
SECURITY
WAIT... WHERE ARE YOU TAKING ME? WHAT ABOUT MY STUFF?!
YOUR BELONGINGS WILL BE HANDLED WITH THE UTMOST CARE.
SECURITY
SECURITY
OKAY, THIS IS WEIRD. AND THOSE ARE SOME TOUGH-LOOKING NERDS.
'COURSE, I'M NOT EXACTLY YOUR TYPICAL GEEK, EITHER.
TO ME, MY BO STAFF.
SIDENOTE: SOMEDAY I'M GONNA RIG IT SO IT FLIES RIGHT INTO MY HAND WHEN I COMMAND IT TO.

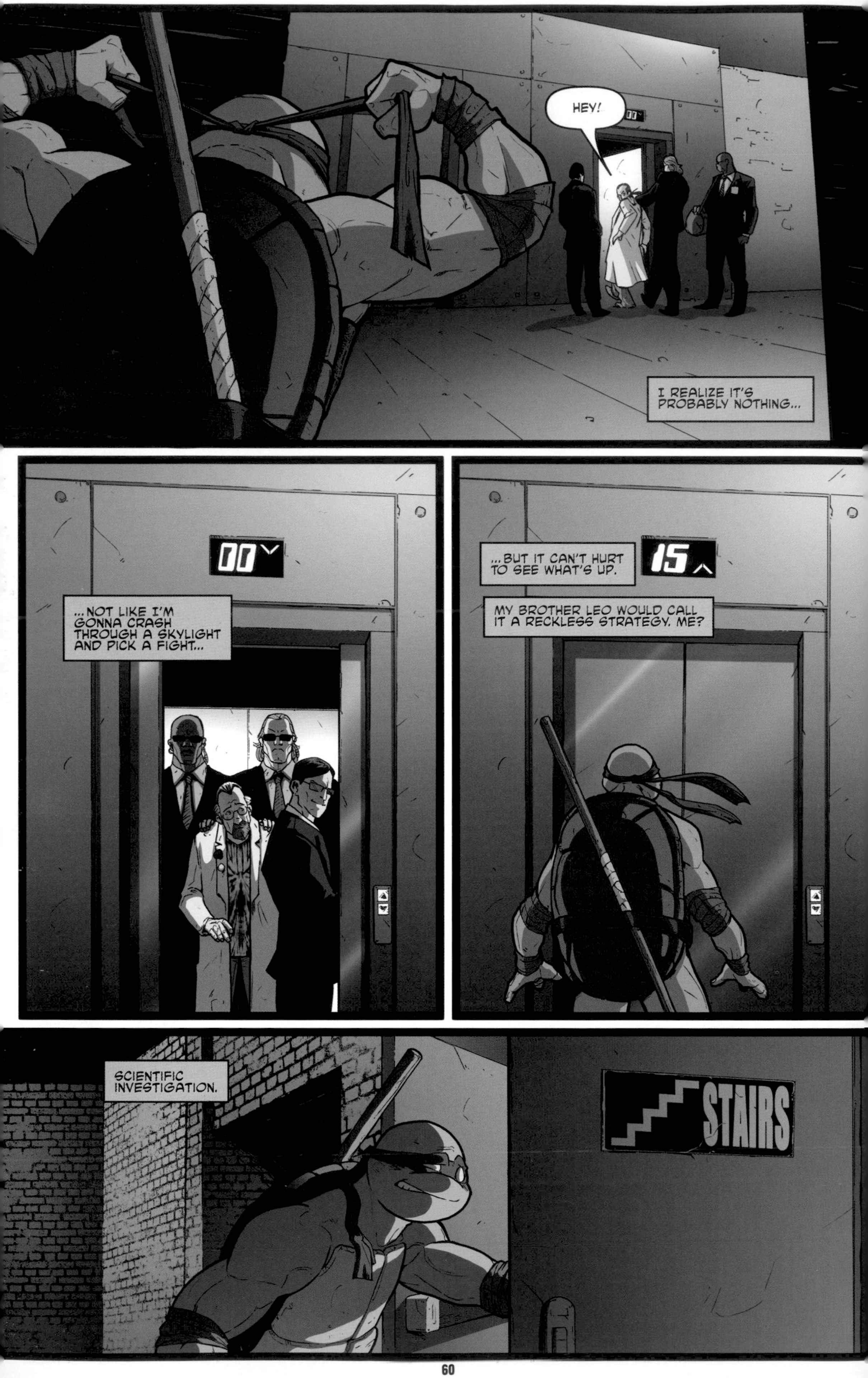
HEY!
I REALIZE IT'S PROBABLY NOTHING...
...NOT LIKE I'M GONNA CRASH THROUGH A SKYLIGHT AND PICK A FIGHT...
...BUT IT CAN'T HURT TO SEE WHAT'S UP.
MY BROTHER LEO WOULD CALL IT A RECKLESS STRATEGY. ME?
SCIENTIFIC INVESTIGATION.
STAIRS

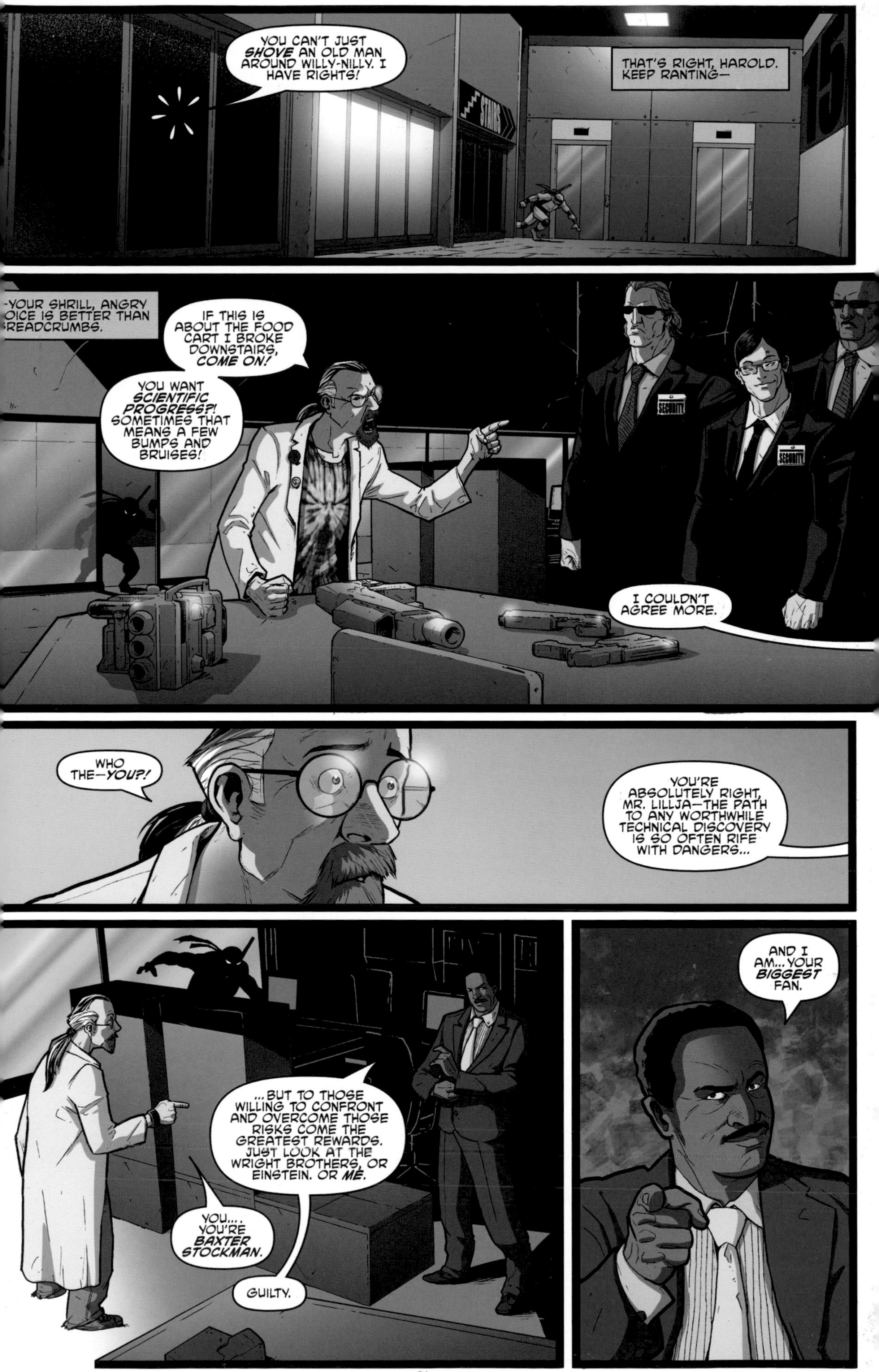

YOU CAN'T JUST SHOVE AN OLD MAN AROUND WILLY-NILLY. I HAVE RIGHTS!
THAT'S RIGHT, HAROLD. KEEP RANTING—
STAIRS
-YOUR SHRILL, ANGRY OICE IS BETTER THAN READCRUMBS.
IF THIS IS ABOUT THE FOOD CART I BROKE DOWNSTAIRS, COME ON!
YOU WANT SCIENTIFIC PROGRESS?! SOMETIMES THAT MEANS A FEW BUMPS AND BRUISES!
SECURITY
SECURITY
I COULDN'T AGREE MORE.
WHO THE—YOU?!
YOU'RE ABSOLUTELY RIGHT, MR. LILLJA—THE PATH TO ANY WORTHWHILE TECHNICAL DISCOVERY IS SO OFTEN RIFE WITH DANGERS...
...BUT TO THOSE WILLING TO CONFRONT AND OVERCOME THOSE RISKS COME THE GREATEST REWARDS. JUST LOOK AT THE WRIGHT BROTHERS, OR EINSTEIN. OR ME.
YOU... YOU'RE BAXTER STOCKMAN.
GUILTY.
AND I AM...YOUR BIGGEST FAN.

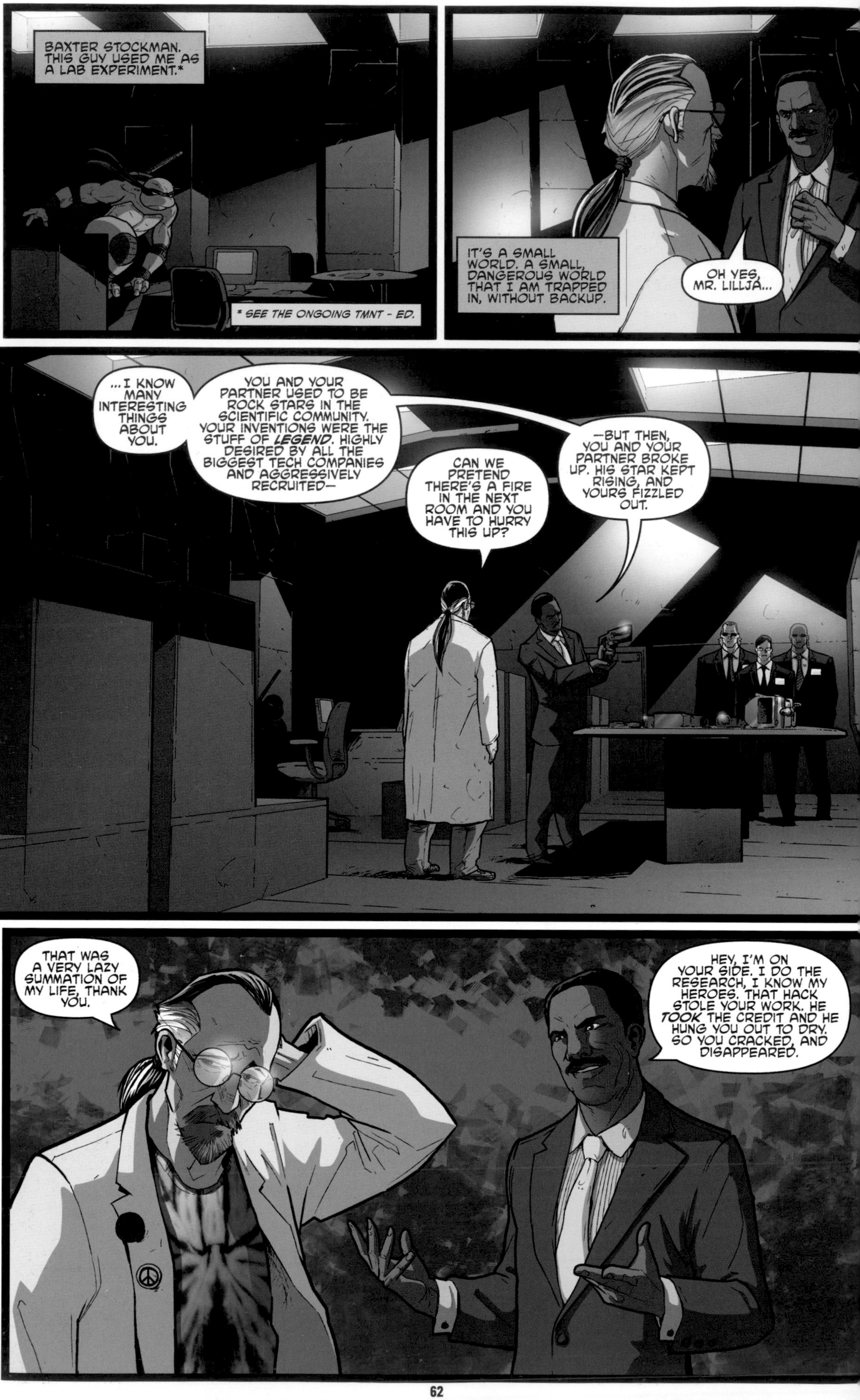
BAXTER STOCKMAN. THIS GUY USED ME AS A LAB EXPERIMENT.*
* SEE THE ONGOING TMNT - ED.
IT'S A SMALL WORLD. A SMALL, DANGEROUS WORLD THAT I AM TRAPPED IN, WITHOUT BACKUP.
OH YES, MR. LILLJA...
...I KNOW MANY INTERESTING THINGS ABOUT YOU.
YOU AND YOUR PARTNER USED TO BE ROCK STARS IN THE SCIENTIFIC COMMUNITY. YOUR INVENTIONS WERE THE STUFF OF *LEGEND*. HIGHLY DESIRED BY ALL THE BIGGEST TECH COMPANIES AND AGGRESSIVELY RECRUITED—
—BUT THEN, YOU AND YOUR PARTNER BROKE UP. HIS STAR KEPT RISING, AND YOURS FIZZLED OUT.
CAN WE PRETEND THERE'S A FIRE IN THE NEXT ROOM AND YOU HAVE TO HURRY THIS UP?
THAT WAS A VERY LAZY SUMMATION OF MY LIFE, THANK YOU.
HEY, I'M ON YOUR SIDE. I DO THE RESEARCH, I KNOW MY HEROES. THAT HACK STOLE YOUR WORK. HE *TOOK* THE CREDIT AND HE HUNG YOU OUT TO DRY. SO YOU CRACKED, AND DISAPPEARED.

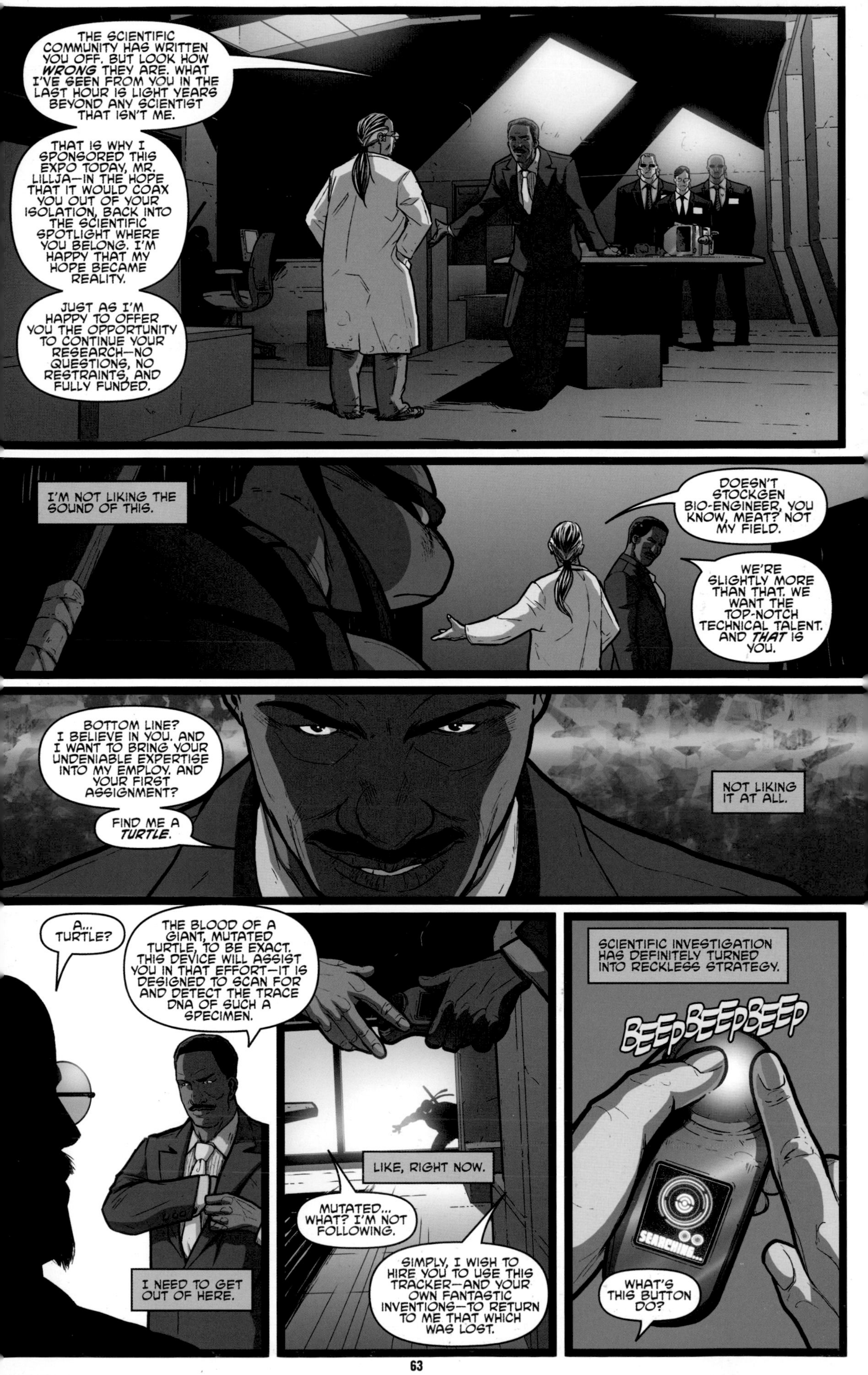
THE SCIENTIFIC COMMUNITY HAS WRITTEN YOU OFF. BUT LOOK HOW WRONG THEY ARE. WHAT I'VE SEEN FROM YOU IN THE LAST HOUR IS LIGHT YEARS BEYOND ANY SCIENTIST THAT ISN'T ME.
THAT IS WHY I SPONSORED THIS EXPO TODAY, MR. LILLJA—IN THE HOPE THAT IT WOULD COAX YOU OUT OF YOUR ISOLATION, BACK INTO THE SCIENTIFIC SPOTLIGHT WHERE YOU BELONG. I'M HAPPY THAT MY HOPE BECAME REALITY.
JUST AS I'M HAPPY TO OFFER YOU THE OPPORTUNITY TO CONTINUE YOUR RESEARCH—NO QUESTIONS, NO RESTRAINTS, AND FULLY FUNDED.
I'M NOT LIKING THE SOUND OF THIS.
DOESN'T STOCKGEN BIO-ENGINEER, YOU KNOW, MEAT? NOT MY FIELD.
WE'RE SLIGHTLY MORE THAN THAT. WE WANT THE TOP-NOTCH TECHNICAL TALENT. AND THAT IS YOU.
BOTTOM LINE? I BELIEVE IN YOU. AND I WANT TO BRING YOUR UNDENIABLE EXPERTISE INTO MY EMPLOY. AND YOUR FIRST ASSIGNMENT?
FIND ME A TURTLE.
NOT LIKING IT AT ALL.
A... TURTLE?
THE BLOOD OF A GIANT, MUTATED TURTLE, TO BE EXACT. THIS DEVICE WILL ASSIST YOU IN THAT EFFORT—IT IS DESIGNED TO SCAN FOR AND DETECT THE TRACE DNA OF SUCH A SPECIMEN.
I NEED TO GET OUT OF HERE.
LIKE, RIGHT NOW.
MUTATED... WHAT? I'M NOT FOLLOWING.
SIMPLY, I WISH TO HIRE YOU TO USE THIS TRACKER—AND YOUR OWN FANTASTIC INVENTIONS—TO RETURN TO ME THAT WHICH WAS LOST.
SCIENTIFIC INVESTIGATION HAS DEFINITELY TURNED INTO RECKLESS STRATEGY.
BEEPBEEPBEEP
SEARCHING...
WHAT'S THIS BUTTON DO?

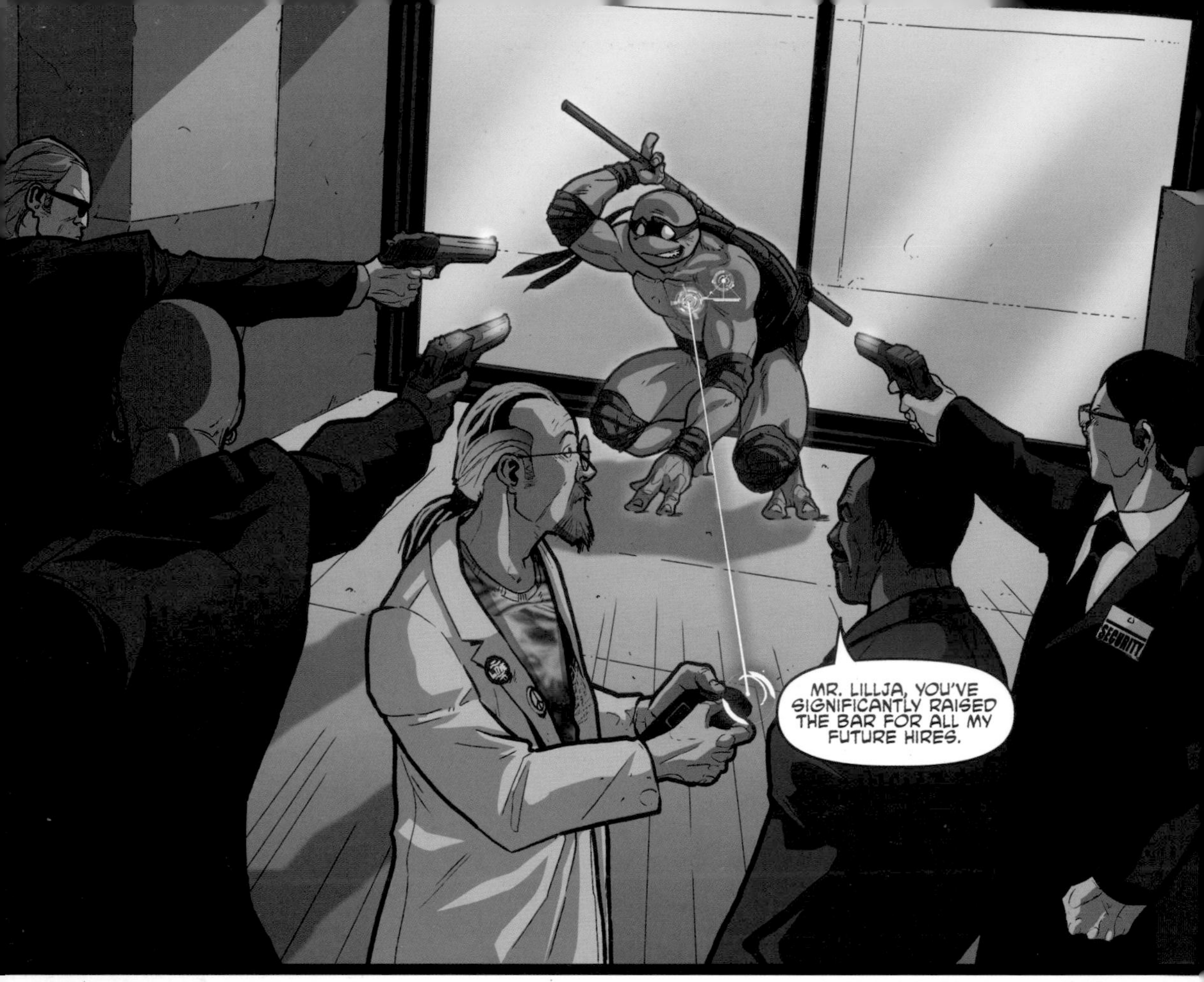
MR. LILLJA, YOU'VE SIGNIFICANTLY RAISED THE BAR FOR ALL MY FUTURE HIRES.
SECURITY

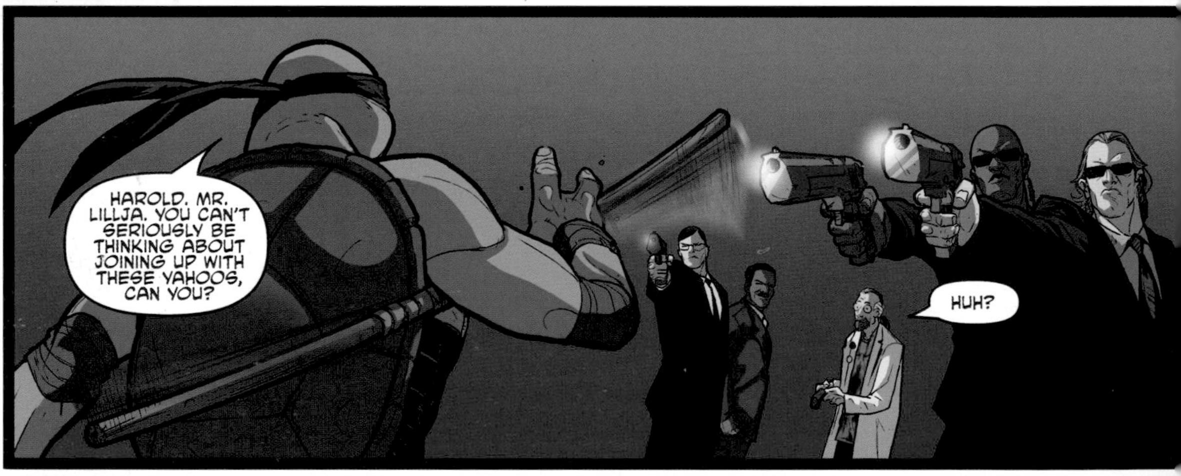
HAROLD. MR. LILLJA. YOU CAN'T SERIOUSLY BE THINKING ABOUT JOINING UP WITH THESE YAHOOS, CAN YOU?
HUH?

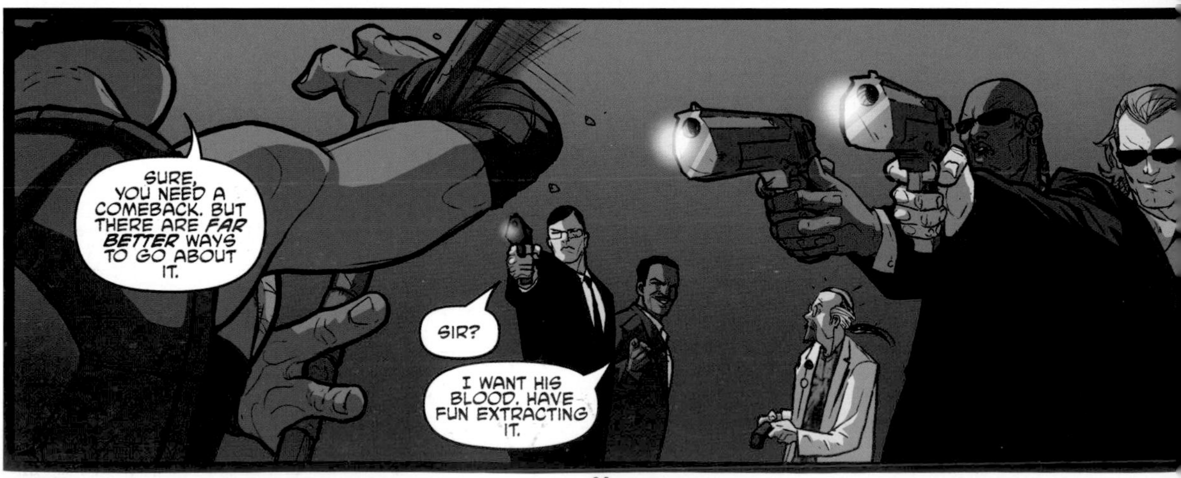
SURE, YOU NEED A COMEBACK. BUT THERE ARE *FAR BETTER* WAYS TO GO ABOUT IT.
SIR?
I WANT HIS BLOOD. HAVE FUN EXTRACTING IT.

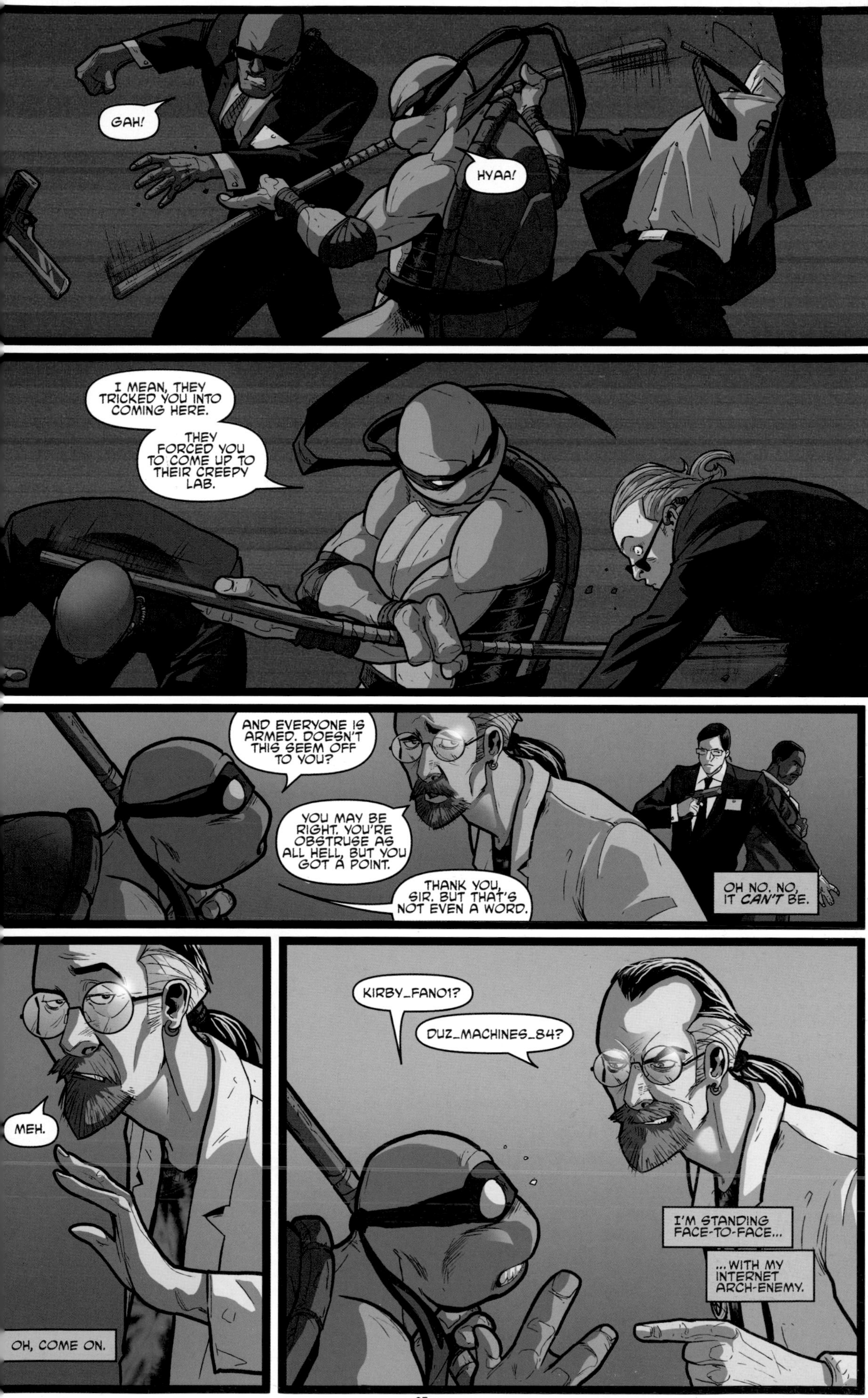
GAH!
HYAA!
I MEAN, THEY TRICKED YOU INTO COMING HERE.
THEY FORCED YOU TO COME UP TO THEIR CREEPY LAB.
AND EVERYONE IS ARMED. DOESN'T THIS SEEM OFF TO YOU?
YOU MAY BE RIGHT. YOU'RE OBSTRUSE AS ALL HELL, BUT YOU GOT A POINT.
THANK YOU, SIR. BUT THAT'S NOT EVEN A WORD.
OH NO. NO, IT *CAN'T* BE.
MEH.
OH, COME ON.
KIRBY_FAN01?
DUZ_MACHINES_84?
I'M STANDING FACE-TO-FACE...
...WITH MY INTERNET ARCH-ENEMY.

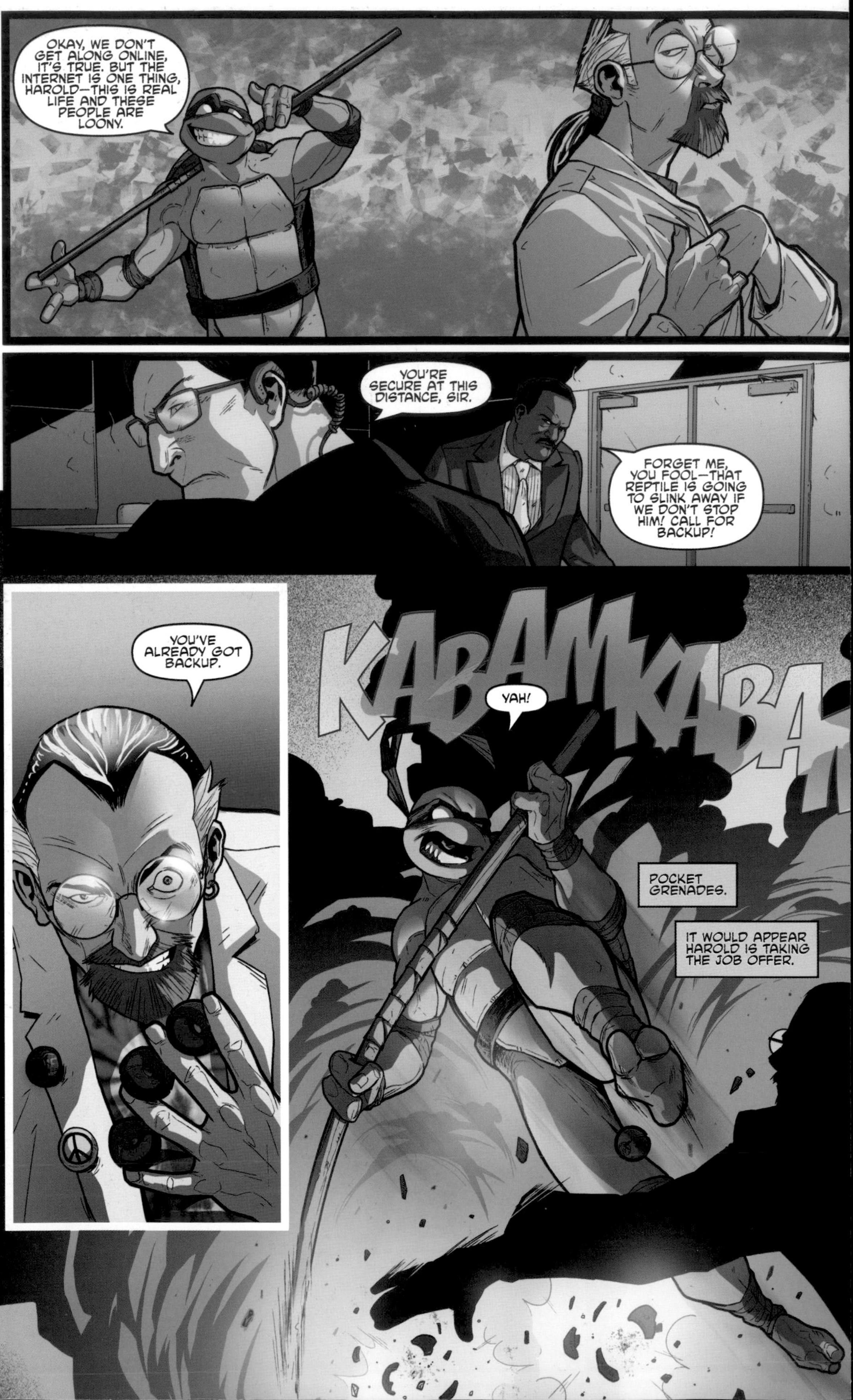
OKAY, WE DON'T GET ALONG ONLINE, IT'S TRUE. BUT THE INTERNET IS ONE THING, HAROLD—THIS IS REAL LIFE AND THESE PEOPLE ARE LOONY.
YOU'RE SECURE AT THIS DISTANCE, SIR.
FORGET ME, YOU FOOL—THAT REPTILE IS GOING TO SLINK AWAY IF WE DON'T STOP HIM! CALL FOR BACKUP!
YOU'VE ALREADY GOT BACKUP.
KABAM
YAH!
POCKET GRENADES.
IT WOULD APPEAR HAROLD IS TAKING THE JOB OFFER.

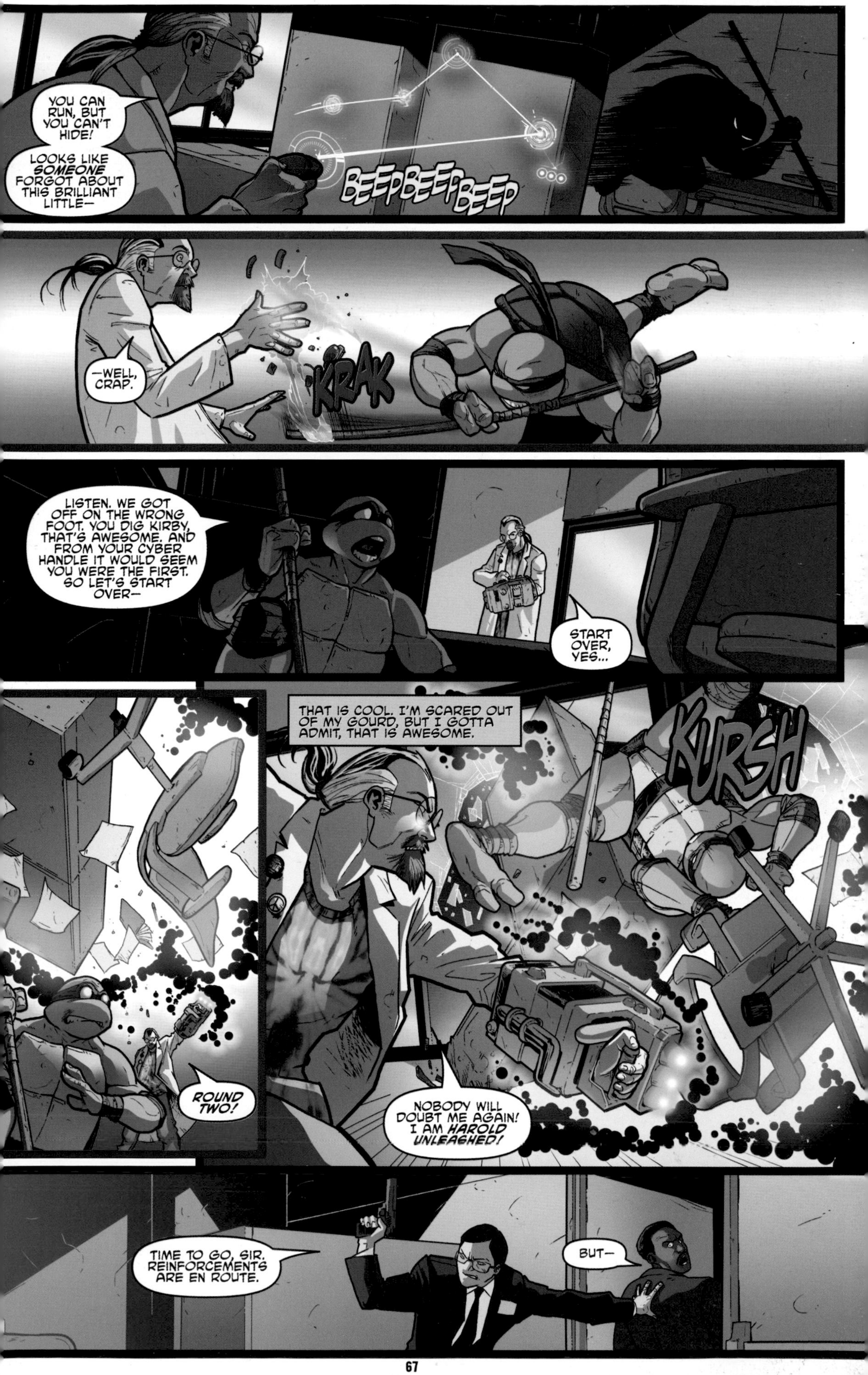
YOU CAN RUN, BUT YOU CAN'T HIDE!
LOOKS LIKE SOMEONE FORGOT ABOUT THIS BRILLIANT LITTLE—
BEEPBEEPBEEP
—WELL, CRAP.
KRAK
LISTEN. WE GOT OFF ON THE WRONG FOOT. YOU DIG KIRBY, THAT'S AWESOME. AND FROM YOUR CYBER HANDLE IT WOULD SEEM YOU WERE THE FIRST. SO LET'S START OVER—
START OVER, YES...
ROUND TWO!
THAT IS COOL. I'M SCARED OUT OF MY GOURD, BUT I GOTTA ADMIT, THAT IS AWESOME.
KURSH
NOBODY WILL DOUBT ME AGAIN! I AM HAROLD UNLEASHED!
TIME TO GO, SIR. REINFORCEMENTS ARE EN ROUTE.
BUT—

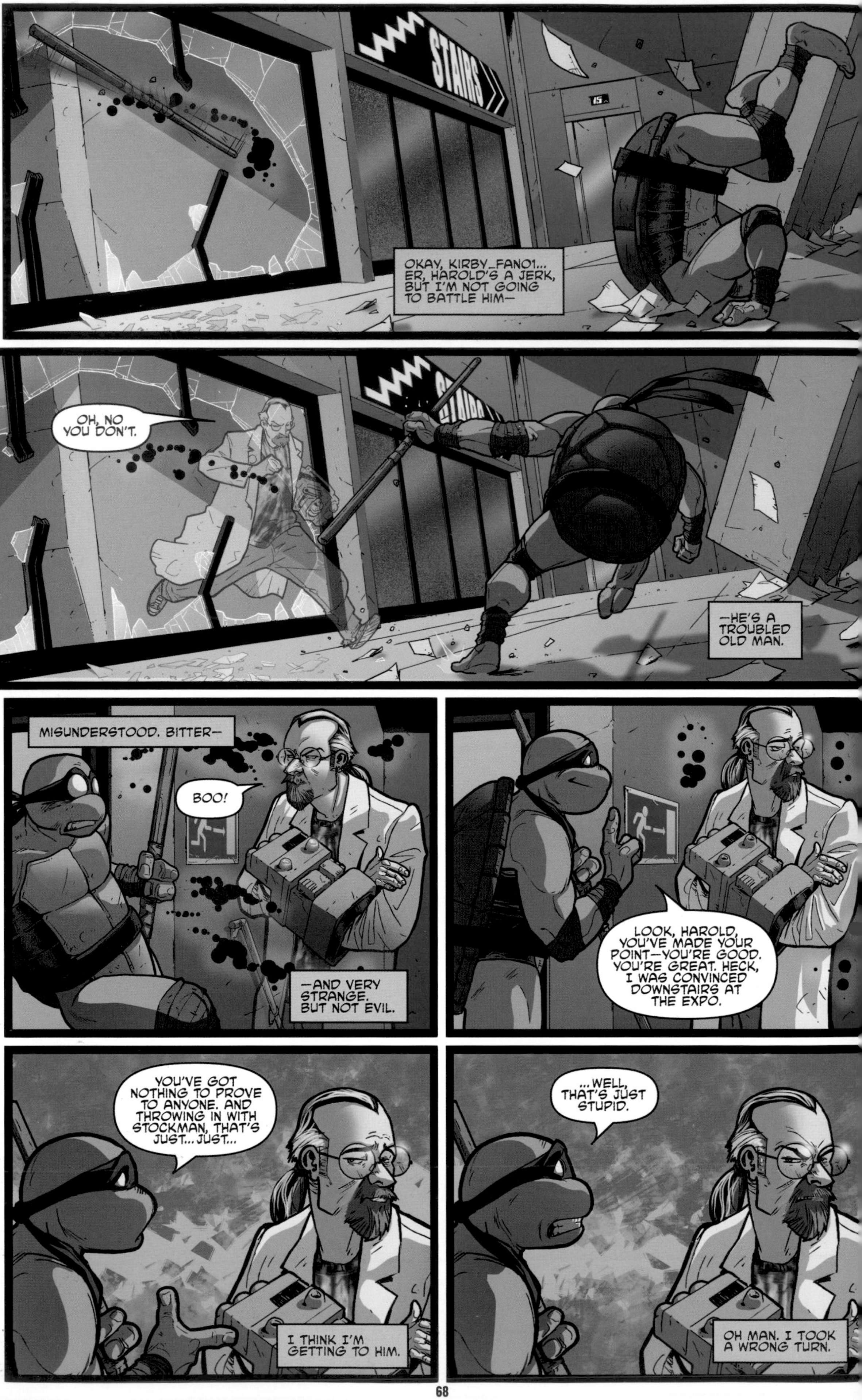

STAIRS
OKAY, KIRBY_FAN01... ER, HAROLD'S A JERK, BUT I'M NOT GOING TO BATTLE HIM—
OH, NO YOU DON'T.
—HE'S A TROUBLED OLD MAN.
MISUNDERSTOOD. BITTER—
BOO!
—AND VERY STRANGE. BUT NOT EVIL.
LOOK, HAROLD, YOU'VE MADE YOUR POINT—YOU'RE GOOD. YOU'RE GREAT. HECK, I WAS CONVINCED DOWNSTAIRS AT THE EXPO.
YOU'VE GOT NOTHING TO PROVE TO ANYONE. AND THROWING IN WITH STOCKMAN, THAT'S JUST... JUST...
I THINK I'M GETTING TO HIM.
...WELL, THAT'S JUST STUPID.
OH MAN. I TOOK A WRONG TURN.

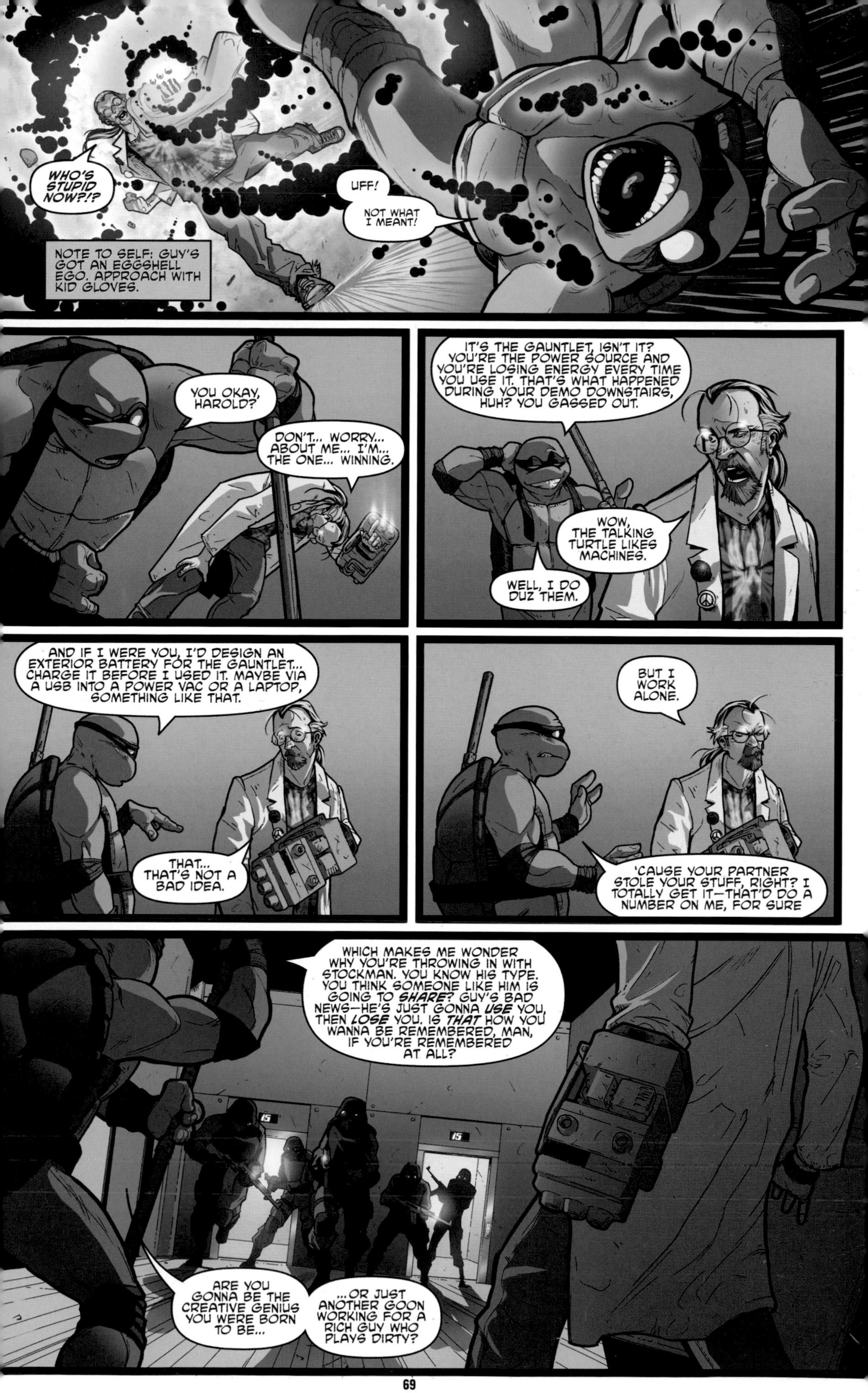
WHO'S STUPID NOW?!?
UFF!
NOT WHAT I MEANT!
NOTE TO SELF: GUY'S GOT AN EGGSHELL EGO. APPROACH WITH KID GLOVES.
YOU OKAY, HAROLD?
DON'T... WORRY... ABOUT ME... I'M... THE ONE... WINNING.
IT'S THE GAUNTLET, ISN'T IT? YOU'RE THE POWER SOURCE AND YOU'RE LOSING ENERGY EVERY TIME YOU USE IT. THAT'S WHAT HAPPENED DURING YOUR DEMO DOWNSTAIRS, HUH? YOU GASSED OUT.
WOW, THE TALKING TURTLE LIKES MACHINES.
WELL, I DO DUZ THEM.
AND IF I WERE YOU, I'D DESIGN AN EXTERIOR BATTERY FOR THE GAUNTLET... CHARGE IT BEFORE I USED IT. MAYBE VIA A USB INTO A POWER VAC OR A LAPTOP, SOMETHING LIKE THAT.
THAT... THAT'S NOT A BAD IDEA.
BUT I WORK ALONE.
'CAUSE YOUR PARTNER STOLE YOUR STUFF, RIGHT? I TOTALLY GET IT—THAT'D DO A NUMBER ON ME, FOR SURE
WHICH MAKES ME WONDER WHY YOU'RE THROWING IN WITH STOCKMAN. YOU KNOW HIS TYPE. YOU THINK SOMEONE LIKE HIM IS GOING TO SHARE? GUY'S BAD NEWS—HE'S JUST GONNA USE YOU, THEN LOSE YOU. IS THAT HOW YOU WANNA BE REMEMBERED, MAN, IF YOU'RE REMEMBERED AT ALL?
ARE YOU GONNA BE THE CREATIVE GENIUS YOU WERE BORN TO BE...
...OR JUST ANOTHER GOON WORKING FOR A RICH GUY WHO PLAYS DIRTY?

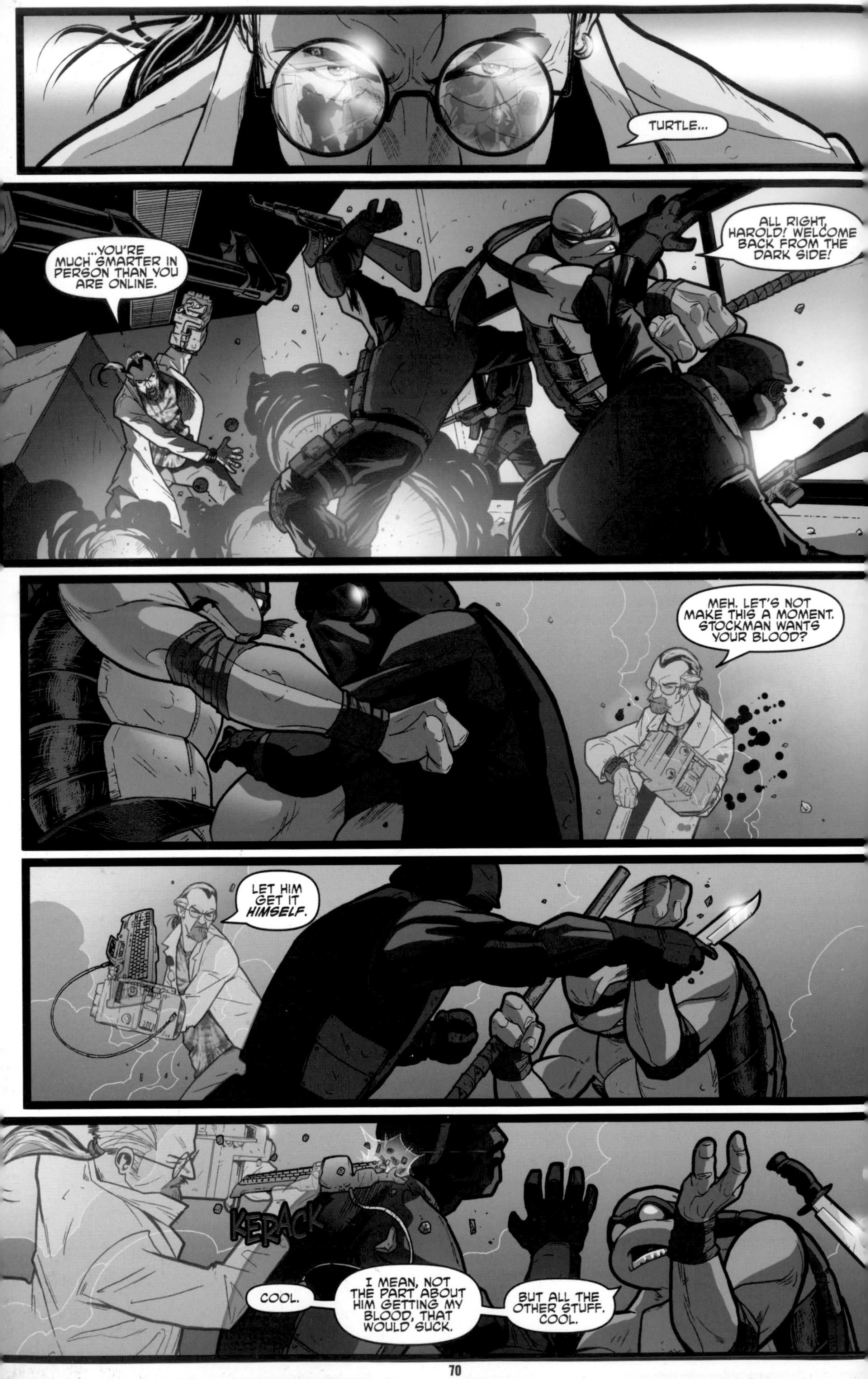

TURTLE...
...YOU'RE MUCH SMARTER IN PERSON THAN YOU ARE ONLINE.
ALL RIGHT, HAROLD! WELCOME BACK FROM THE DARK SIDE!
MEH. LET'S NOT MAKE THIS A MOMENT. STOCKMAN WANTS YOUR BLOOD?
LET HIM GET IT *HIMSELF*.
KERACK
COOL.
I MEAN, NOT THE PART ABOUT HIM GETTING MY BLOOD, THAT WOULD SUCK.
BUT ALL THE OTHER STUFF. COOL.

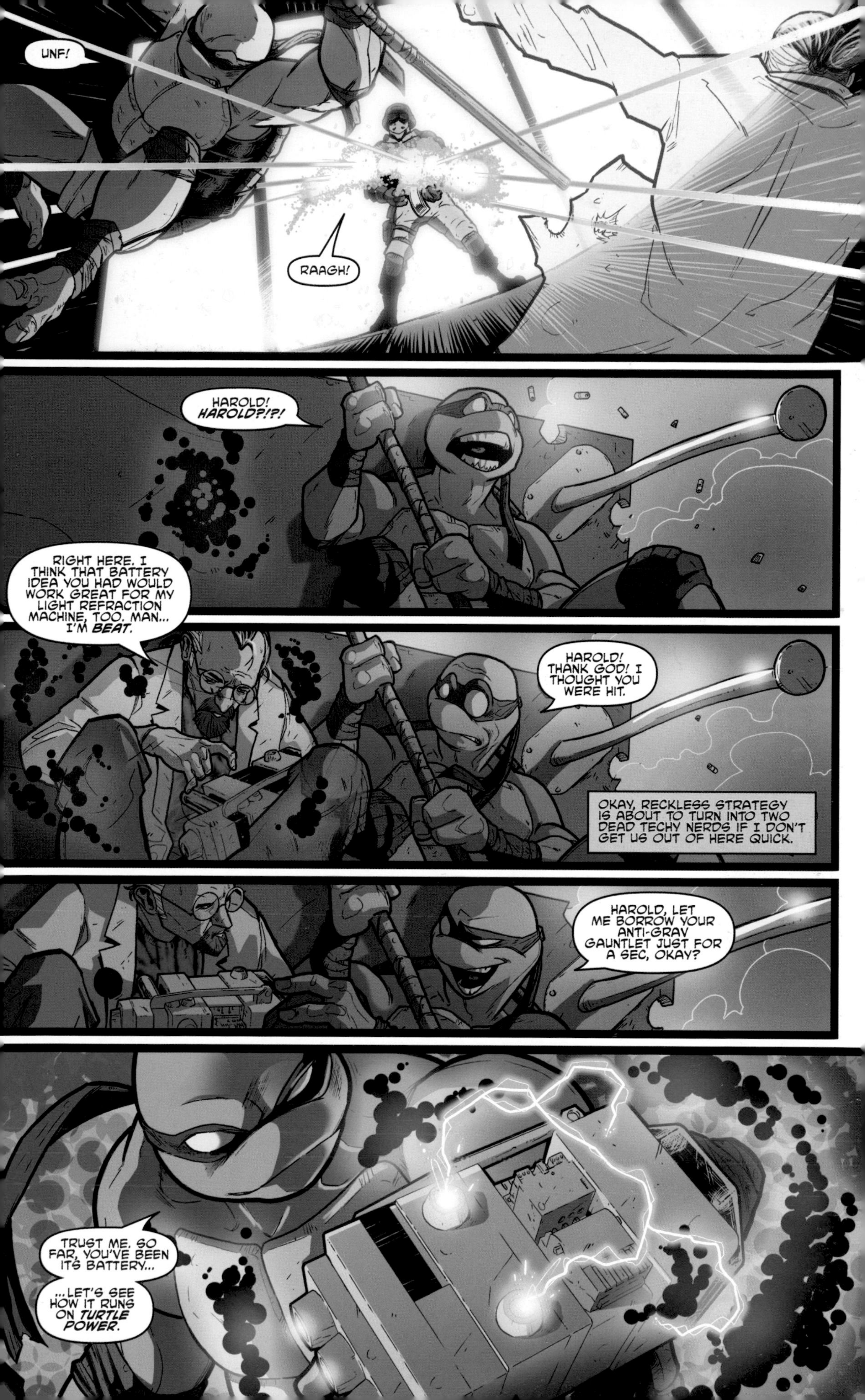
UNF!
RAAGH!
HAROLD! HAROLD?!?!
RIGHT HERE. I THINK THAT BATTERY IDEA YOU HAD WOULD WORK GREAT FOR MY LIGHT REFRACTION MACHINE, TOO. MAN... I'M BEAT.
HAROLD! THANK GOD! I THOUGHT YOU WERE HIT.
OKAY, RECKLESS STRATEGY IS ABOUT TO TURN INTO TWO DEAD TECHY NERDS IF I DON'T GET US OUT OF HERE QUICK.
HAROLD, LET ME BORROW YOUR ANTI-GRAV GAUNTLET JUST FOR A SEC, OKAY?
TRUST ME. SO FAR, YOU'VE BEEN ITS BATTERY...
...LET'S SEE HOW IT RUNS ON TURTLE POWER.

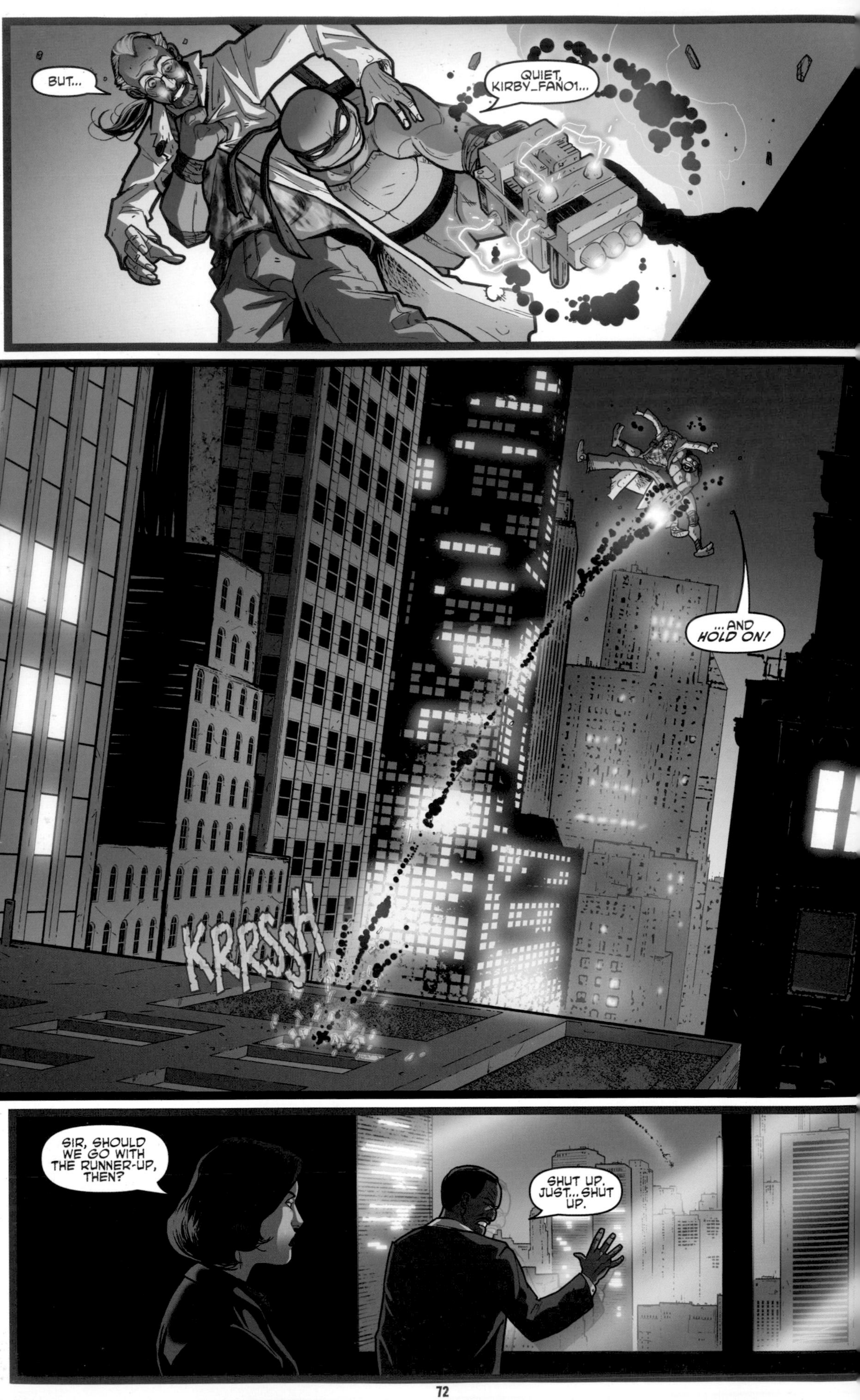
BUT...
QUIET, KIRBY_FAN01...
...AND HOLD ON!
KRRSSH
SIR, SHOULD WE GO WITH THE RUNNER-UP, THEN?
SHUT UP. JUST... SHUT UP.

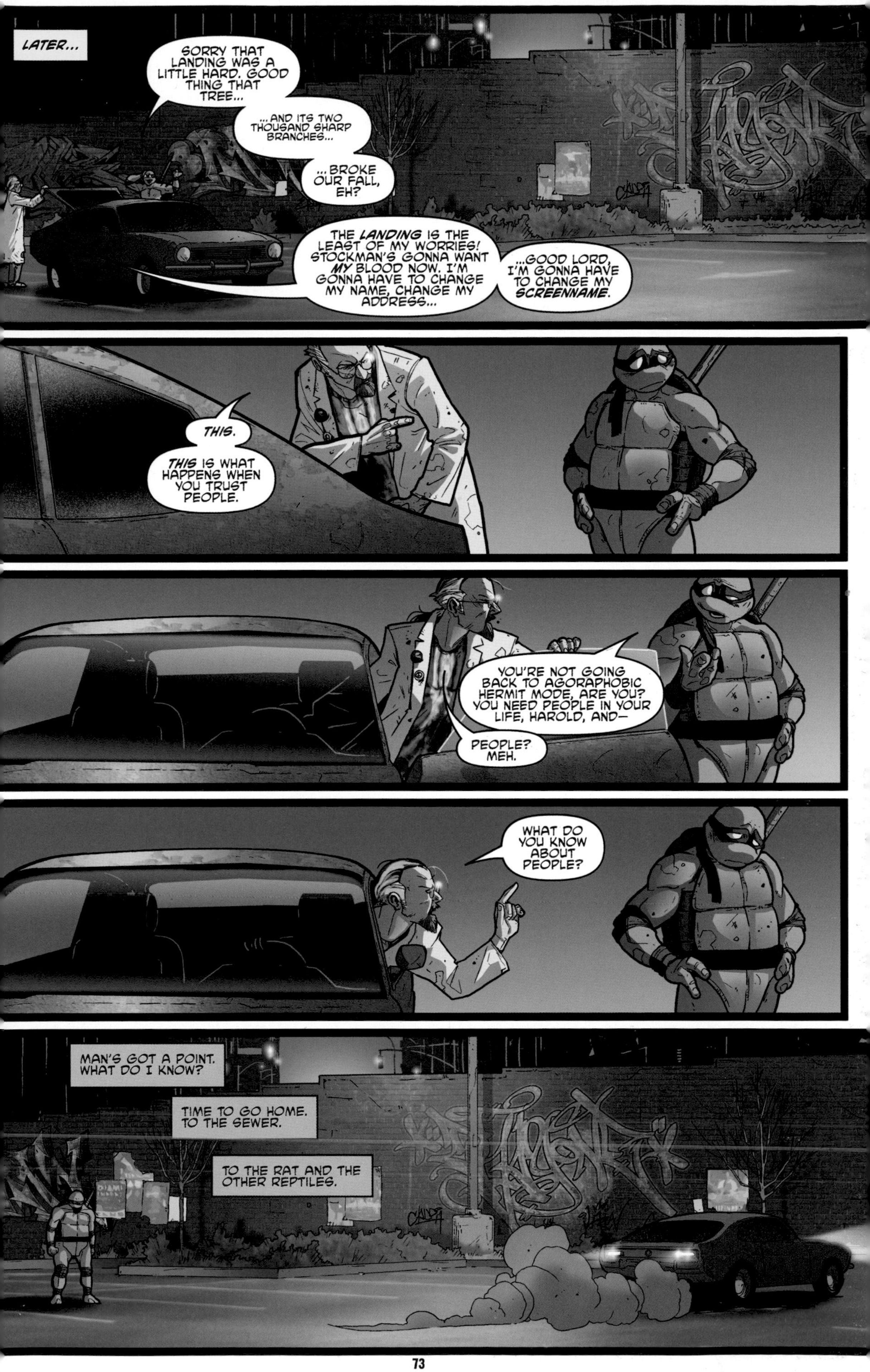
LATER...
SORRY THAT LANDING WAS A LITTLE HARD. GOOD THING THAT TREE...
...AND ITS TWO THOUSAND SHARP BRANCHES...
...BROKE OUR FALL, EH?
THE LANDING IS THE LEAST OF MY WORRIES! STOCKMAN'S GONNA WANT MY BLOOD NOW. I'M GONNA HAVE TO CHANGE MY NAME, CHANGE MY ADDRESS...
...GOOD LORD, I'M GONNA HAVE TO CHANGE MY SCREENNAME.
THIS.
THIS IS WHAT HAPPENS WHEN YOU TRUST PEOPLE.
YOU'RE NOT GOING BACK TO AGORAPHOBIC HERMIT MODE, ARE YOU? YOU NEED PEOPLE IN YOUR LIFE, HAROLD, AND—
PEOPLE? MEH.
WHAT DO YOU KNOW ABOUT PEOPLE?
MAN'S GOT A POINT. WHAT DO I KNOW?
TIME TO GO HOME. TO THE SEWER.
TO THE RAT AND THE OTHER REPTILES.

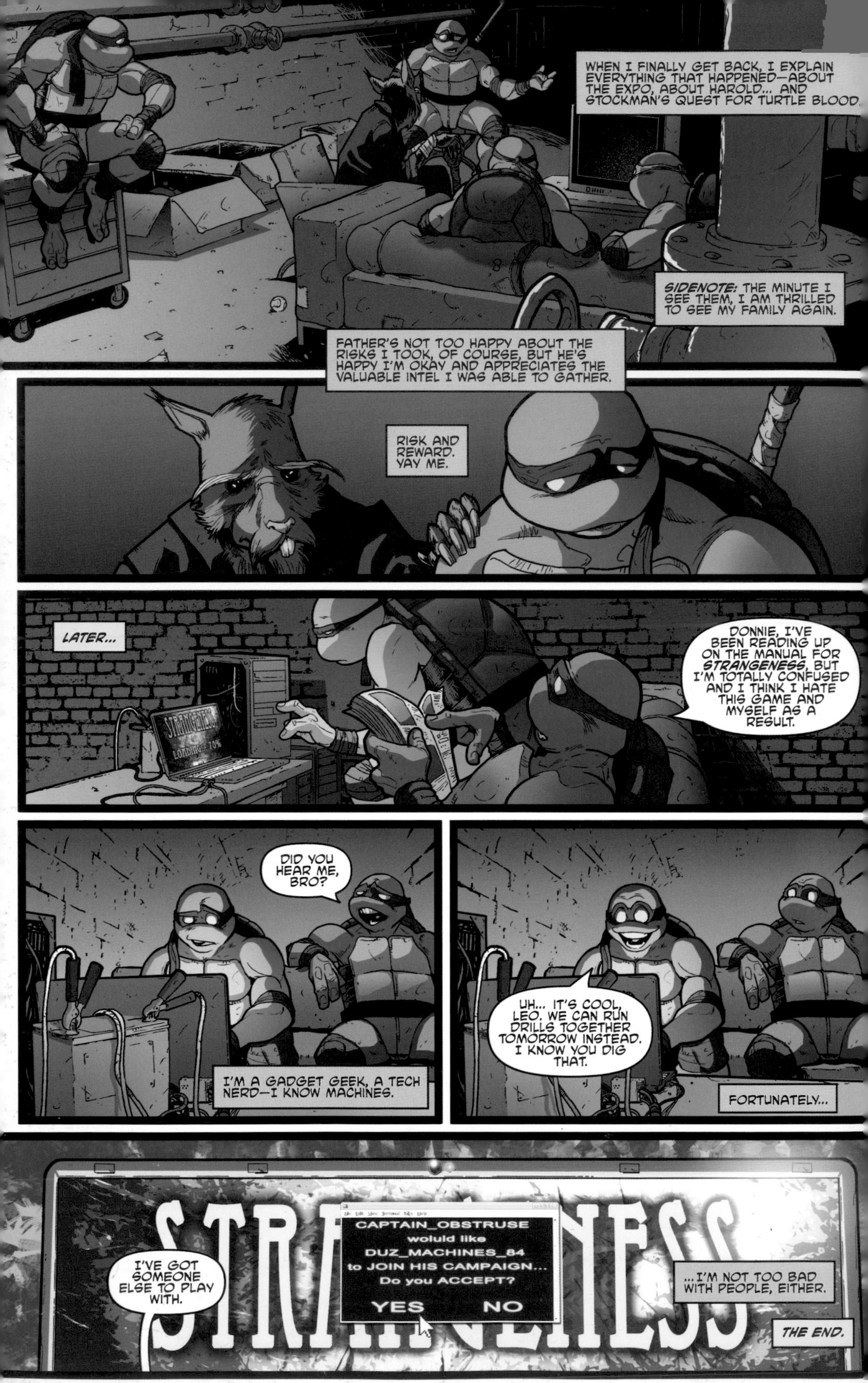
WHEN I FINALLY GET BACK, I EXPLAIN EVERYTHING THAT HAPPENED—ABOUT THE EXPO, ABOUT HAROLD... AND STOCKMAN'S QUEST FOR TURTLE BLOOD.
SIDENOTE: THE MINUTE I SEE THEM, I AM THRILLED TO SEE MY FAMILY AGAIN.
FATHER'S NOT TOO HAPPY ABOUT THE RISKS I TOOK, OF COURSE, BUT HE'S HAPPY I'M OKAY AND APPRECIATES THE VALUABLE INTEL I WAS ABLE TO GATHER.
RISK AND REWARD. YAY ME.
LATER...
DONNIE, I'VE BEEN READING UP ON THE MANUAL FOR STRANGENESS, BUT I'M TOTALLY CONFUSED AND I THINK I HATE THIS GAME AND MYSELF AS A RESULT.
DID YOU HEAR ME, BRO?
I'M A GADGET GEEK, A TECH NERD—I KNOW MACHINES.
UH... IT'S COOL, LEO. WE CAN RUN DRILLS TOGETHER TOMORROW INSTEAD. I KNOW YOU DIG THAT.
FORTUNATELY...
CAPTAIN_OBSTRUSE woluld like DUZ_MACHINES_84 to JOIN HIS CAMPAIGN... Do you ACCEPT?
YES NO
I'VE GOT SOMEONE ELSE TO PLAY WITH.
...I'M NOT TOO BAD WITH PEOPLE, EITHER.
THE END.

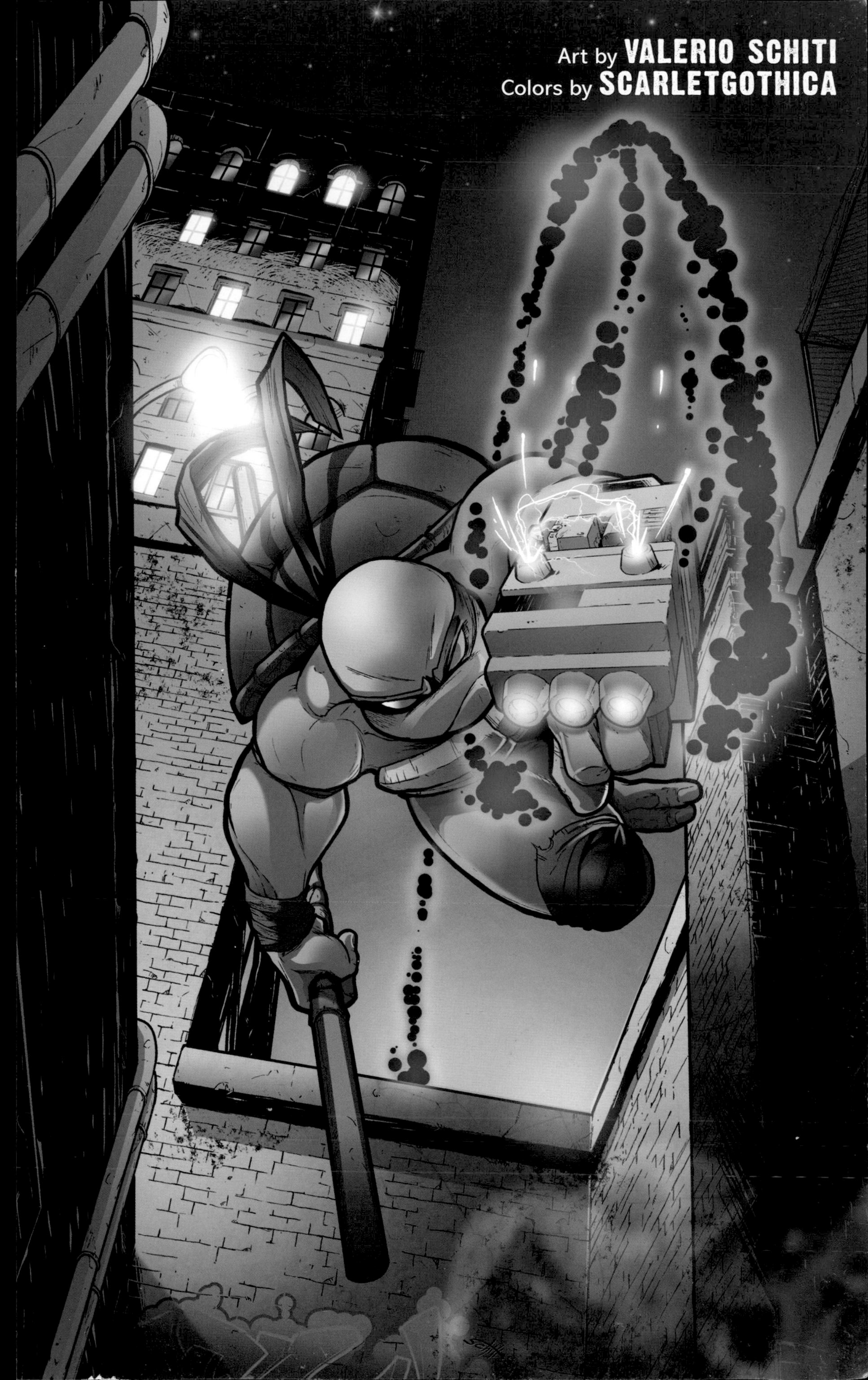

Art by **VALERIO SCHITI**
Colors by **SCARLETGOTHICA**

Art by **DAVID PETERSEN**

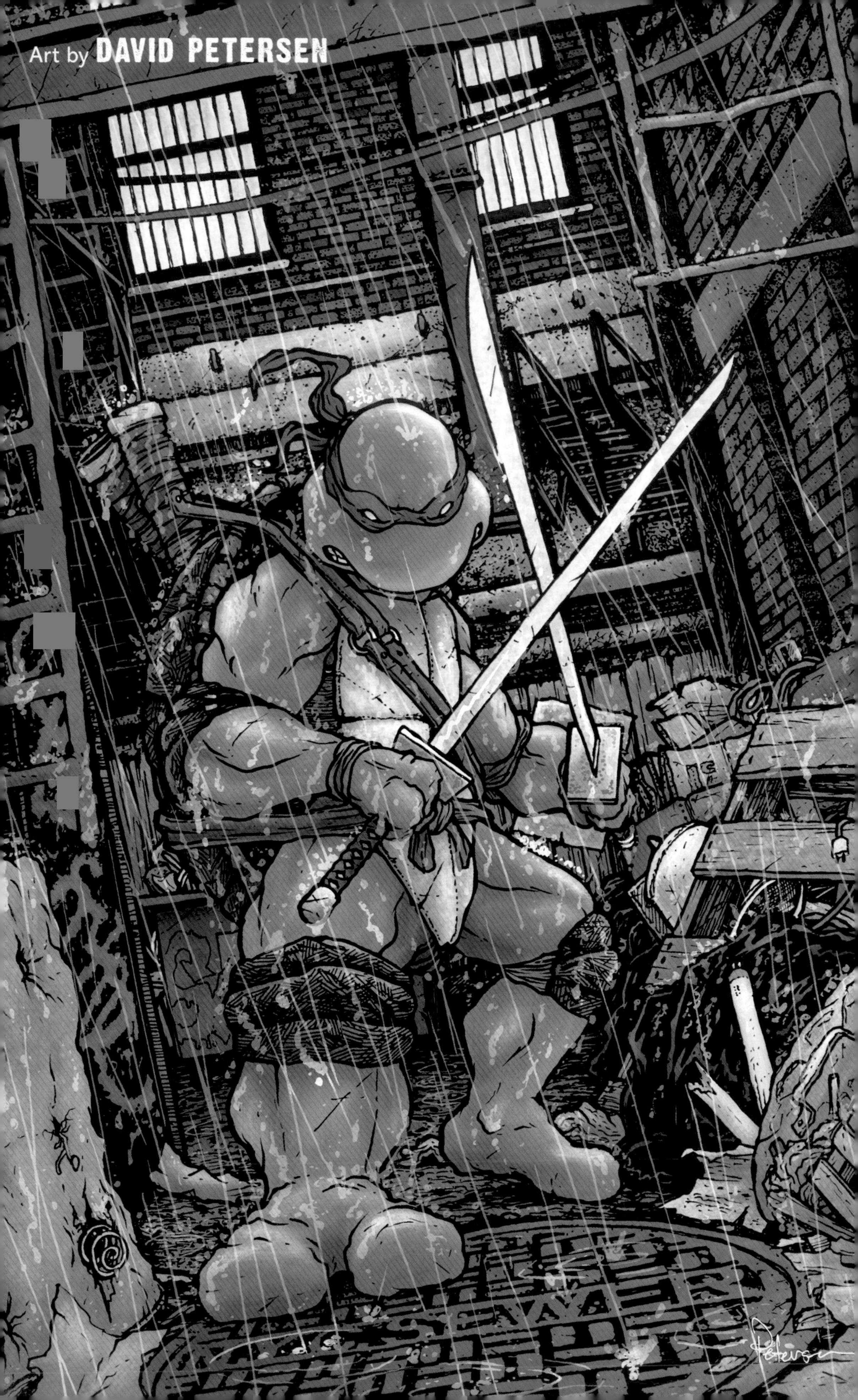

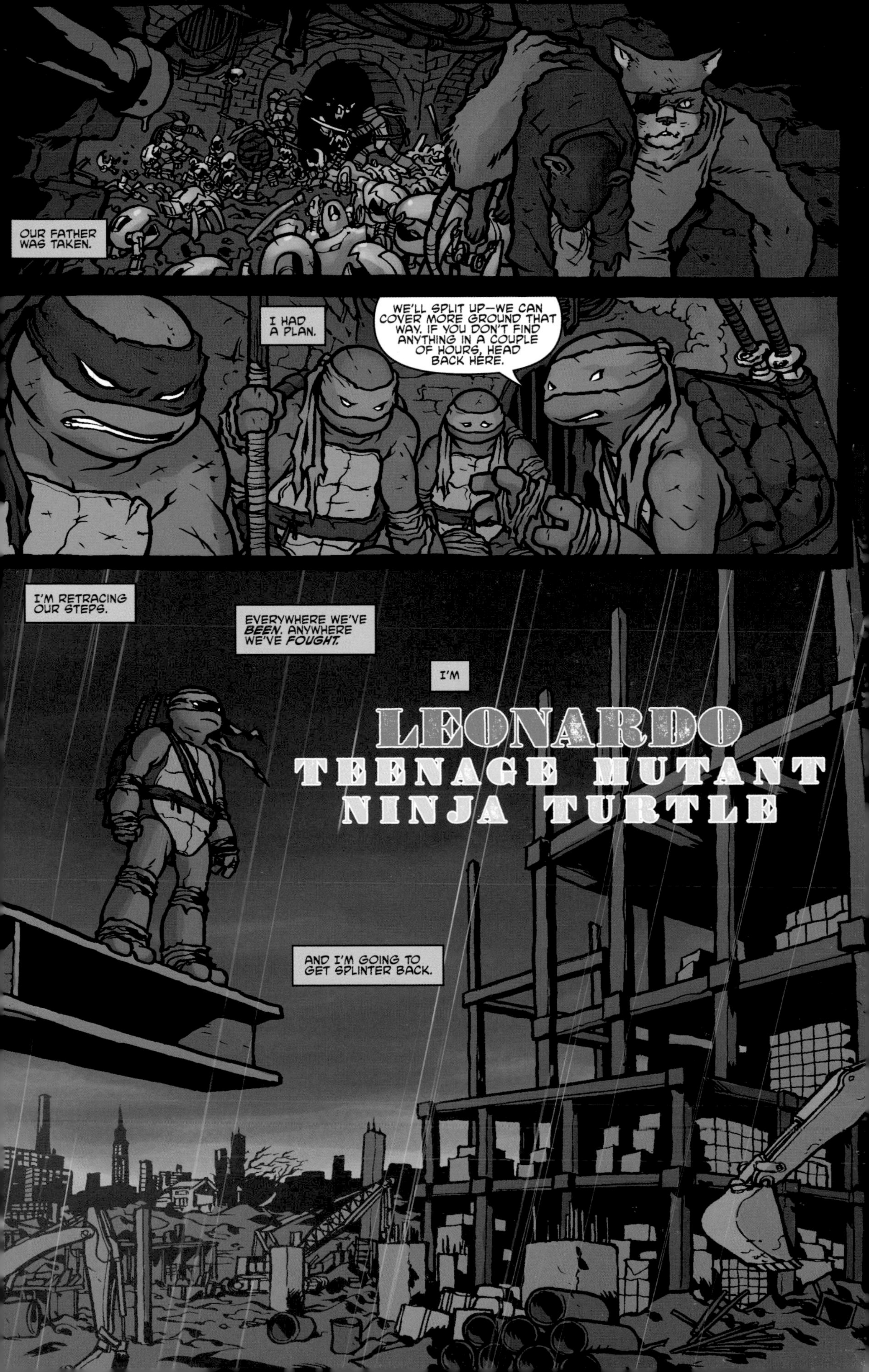
OUR FATHER WAS TAKEN.
I HAD A PLAN.
WE'LL SPLIT UP—WE CAN COVER MORE GROUND THAT WAY. IF YOU DON'T FIND ANYTHING IN A COUPLE OF HOURS, HEAD BACK HERE.
I'M RETRACING OUR STEPS.
EVERYWHERE WE'VE *BEEN*. ANYWHERE WE'VE *FOUGHT*.
I'M
LEONARDO
TEENAGE MUTANT NINJA TURTLE
AND I'M GOING TO GET SPLINTER BACK.

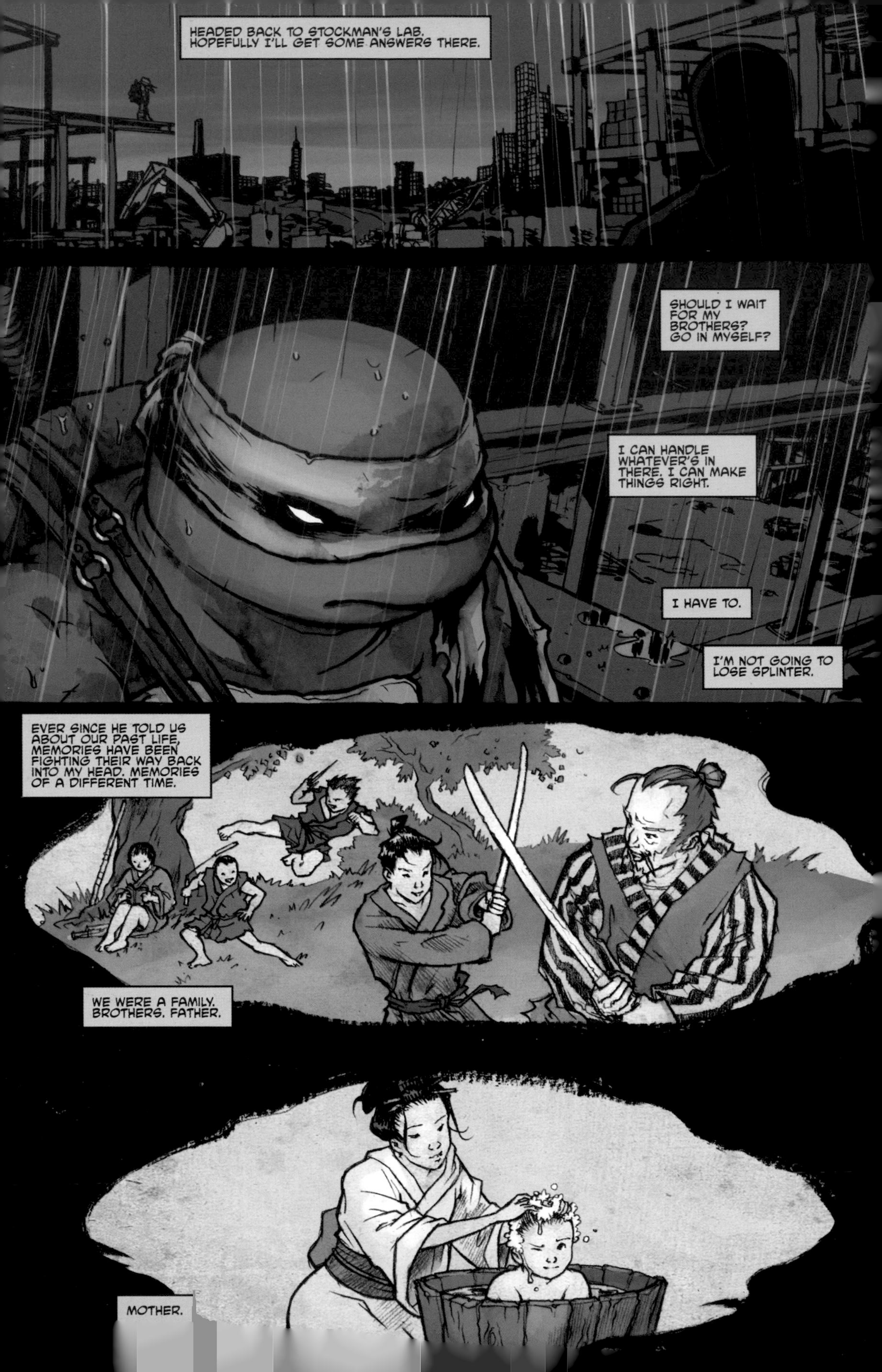
HEADED BACK TO STOCKMAN'S LAB. HOPEFULLY I'LL GET SOME ANSWERS THERE.
SHOULD I WAIT FOR MY BROTHERS? GO IN MYSELF?
I CAN HANDLE WHATEVER'S IN THERE. I CAN MAKE THINGS RIGHT.
I HAVE TO.
I'M NOT GOING TO LOSE SPLINTER.
EVER SINCE HE TOLD US ABOUT OUR PAST LIFE, MEMORIES HAVE BEEN FIGHTING THEIR WAY BACK INTO MY HEAD. MEMORIES OF A DIFFERENT TIME.
WE WERE A FAMILY. BROTHERS. FATHER.
MOTHER.

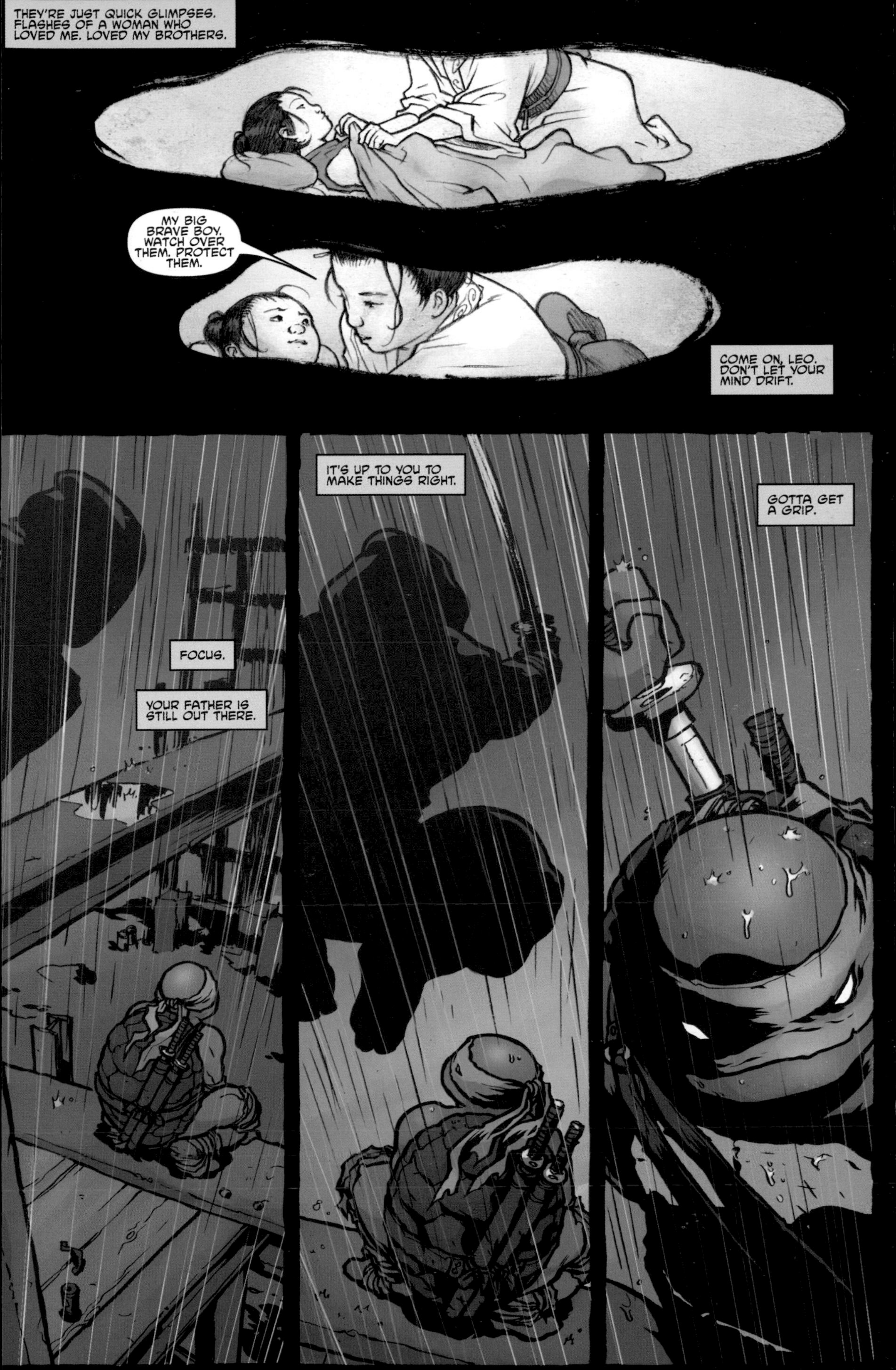
THEY'RE JUST QUICK GLIMPSES. FLASHES OF A WOMAN WHO LOVED ME. LOVED MY BROTHERS.
MY BIG BRAVE BOY. WATCH OVER THEM. PROTECT THEM.
COME ON, LEO. DON'T LET YOUR MIND DRIFT.
FOCUS.
YOUR FATHER IS STILL OUT THERE.
IT'S UP TO YOU TO MAKE THINGS RIGHT.
GOTTA GET A GRIP.

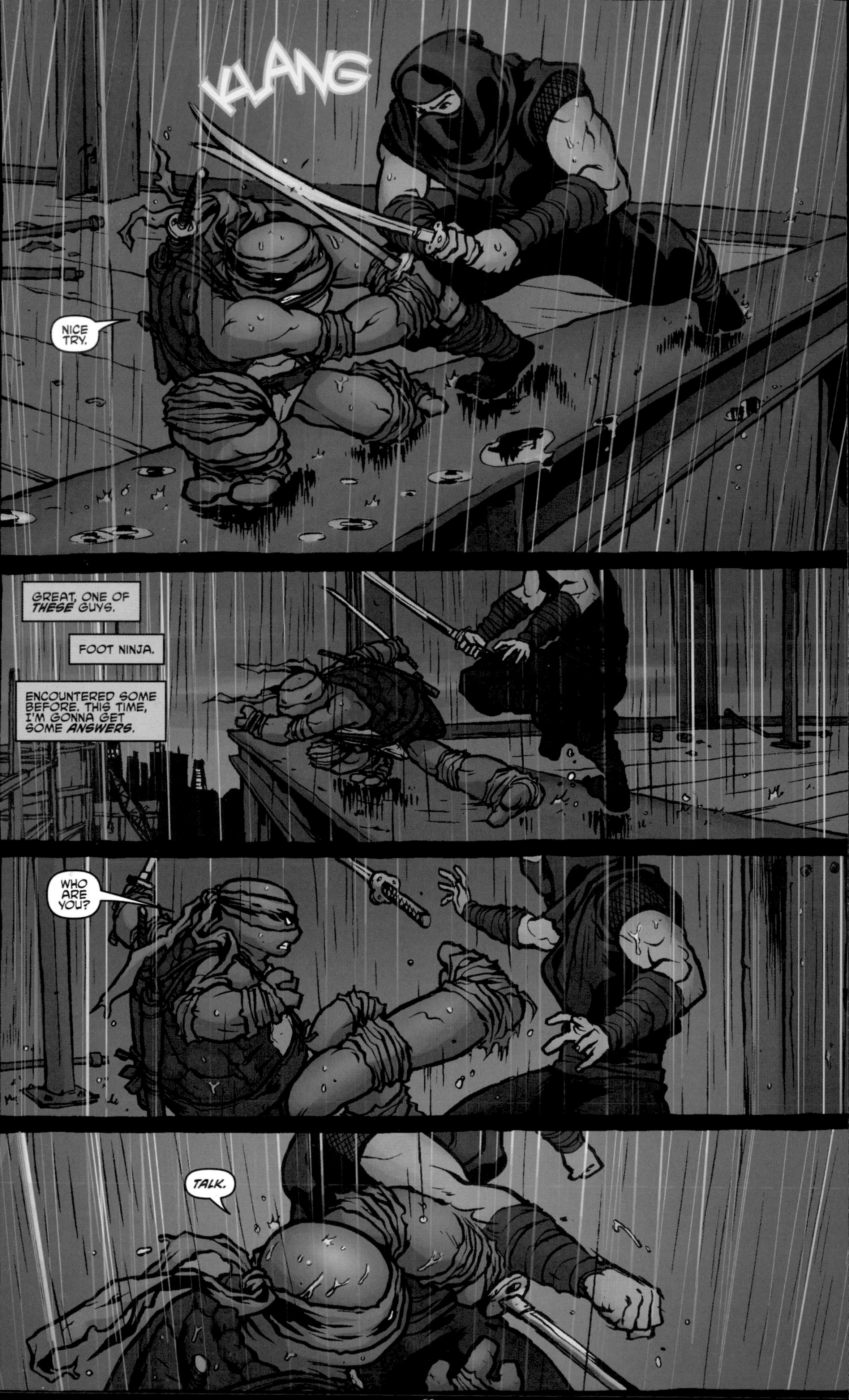
KLANG
NICE TRY.
GREAT, ONE OF *THESE* GUYS.
FOOT NINJA.
ENCOUNTERED SOME BEFORE. THIS TIME, I'M GONNA GET SOME *ANSWERS*.
WHO ARE YOU?
TALK.

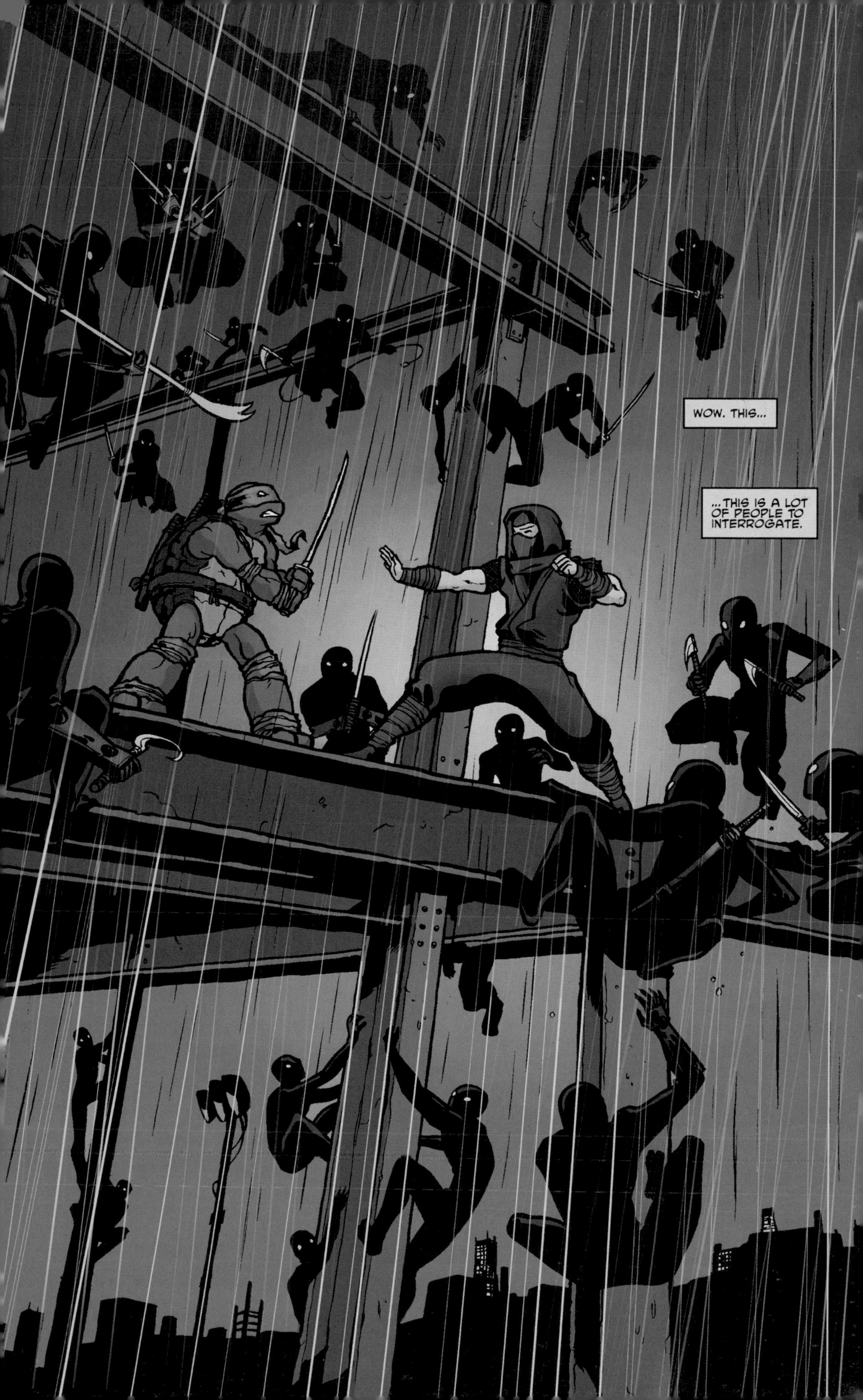
WOW. THIS...
...THIS IS A LOT OF PEOPLE TO INTERROGATE.

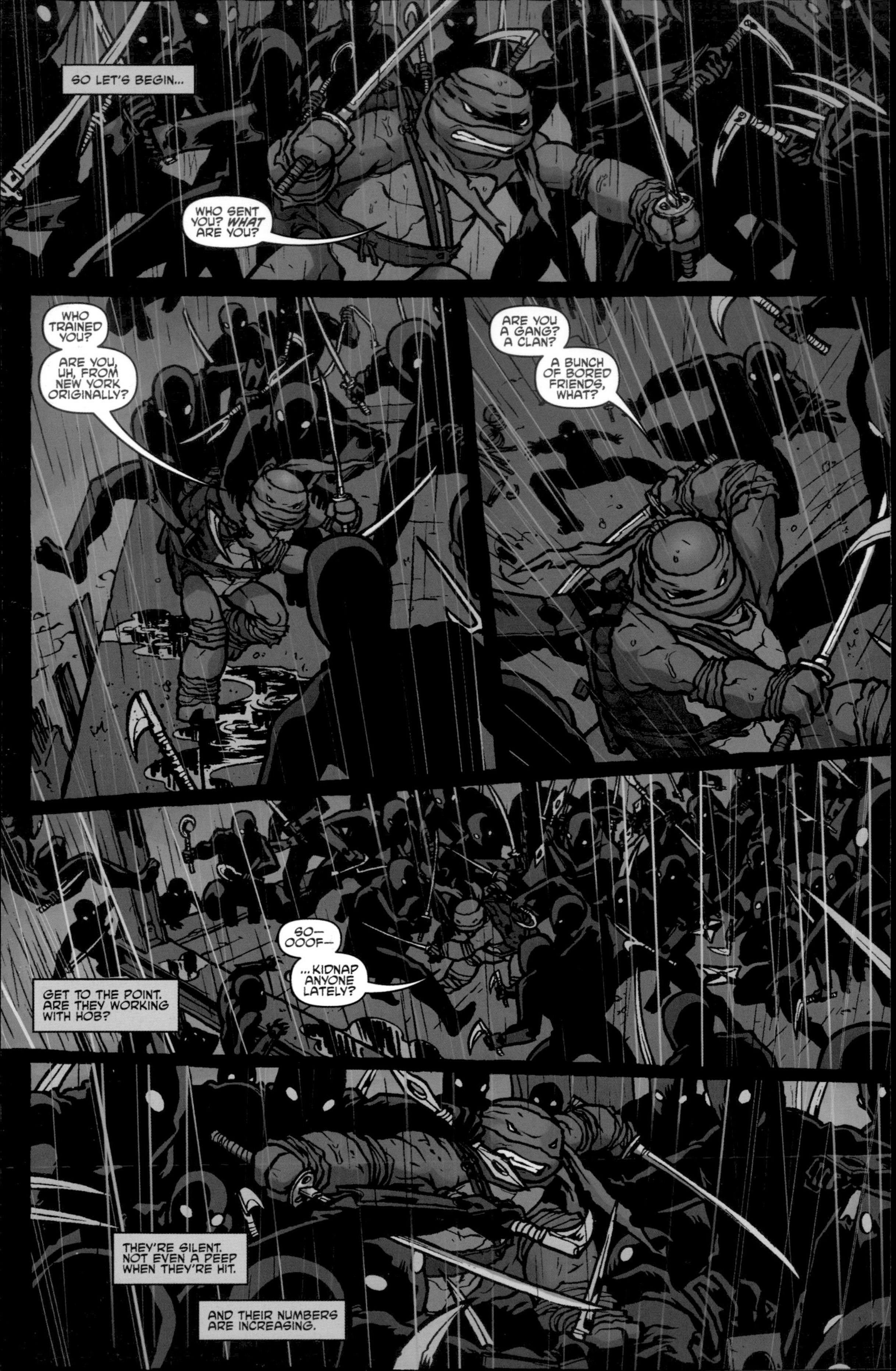

SO LET'S BEGIN...
WHO SENT YOU? WHAT ARE YOU?
WHO TRAINED YOU?
ARE YOU, UH, FROM NEW YORK ORIGINALLY?
ARE YOU A GANG? A CLAN?
A BUNCH OF BORED FRIENDS, WHAT?
SO— OOOF—
...KIDNAP ANYONE LATELY?
GET TO THE POINT. ARE THEY WORKING WITH HOB?
THEY'RE SILENT. NOT EVEN A PEEP WHEN THEY'RE HIT.
AND THEIR NUMBERS ARE INCREASING.

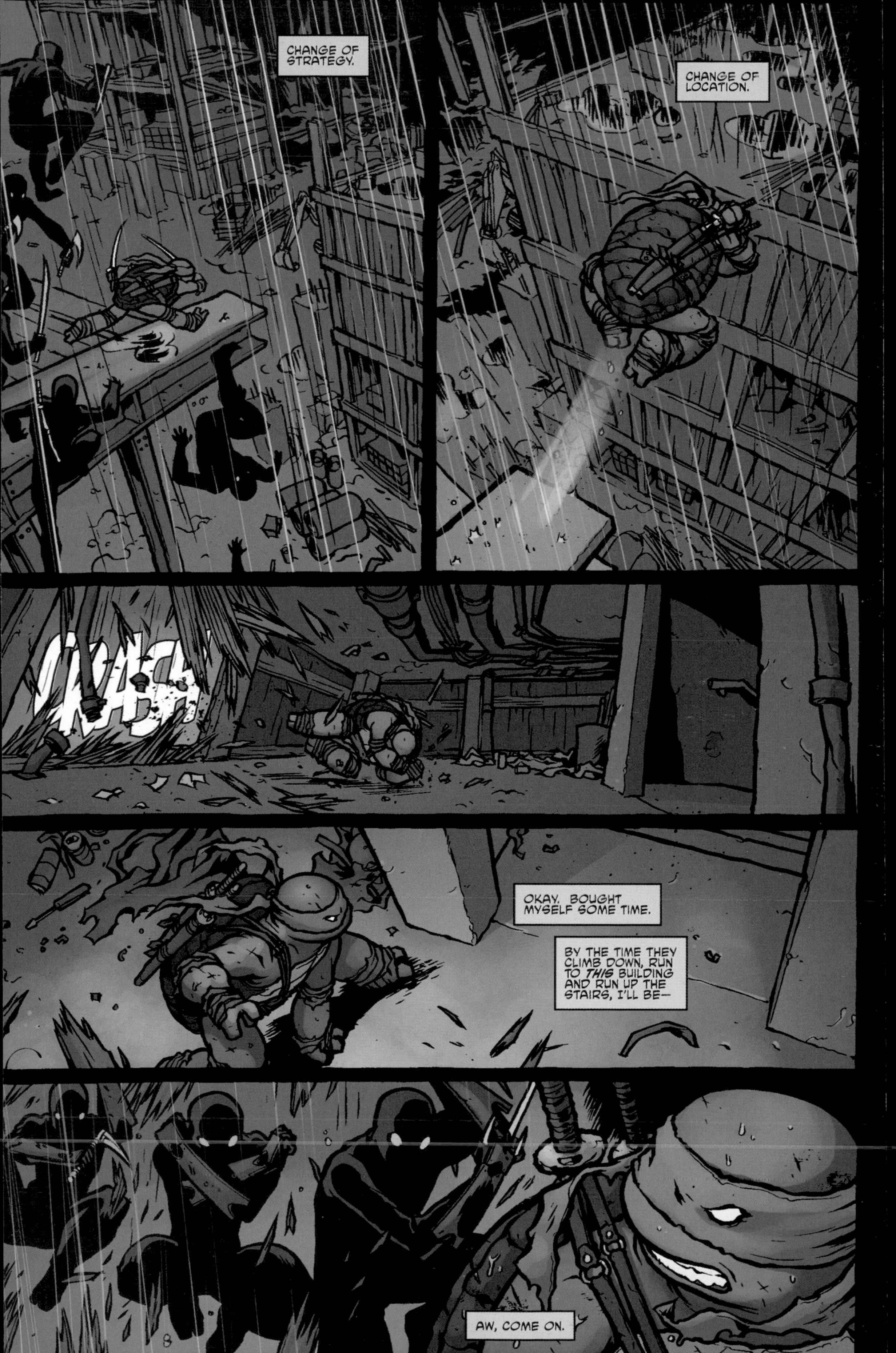
CHANGE OF STRATEGY.
CHANGE OF LOCATION.
OKAY. BOUGHT MYSELF SOME TIME.
BY THE TIME THEY CLIMB DOWN, RUN TO *THIS* BUILDING AND RUN UP THE STAIRS, I'LL BE—
AW, COME ON.

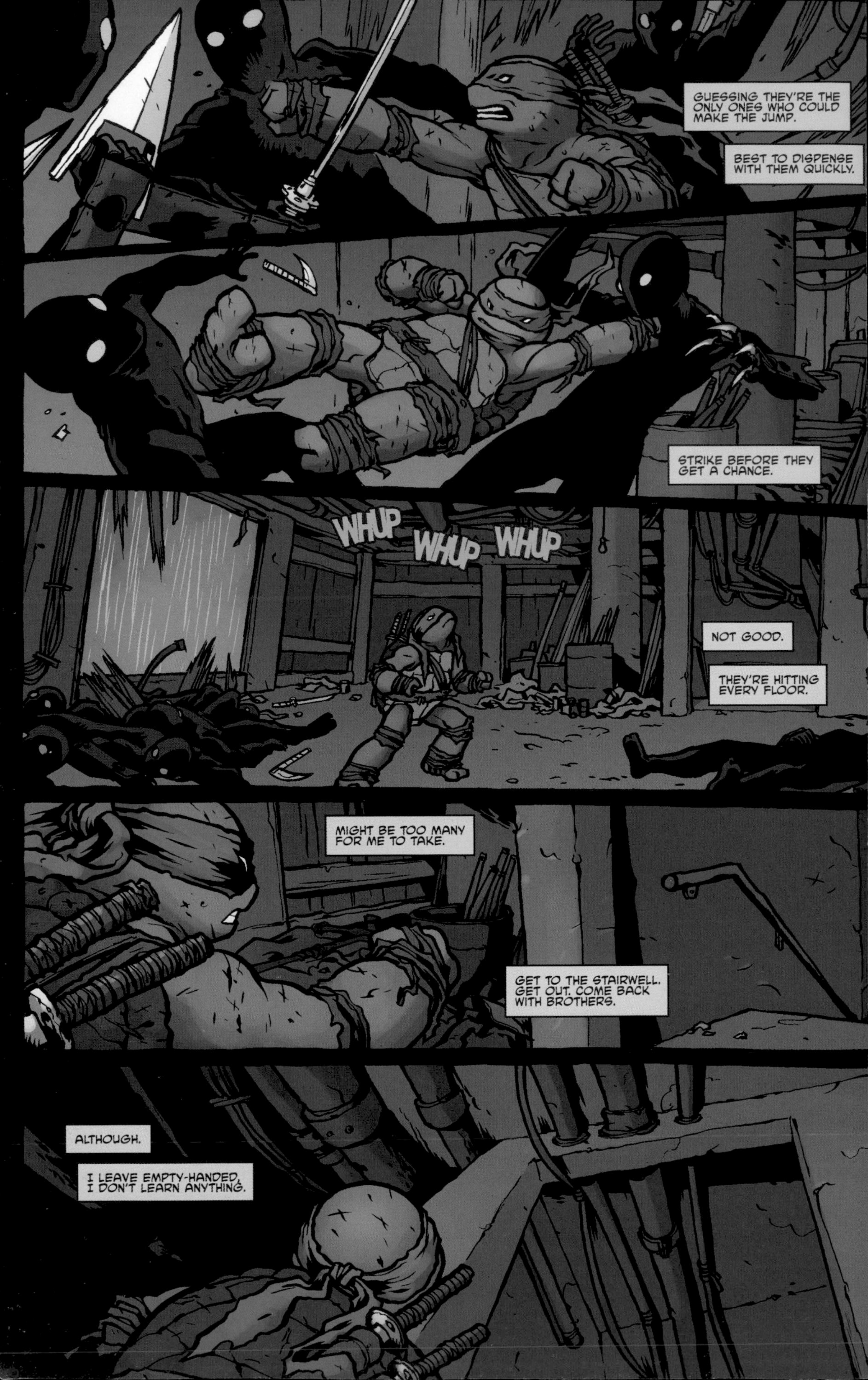
GUESSING THEY'RE THE ONLY ONES WHO COULD MAKE THE JUMP.
BEST TO DISPENSE WITH THEM QUICKLY.
STRIKE BEFORE THEY GET A CHANCE.
WHUP
WHUP
WHUP
NOT GOOD.
THEY'RE HITTING EVERY FLOOR.
MIGHT BE TOO MANY FOR ME TO TAKE.
GET TO THE STAIRWELL. GET OUT. COME BACK WITH BROTHERS.
ALTHOUGH.
I LEAVE EMPTY-HANDED, I DON'T LEARN ANYTHING.

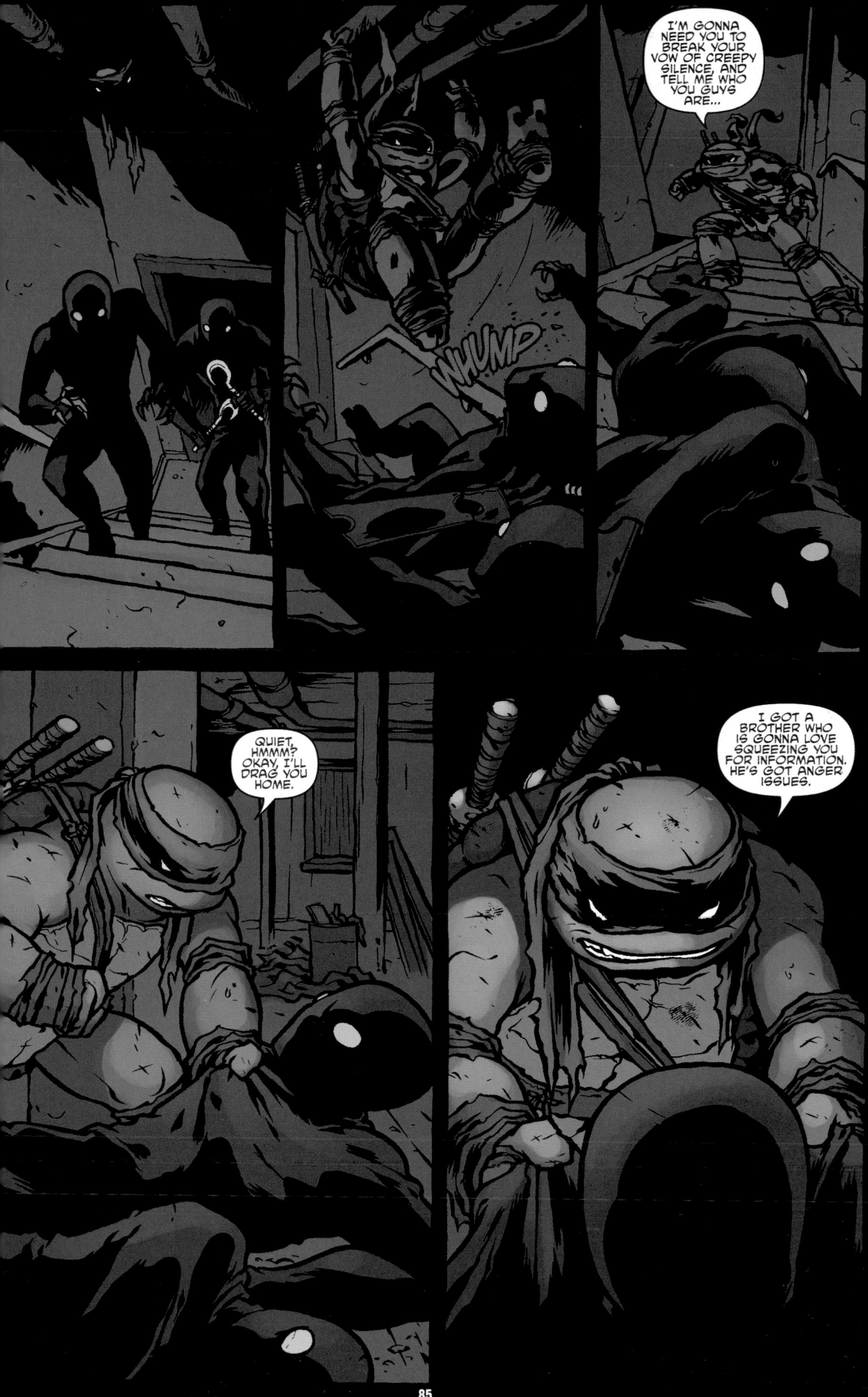
WHUMP
I'M GONNA NEED YOU TO BREAK YOUR VOW OF CREEPY SILENCE, AND TELL ME WHO YOU GUYS ARE...
QUIET, HMMM? OKAY, I'LL DRAG YOU HOME.
I GOT A BROTHER WHO IS GONNA LOVE SQUEEZING YOU FOR INFORMATION. HE'S GOT ANGER ISSUES.

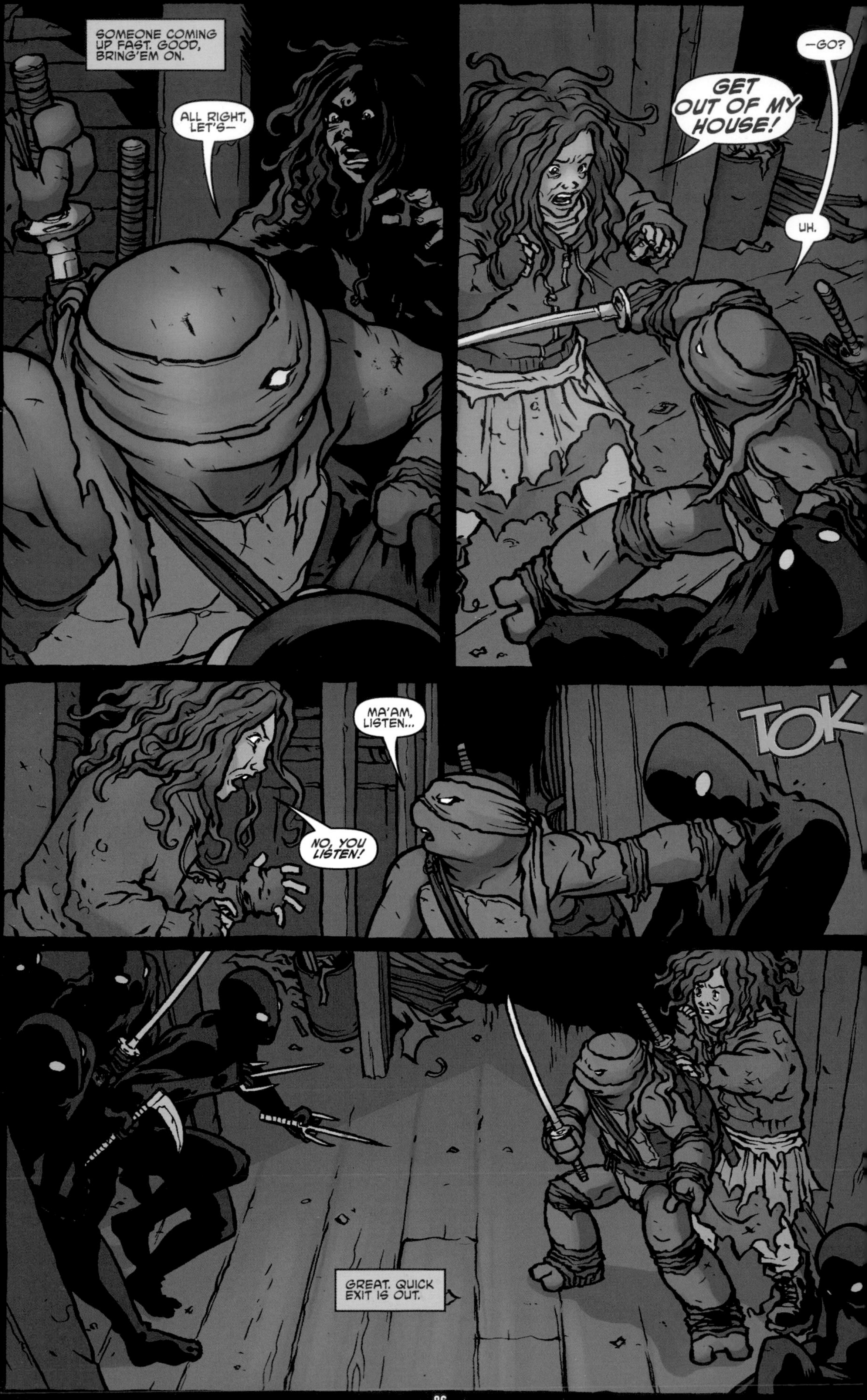
SOMEONE COMING UP FAST. GOOD, BRING'EM ON.
ALL RIGHT, LET'S—
GET OUT OF MY HOUSE!
—GO?
UH.
MA'AM, LISTEN...
NO, YOU LISTEN!
TOK
GREAT. QUICK EXIT IS OUT.

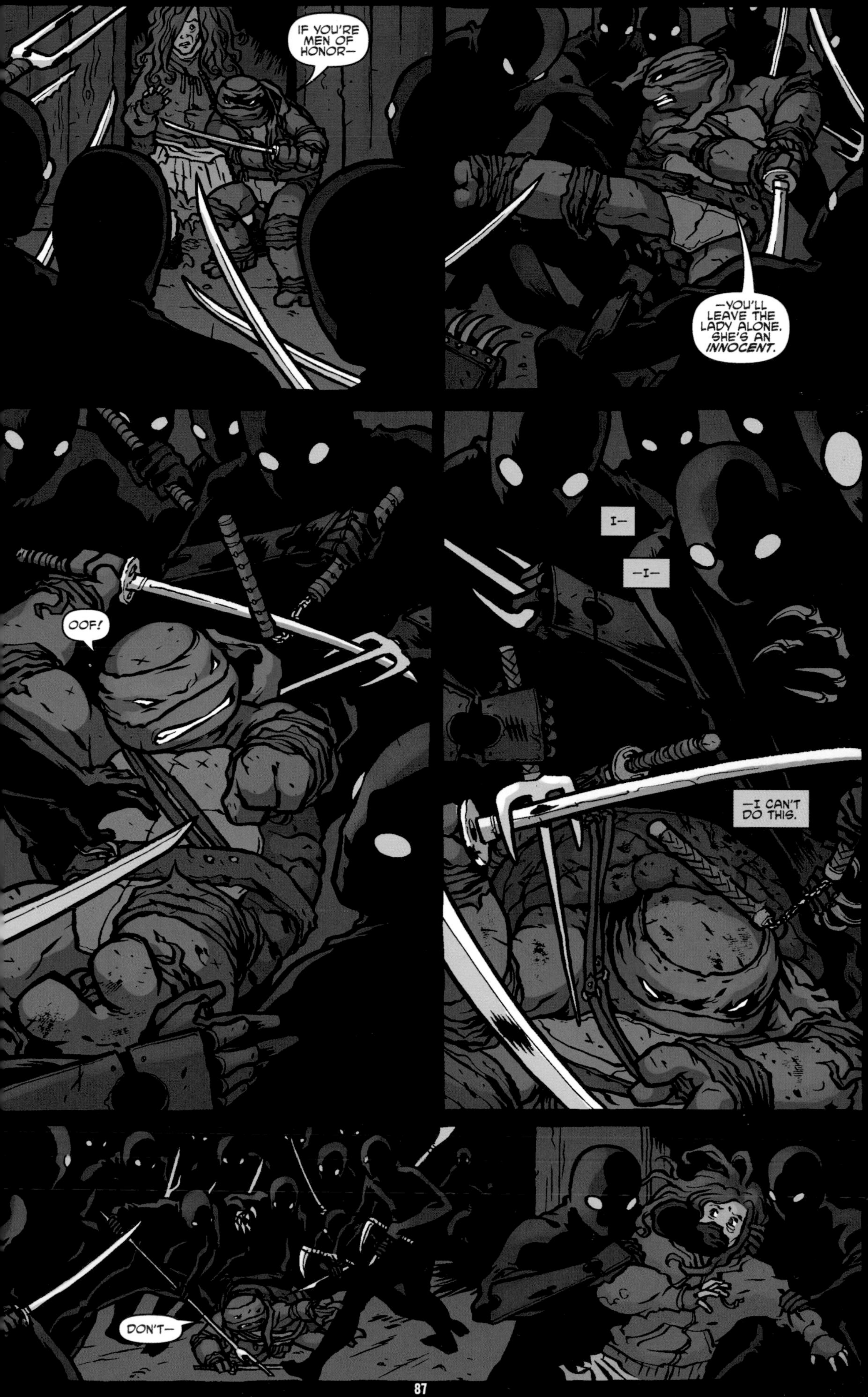
IF YOU'RE MEN OF HONOR—
—YOU'LL LEAVE THE LADY ALONE. SHE'S AN *INNOCENT*.
OOF!
I—
—I—
—I CAN'T DO THIS.
DON'T—

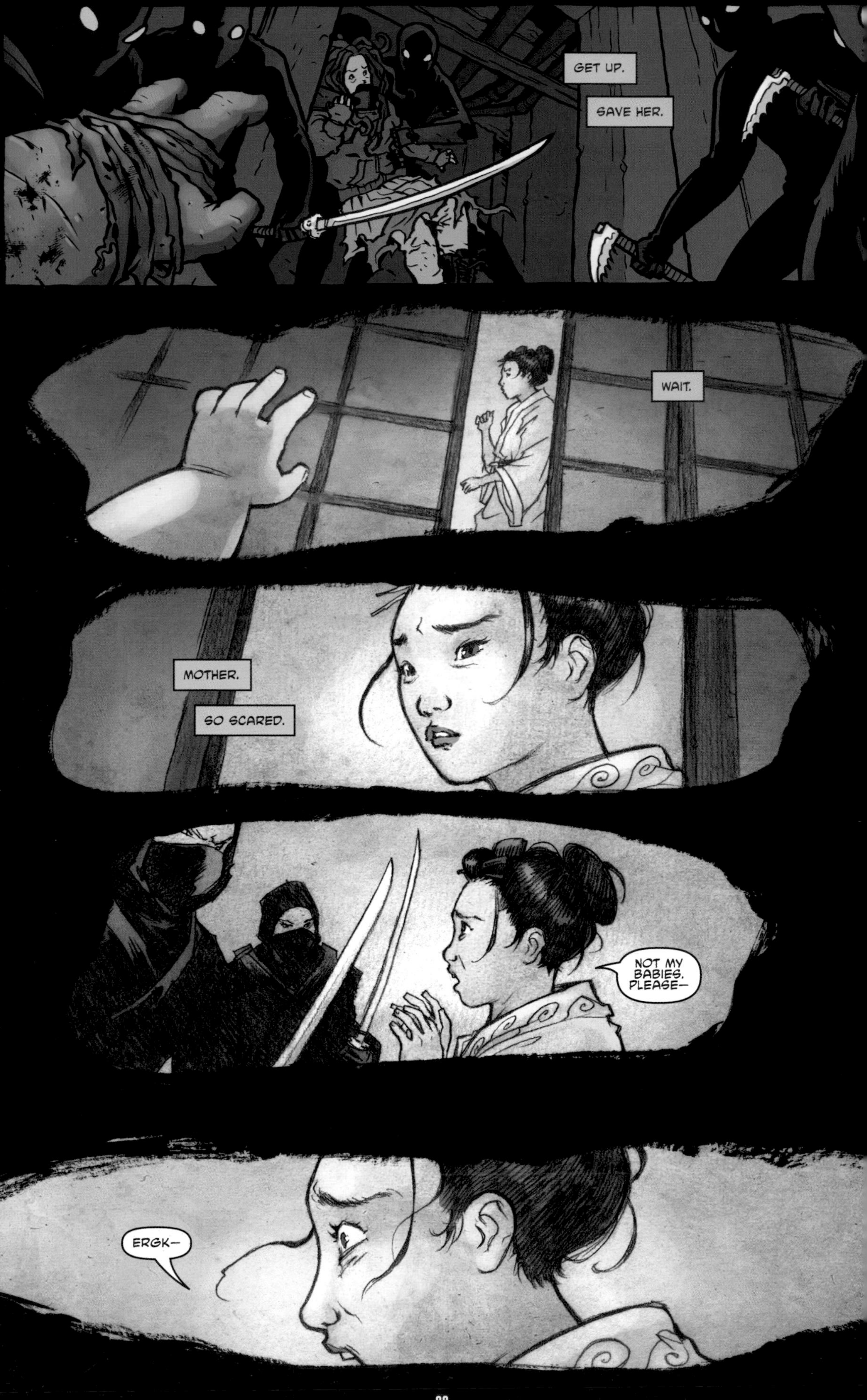
GET UP.
SAVE HER.
WAIT.
MOTHER.
SO SCARED.
NOT MY BABIES. PLEASE—
ERGK—

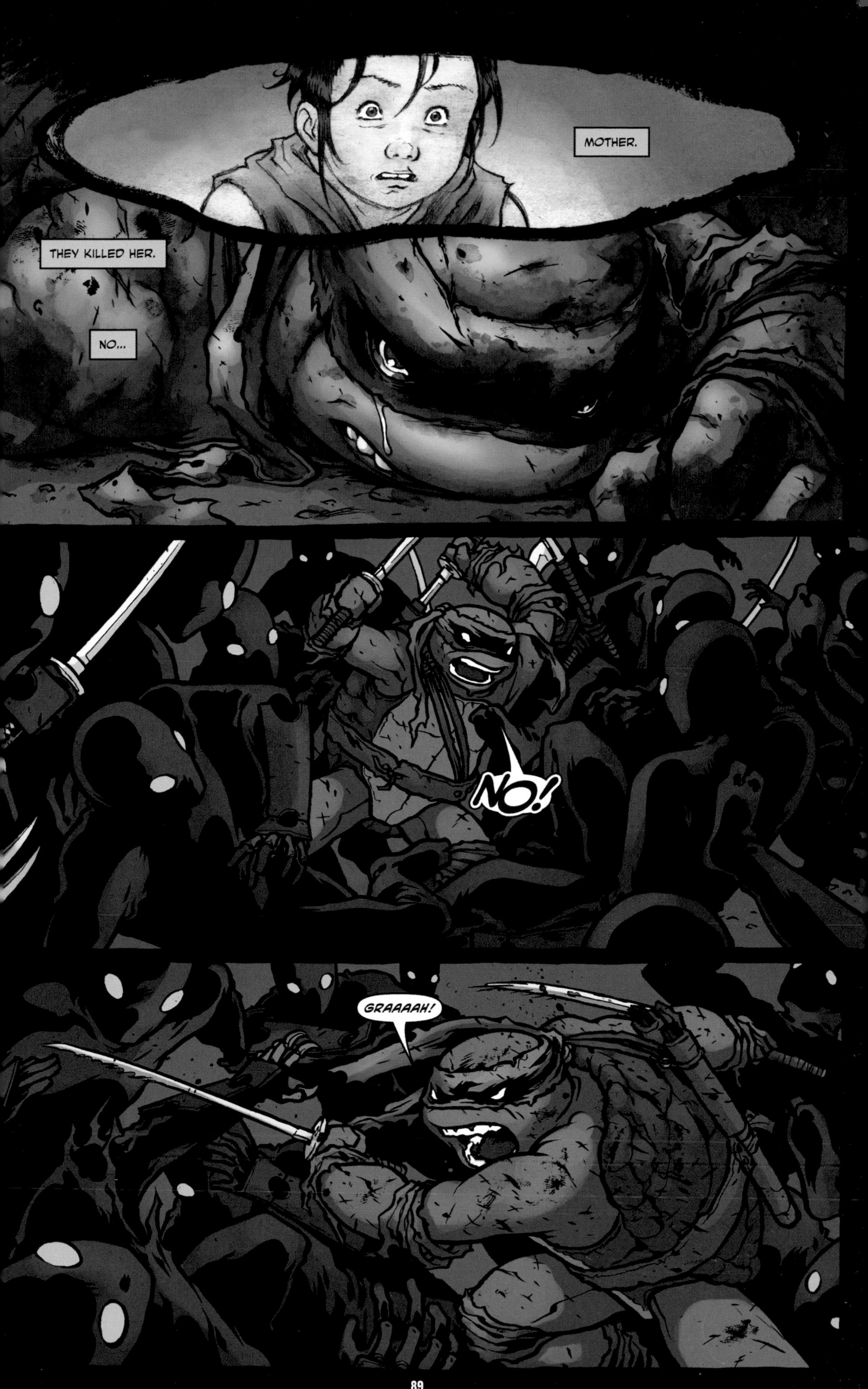
MOTHER.
THEY KILLED HER.
NO...
NO!
GRAAAAH!

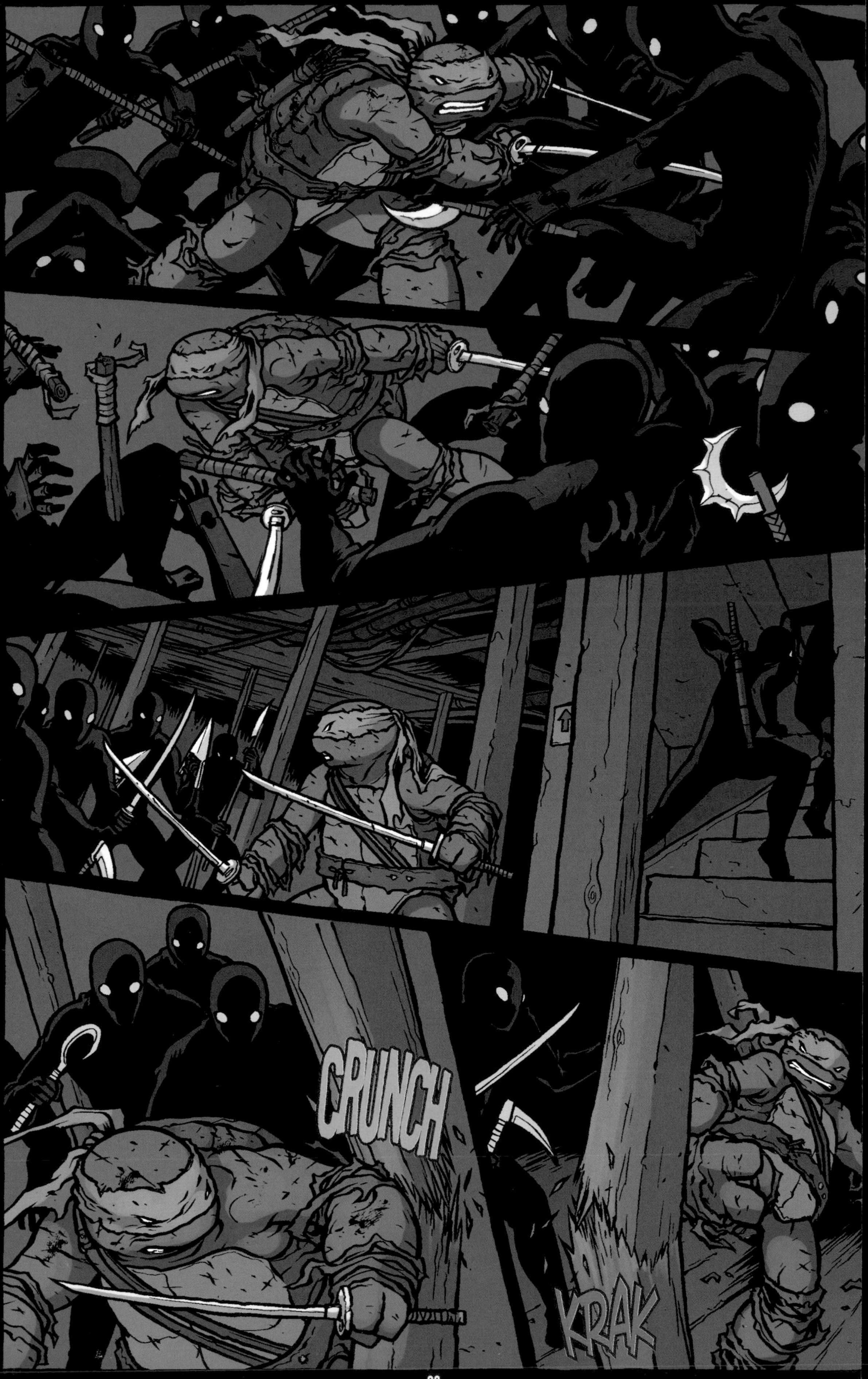
CRUNCH
KRAK

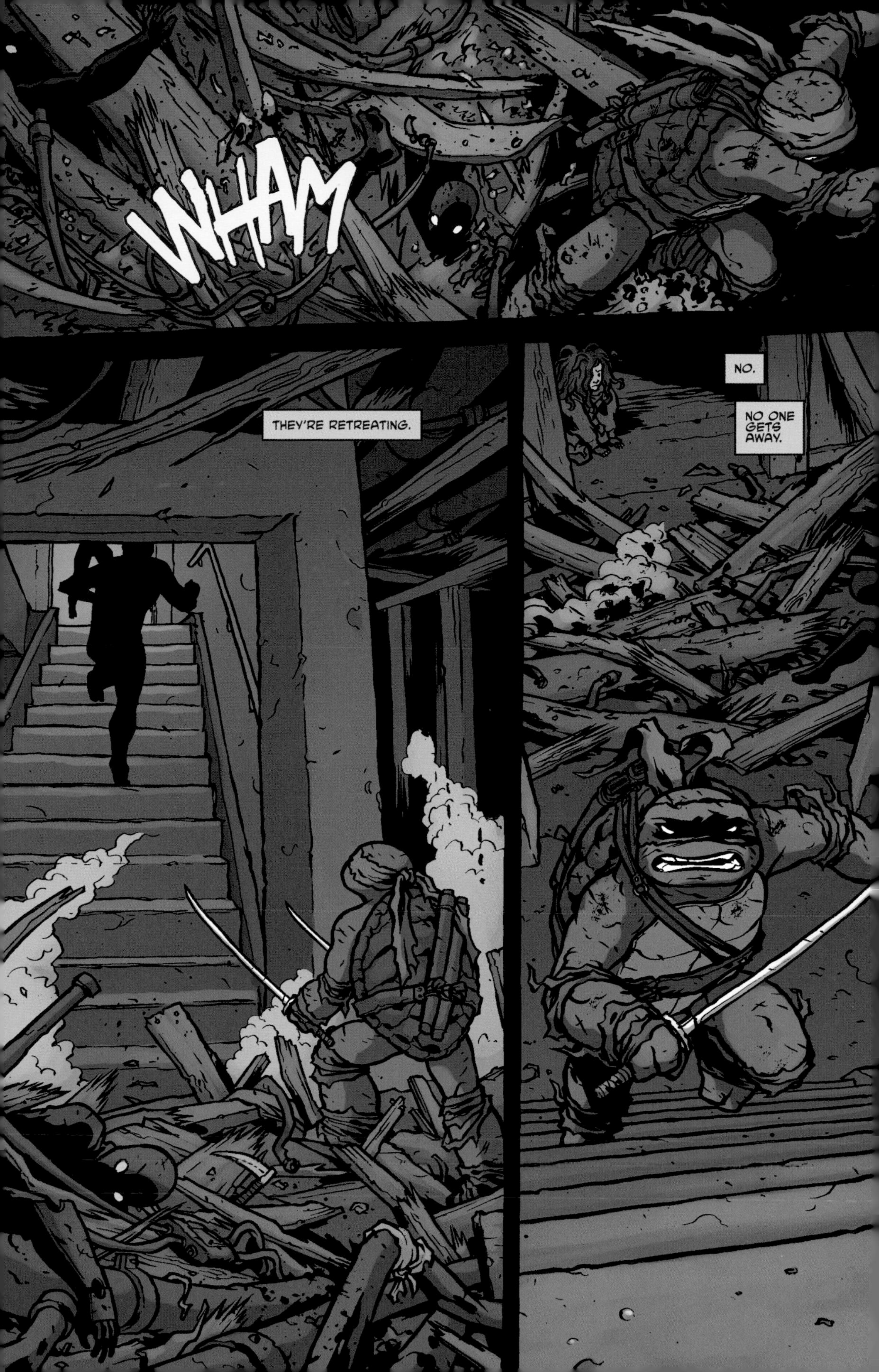
WHAM
THEY'RE RETREATING.
NO.
NO ONE GETS AWAY.

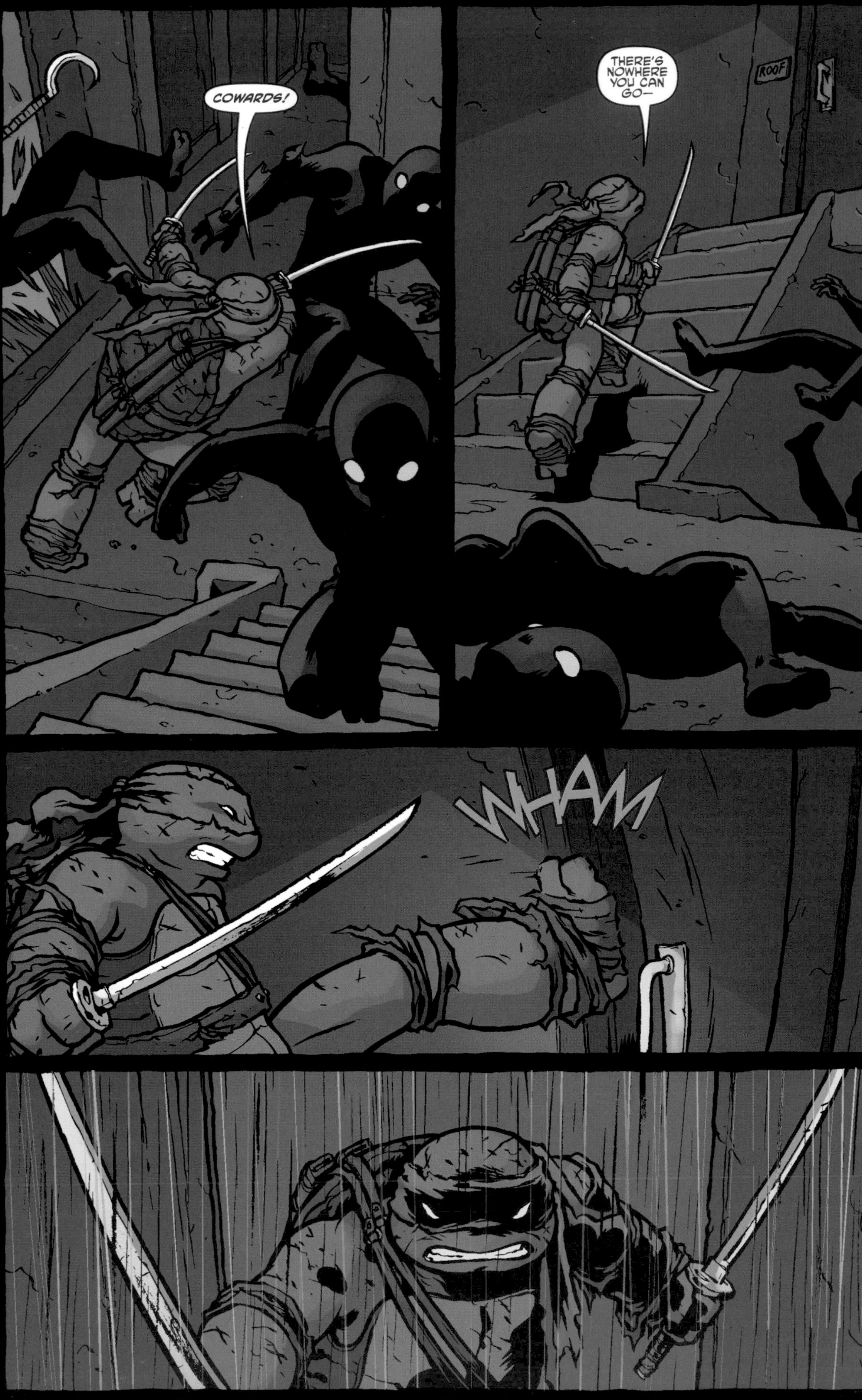
COWARDS!
THERE'S NOWHERE YOU CAN GO—
ROOF
WHAM

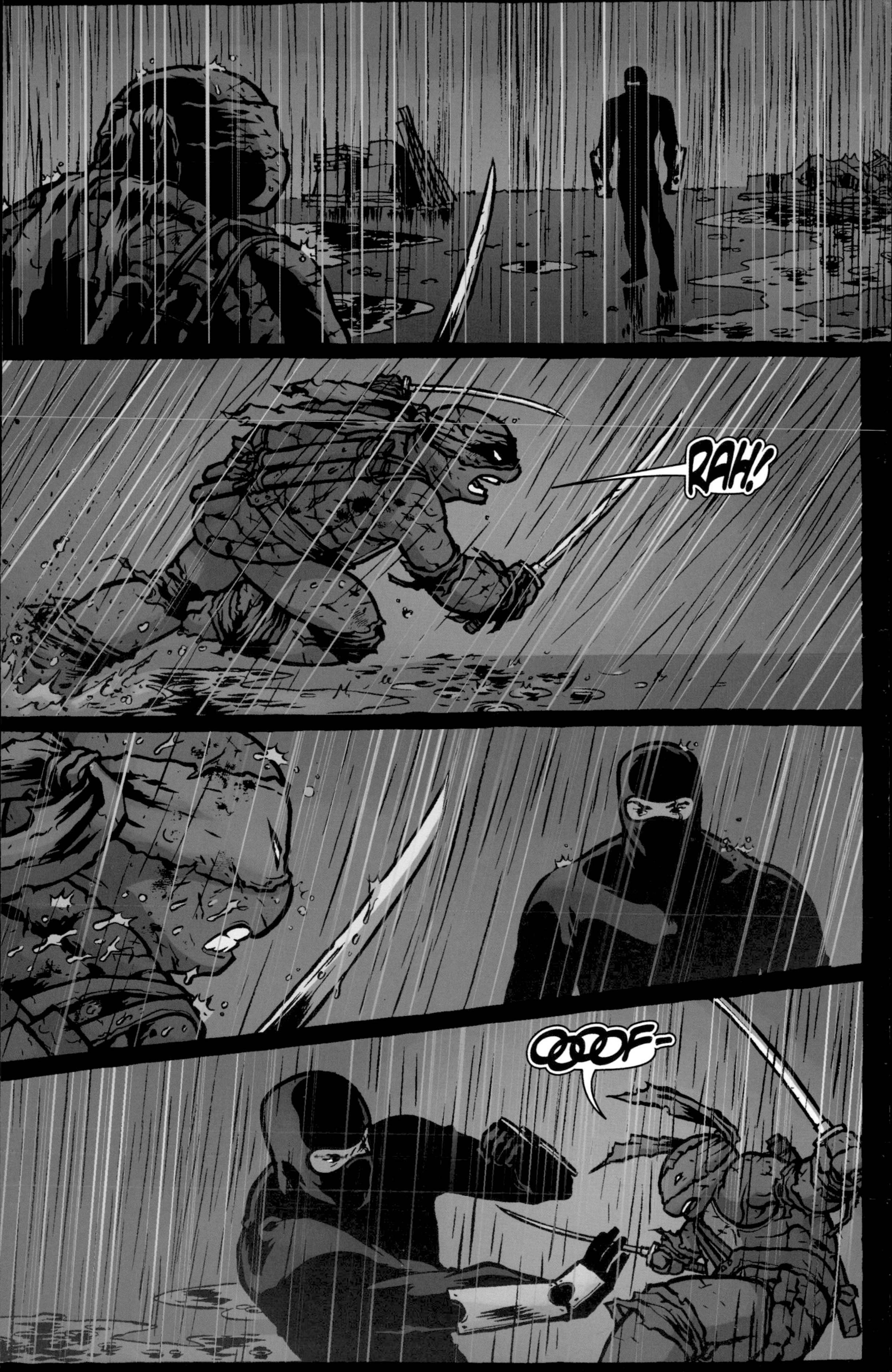
RAH!
OOOOF-

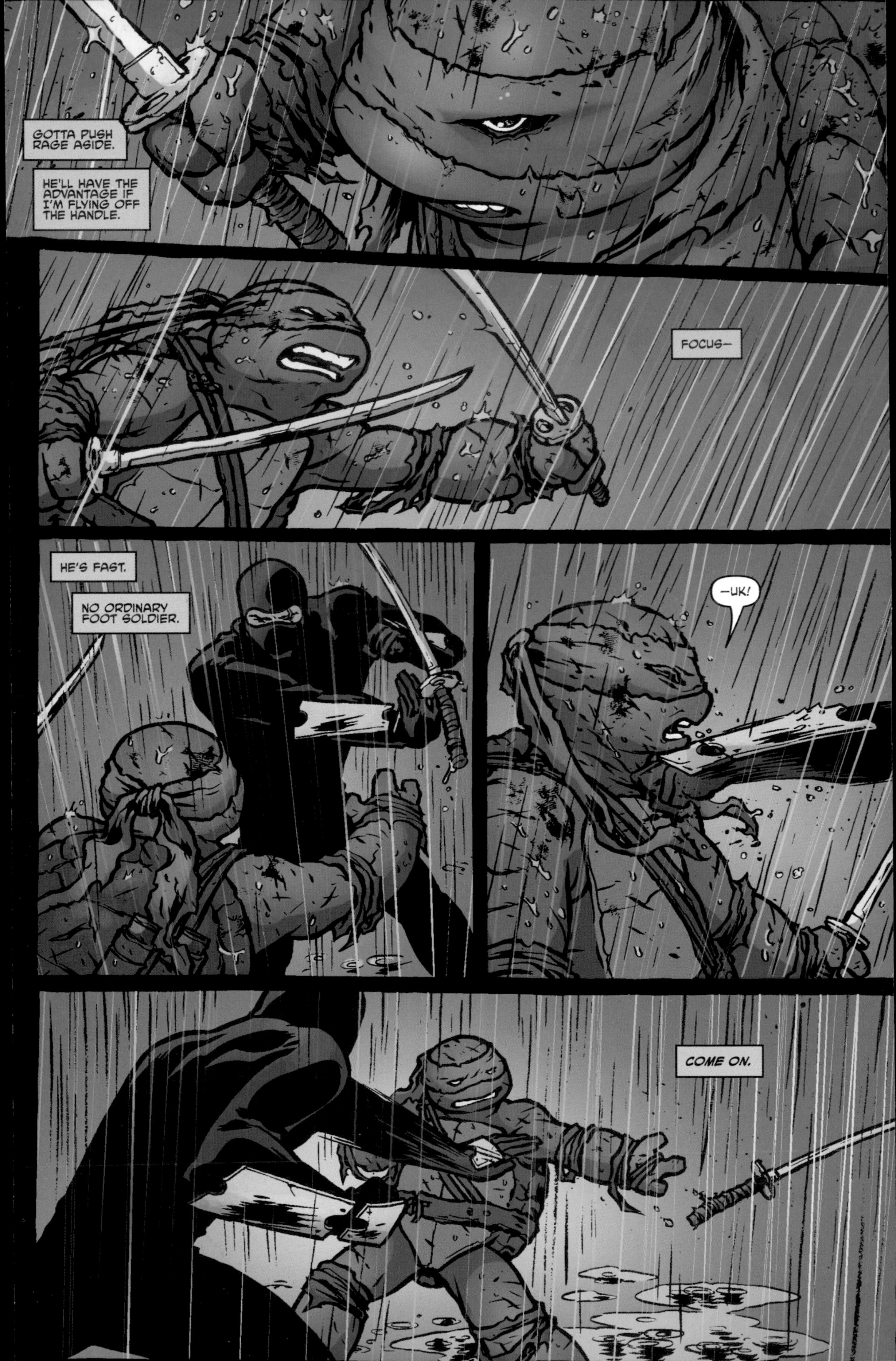
GOTTA PUSH RAGE ASIDE.
HE'LL HAVE THE ADVANTAGE IF I'M FLYING OFF THE HANDLE.
FOCUS—
HE'S FAST.
NO ORDINARY FOOT SOLDIER.
—UK!
COME ON.

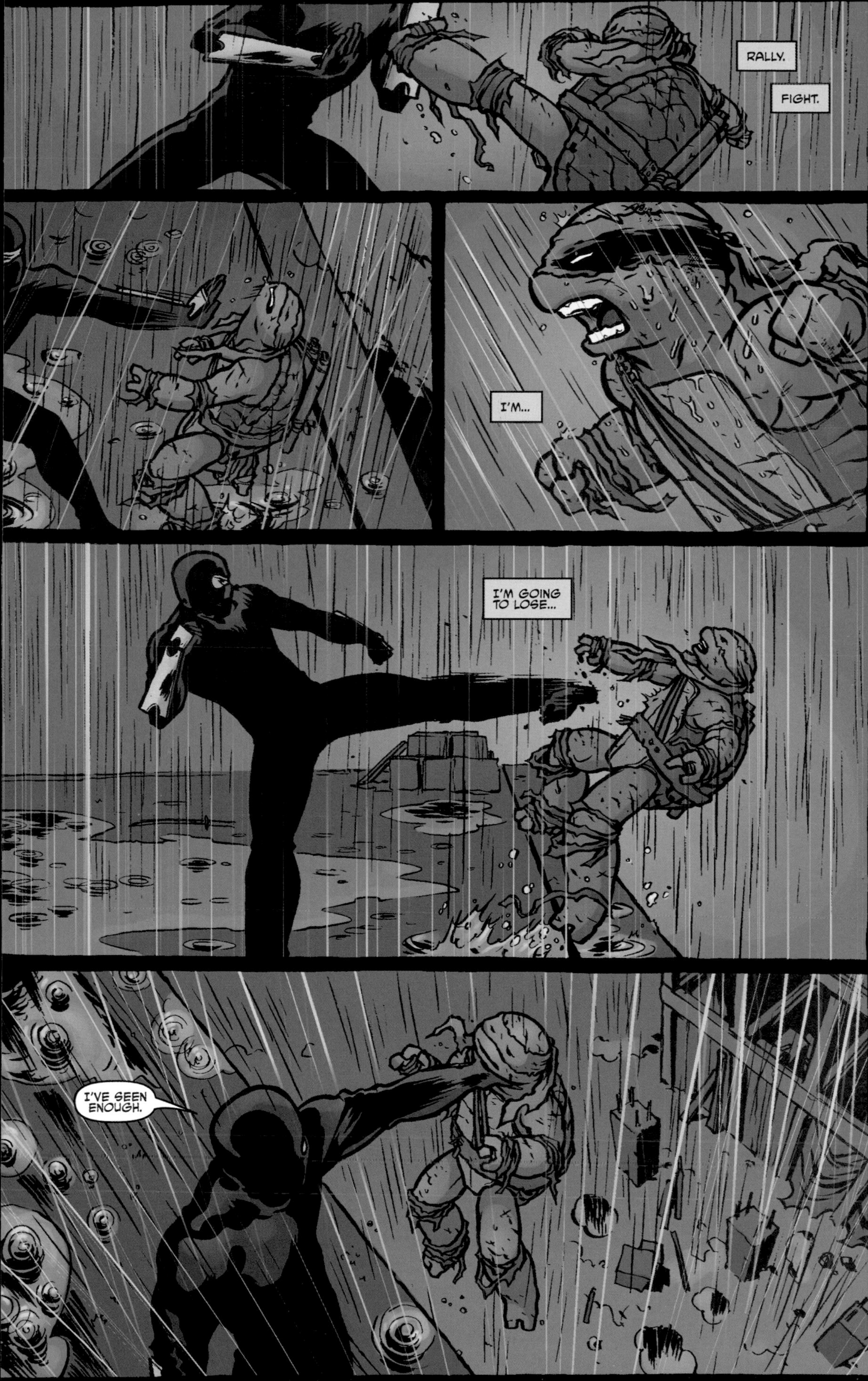
RALLY.
FIGHT.
I'M...
I'M GOING TO LOSE...
I'VE SEEN ENOUGH.

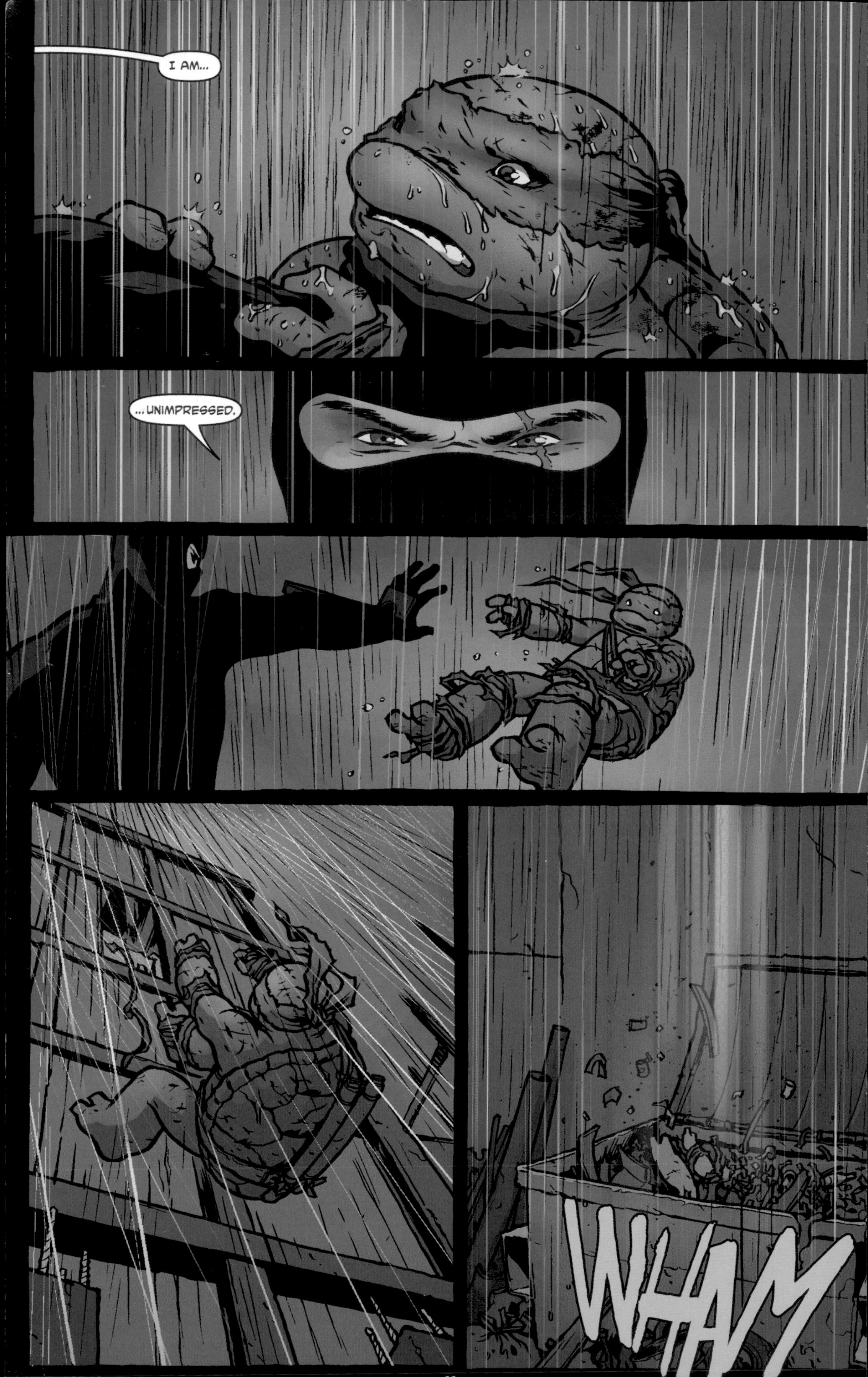
I AM...
...UNIMPRESSED.
WHAM

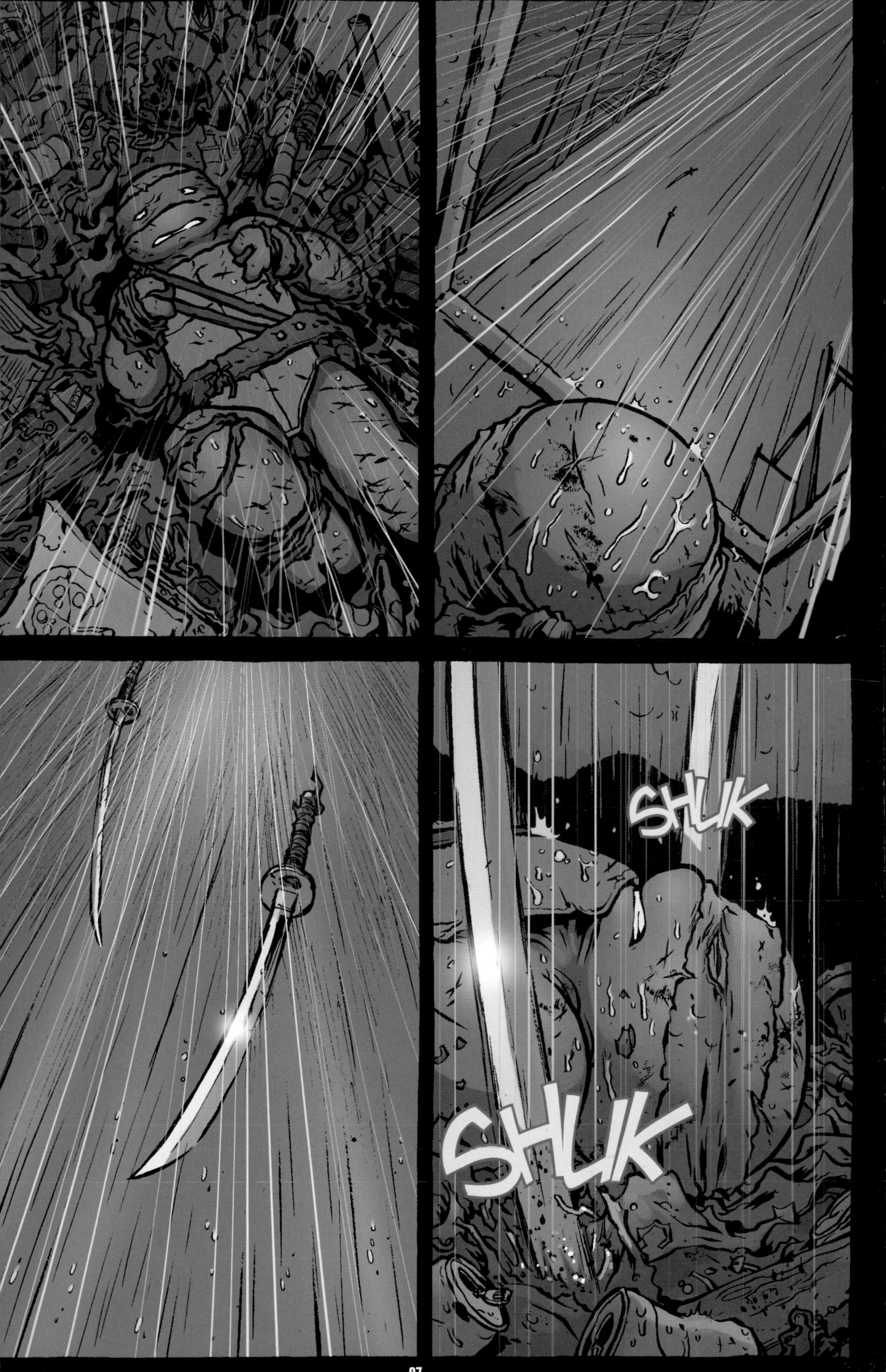
SHUK
SHUK

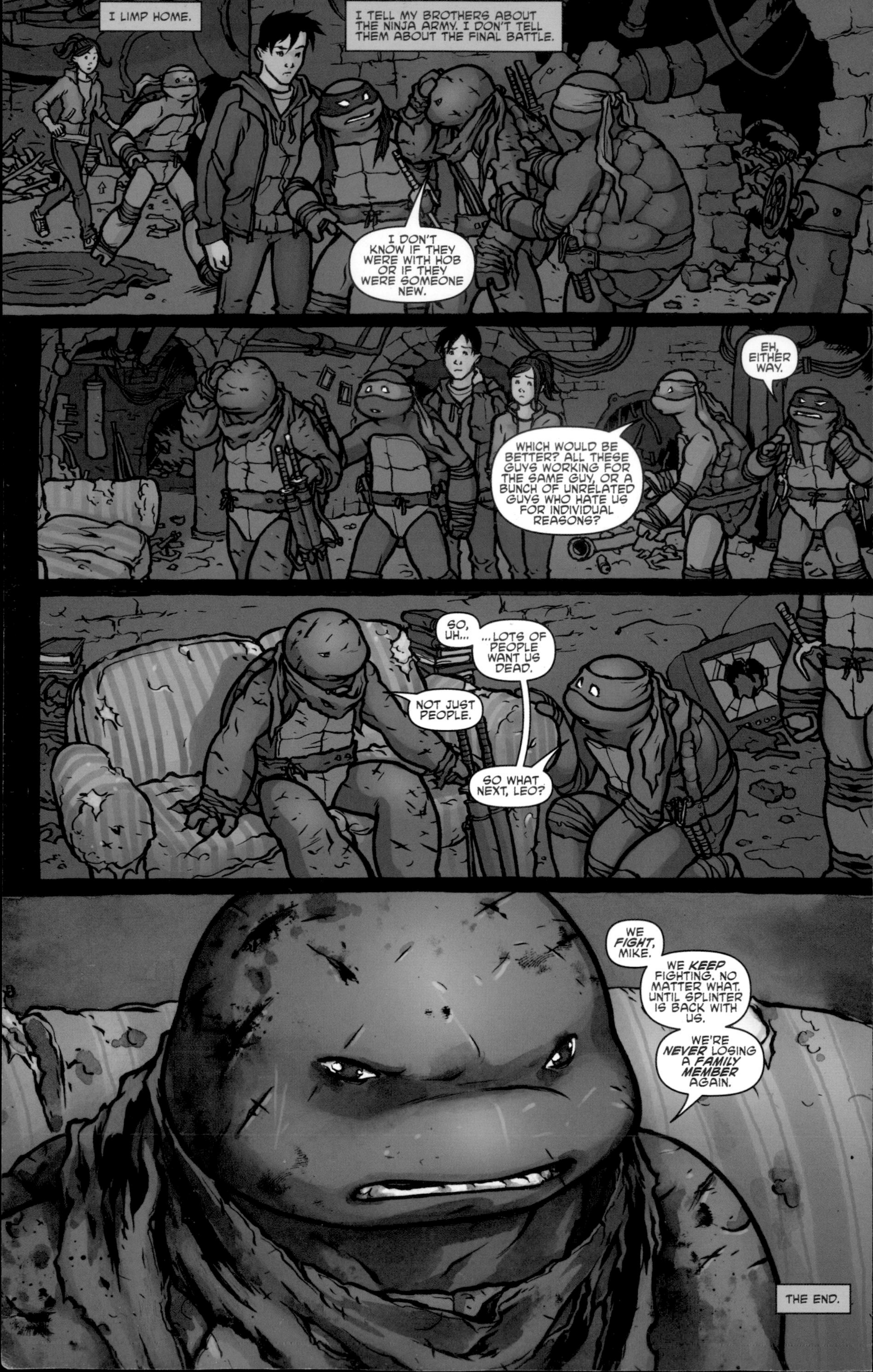
I LIMP HOME.
I TELL MY BROTHERS ABOUT THE NINJA ARMY. I DON'T TELL THEM ABOUT THE FINAL BATTLE.
I DON'T KNOW IF THEY WERE WITH HOB OR IF THEY WERE SOMEONE NEW.
WHICH WOULD BE BETTER? ALL THESE GUYS WORKING FOR THE SAME GUY, OR A BUNCH OF UNRELATED GUYS WHO HATE US FOR INDIVIDUAL REASONS?
EH, EITHER WAY.
SO, UH...
...LOTS OF PEOPLE WANT US DEAD.
NOT JUST PEOPLE.
SO WHAT NEXT, LEO?
WE FIGHT, MIKE.
WE KEEP FIGHTING. NO MATTER WHAT. UNTIL SPLINTER IS BACK WITH US.
WE'RE NEVER LOSING A FAMILY MEMBER AGAIN.
THE END.

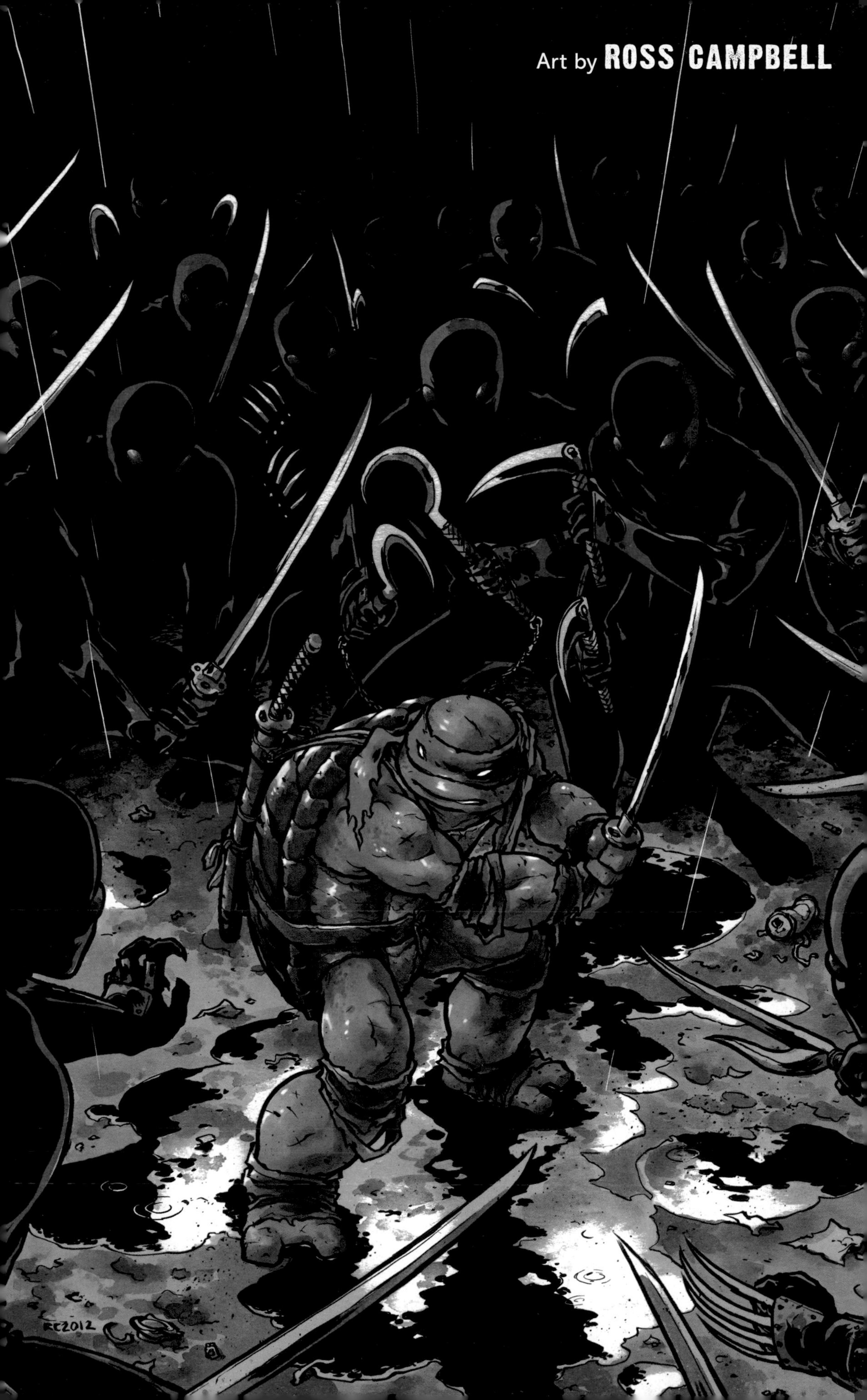
RC2012

Art by **ROSS CAMPBELL**

Art by **KEVIN EASTMAN**

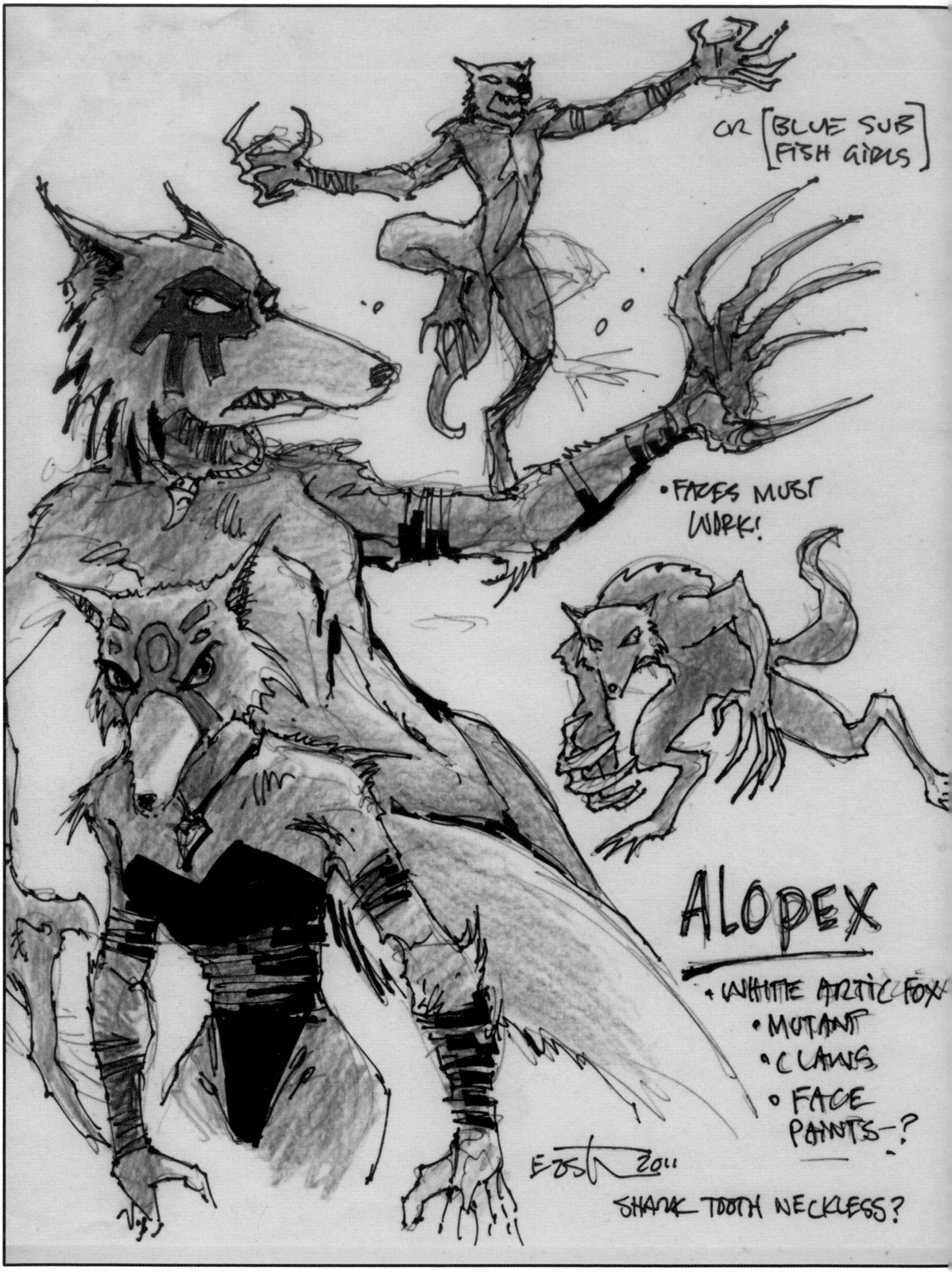

OR [BLUE SUB FISH GIRLS]
• FACES MUST WORK!
ALOPEX
• WHITE ARTIC FOX
• MUTANT
• CLAWS
• FACE PAINTS-?
EASTMAN 2011
SHARK TOOTH NECKLESS?

Art by **KEVIN EASTMAN**

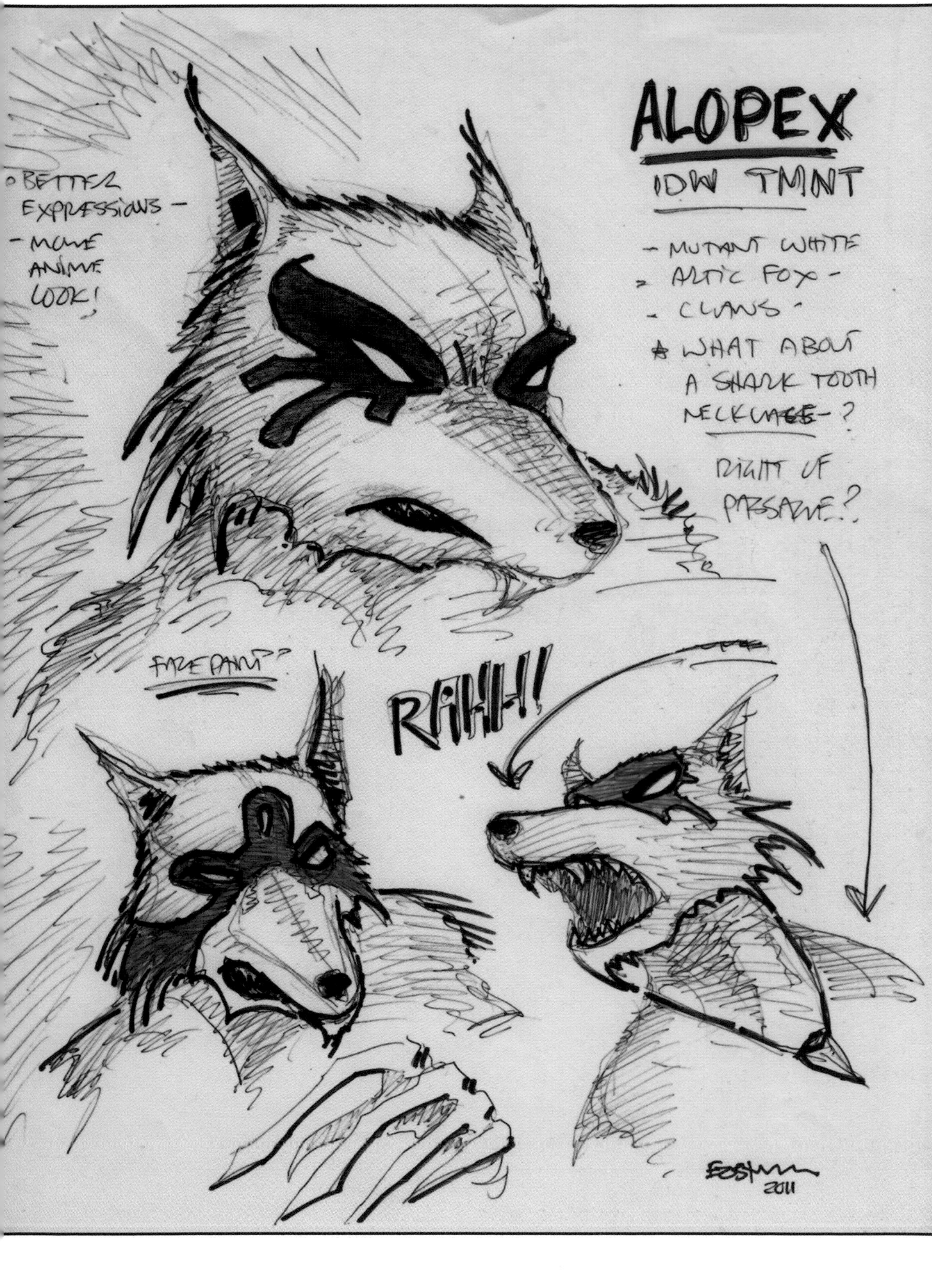
ALOPEX
IDW TMNT
- MUTANT WHITE
- ARTIC FOX -
- CLAWS -
* WHAT ABOUT A SHARK TOOTH NECKLACE - ?
RIGHT OF PASSAGE ?
• BETTER EXPRESSIONS -
- MOVE ANIME LOOK!
FACE PAINT?
RAHH!
EASTMAN 2011

Art by **ANDY KUHN**

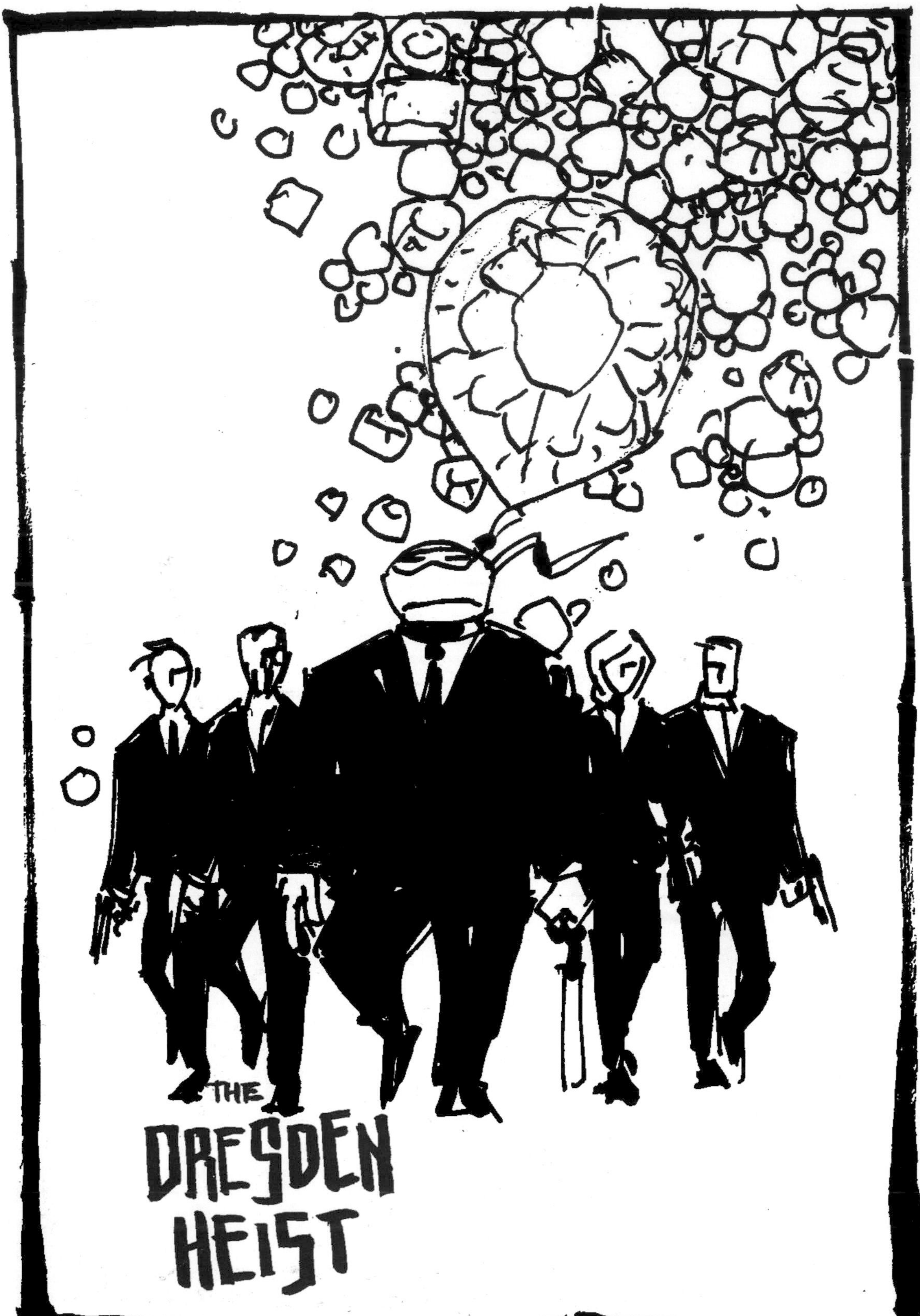
THE
DRESDEN
HEIST

Art by **ANDY KUHN**

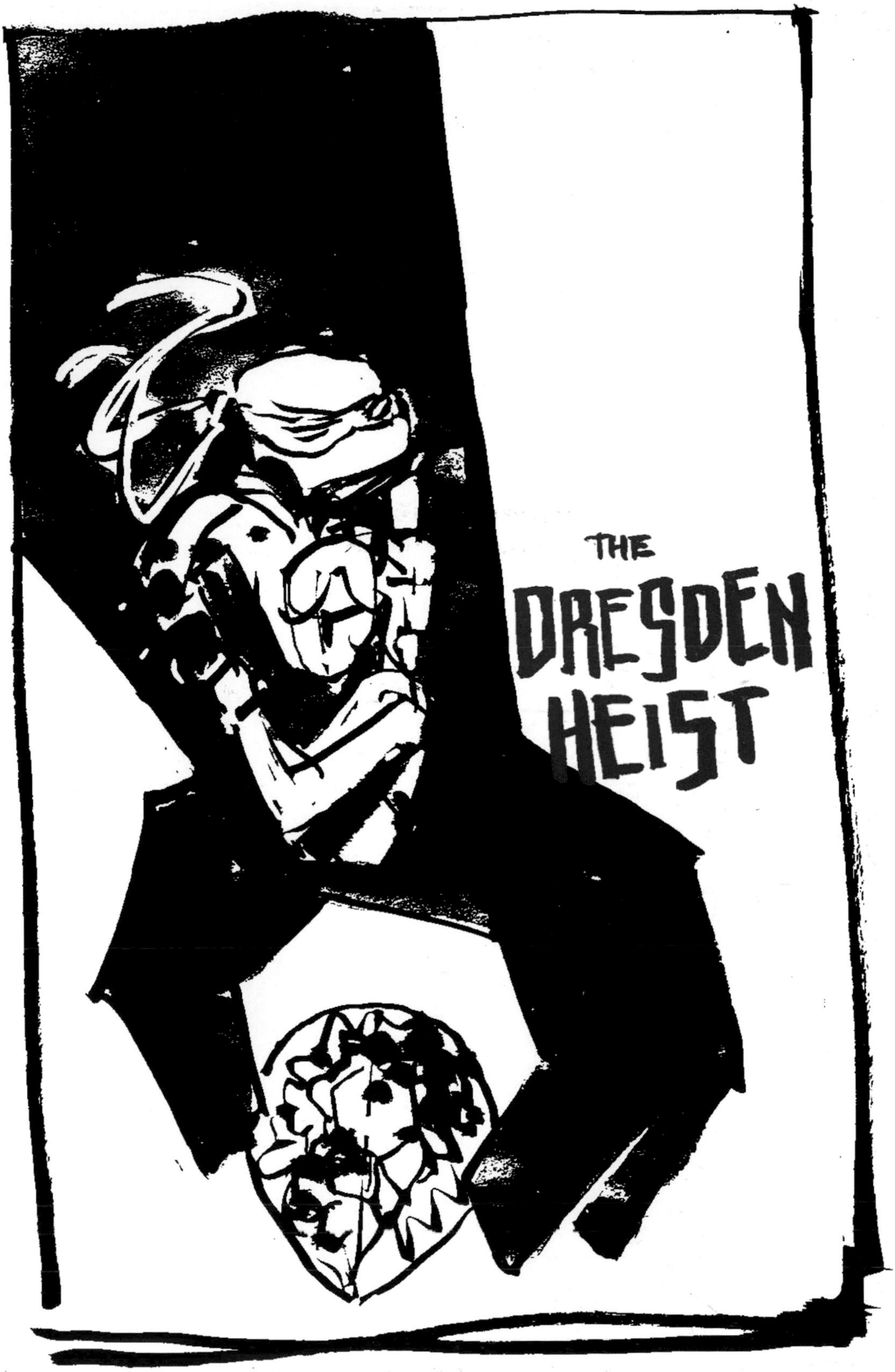
THE
DRESDEN
HEIST

Art by **ROSS CAMPBELL**

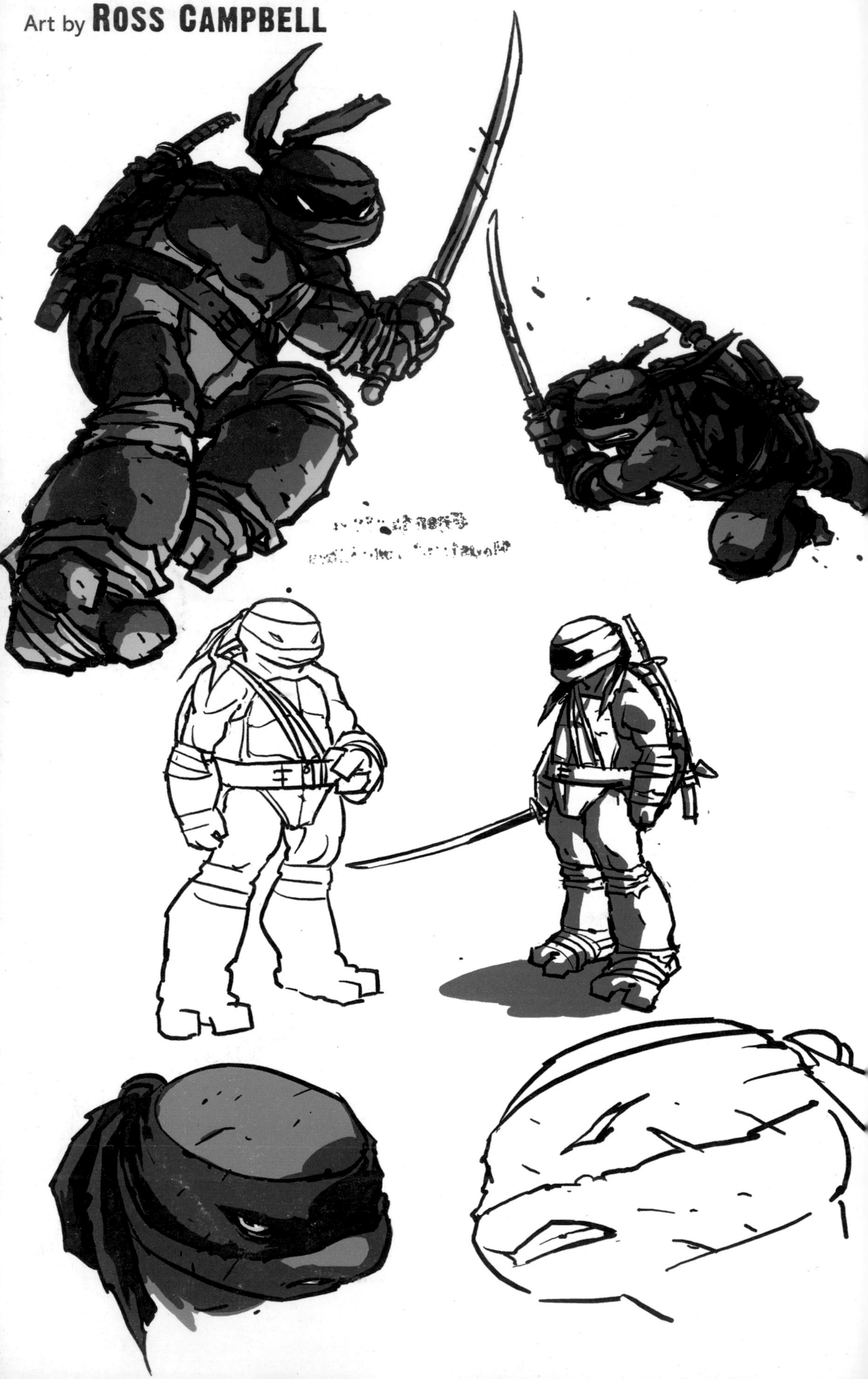